Baby Names 2020

Eleanor Turner

white
LADDER

Acknowledgments

I would like to extend my utmost gratitude to Beth Bishop at Crimson Publishing for her patience and guidance throughout this project. To the many individuals and families I've had the fortune to doula for over the years, and who have graciously allowed me to share their baby names with the world, thank you. Love and appreciation also goes to Michael Turner, who has stuck around and offered endless helpful suggestions while I've worked on these wonderful books for the last nine years. And finally, the greatest thanks go to my own children, Owen Henri, Jasper Hugh, and Josie May. I fall more in love with them, and their names, every day.

This ninth edition published by White Ladder, an imprint of Crimson Publishing Ltd, in 2019.

ISBN 978 1 910336 60 1

Front cover: AMR Image/iStock.com

Printed and bound in England by CPI Books, Chatham, UK.

Contents

Author's note

Baby names vary widely in spelling and pronunciation. To simplify things, this book usually lists each name only once: under the most common initial and spelling. If a name has a common alternate spelling with a different initial, it may also be listed under that letter.

Information relating to statistics and trends in baby names is based on the most recent data at the time of going to press.

Introduction

I first started writing the Baby Names book series a decade ago, and since then they've become something of an annual tradition for me. Throughout the previous year, everyone I know sends me delightful, hilarious, and frequently bizarre snippets of news about baby names, and I pore over them for the best and most interesting bits. For months I work through these to find the funniest or most profound, and compare everything I find to the official data published by the Social Security Administration (SSA). The end result becomes what I hope is a light-hearted, easy-going read for every parent who finds themselves cursing the skies over what to name their new addition.

Inside *Baby Names 2020* you'll find out:

- the nation's favorite names

- what the different states choose as their favorites

- why celebrities pick such unique names

- how politics can shape baby name trends

… and a host of other bizarre facts and figures you never knew you wanted to know.

My goal is to make this decision fun for you! Baby names are fascinating when you dig into the science and statistics of it all, and hugely entertaining when you learn what other people think are great choices … but you privately disagree.

So, grab a pencil and your comfiest yoga pants, dip in, and find some names you like. Use the wealth of suggestions and lists we've given you, and work out whether one of them is your baby's future name.

Good luck!

Eleanor Turner

Part One

1 Current baby-naming trends

What is it about baby names that gets people so excited? We wait with bated breath for the announcement of a new baby's name like it's Christmas Day and we're five years old again. We couldn't wait to hear what Prince Harry and Meghan Markle named their new son just as much as we eagerly awaited news from our best friend or sister. There's a draw to it that we can't escape, and it all boils down to this: will we love it, hate it, laugh at it, or want to copy it? And that very human desire to pass judgment on a new baby's name—for better or worse—is the reason why books like this are written.

So, let's get going, shall we? Let's read up on what parents across the country are currently naming their babies, and practice arranging our faces into "oh, isn't that lovely!" expressions as we go. Somewhere in this little tome is the perfect name for your new baby too, and lots of neat stuff to learn along the way.

Lovely Liam and enduring Emma

We're going to start our journey by looking at the baby names American parents chose more than any others in 2019. For the second year in a row Liam topped the boys' charts, and Emma is also in first place on the girls' list for the fifth year running. More than 18,500 baby girls were given the name Emma in the latest baby names data set (released by the Social Security Administration, SSA), and nearly 20,000 were given the name Liam. Crucially, while Emma was significantly down in numbers from the year before, both managed to keep their prime positions. But why these names? What's going on with these two particular choices that holds such a strong attraction for so many new parents? Well, we have to take a look at some other factors to make that clearer.

Last year was a record low year for birth statistics. Just over 3,788,000 babies were born in the United States, indicating a drop of 2% from the previous year, and was the lowest birth rate in a staggering 32 years. Fertility rates were also down (the number of babies born to each woman in her lifetime), which means that families are choosing to have fewer children, if at all.

> In 2019 there were 132 babies registered as Unknown and 27 named Baby.

What this means for our purposes, is that baby names data is getting really interesting. In the past, if you picked an unusual name it would appear somewhere at the bottom of

The Nation's Top 10

Boys	Girls
1. Liam	1. Emma
2. Noah	2. Olivia
3. William	3. Ava
4. James	4. Isabella
5. Oliver	5. Sophia
6. Benjamin	6. Charlotte
7. Elijah	7. Mia
8. Lucas	8. Amelia
9. Mason	9. Harper
10. Logan	10. Evelyn

the list, having to compete with the thousands and thousands of other folks who chose more traditional names or common spellings. Now though, if you choose something off the beaten track it carries more weight because there are simply fewer other names as competition. There's more shuffling in the ranks now, and names that were stalwarts from a few years ago are moving down, down, down, and others that we might not have even heard of before are up, up, up. I acknowledge that this is very nerdy, but bear with me. I promise it gets even more interesting.

Consider this: until a few years ago, either Jacob or Michael had remained the top choice for parents of newborn baby boys in the US for over 50 years. Jacob has been given to more babies over that period (4.9 million and counting), but Michael has claimed the top spot more often (44 times), so the fact that Liam has rocked the top for two years running is pretty unusual. In fact, Jacob has now been pushed down to position 13 and Michael sits in 14th place, which might say more about broader baby naming and political trends than just about anything else. If the two most popular baby boy names of all time are no longer in the Top 10, then we are surely on the cusp of one of the biggest shakeups in baby names history.

At first glance, the names in the girls' list don't look very different to the year before, but that's only because of the first Top 10. Once we delve a little deeper into the list, you'll see how both the boys' and the girl's lists are changing like never before. Emma, Olivia, and Ava have maintained their positions in the Top 3, while newcomer Harper has pushed Abigail into 11th place. On the boys' side, Lucas is the name responsible for pushing Jacob out of the Top 10 bracket.

The website "Name of the Year" pronounced Canadian ice hockey player Jimbob Ghostkeeper the winner of its annual competition. He beat Dr. Narwhals Mating, Salami Blessing and Princess Nocandy to win the popular vote.

There are a few themes within the Top 10 on both sides, however: Biblical names, which have dominated the American charts for years, are still very much en vogue for baby boys, and Noah, Benjamin, James, and Elijah are all doing very well for themselves. However, long gone are the equivalents for baby girls such as Rebecca, Rachel, and Mary. Instead, parents of little girls are far more likely to choose a name based on sound, rather than historical or religious significance.

In this tradition we now see a run on girls' names with –ah sounds at the end, which accounts for a massive 80% of the Top 10 and 65% of the Top 20. In fact, the only names to not follow the pattern are Charlotte and Evelyn.

Charlotte, once an extremely popular name in the US and appearing consistently in the Top 100 from 1908 to 1953, had dropped dramatically by 1982. However, in the last decade it's seen a sharp uptick in use, and last year popped up as number six. Of course, it has been helped along by a certain Royal princess, who just acquired a new baby cousin in the form of Prince Harry and Meghan Markle's little boy Archie Harrison. See page 14 for more on Harry's son.

> Will Eugenie and Jack be the next royals to make a baby announcement? Will anyone know how to pronounce the name they choose? It took us about 28 years to learn how to pronounce Eugenie. ('YOU-jennee'—sounding like 'use your knees', as her mother Sarah Ferguson, Duchess of York explained.)

Charlotte has now become so fashionable that even shortened versions of it are gaining momentum: Charlie entered the Top 1,000 for baby girls in 2005 and in subsequent years has leaped nearly 800 places to 152nd place. Charlie has also remained a steady favorite for parents of little boys, as it has climbed nearly 250 spots since the year 2000 in the boys' charts, landing last year in position 218.

A name fit for a Duchess

The name Meghan has had a huge resurgence thanks to the popularity of Duchess Meghan Markle. A mere 162 babies were given the name Meghan back in 2017, but last year it appeared in 703rd place—an astonishing climb considering its last heyday was back in the 1990s. In fact, it was the highest-climbing girls' name in 2019, moving up more places in the charts than any other name. Meghan is a Welsh name meaning "pearl," which is rather delightful considering how many jewels the newest duchess will be wearing over the coming years.

The struggle is real

Let's look a little further into what's happening down the lists. I mentioned previously that while the Top 10 for both boys and girls has remained essentially unchanged, things get really interesting once you delve a bit deeper. Names in the Top 100 have seen huge amounts of shuffling within the ranks, with names such as Jayden falling like crazy—even though a few years ago it was the fourth most popular boys' name in the country—while others, such as Luna and Aurora, are skyrocketing.

I think there are two separate things going on here, and the combination is causing this simultaneous effect of the top names going largely unchanged every year, while the ones chasing the rear shuffle up and down like a deck of cards.

Let's start with reason number one: Americans love traditional names. Noah and William have appeared in the Top 20 boys' names every year since 2008, and the girls' names Emma, Ava, Sophia, and Isabella have also stayed put. The world has changed a lot since 2008, but apparently our predominantly traditional taste in names has not.

There are a couple of theories as to why a large number of us are giving our kids the same names, year after year. Personally, I think there's something to be said for the "minimalism" movement. Lately, we've taken to simplifying our lives and streamlining our possessions and choices like never before. We could lay the blame for this at the neat feet of Marie Kondo, but it's been a "thing" for several years now. Well, the same could be said of names: why pick an unusual or complicated one when a classic one will do? Why search among thousands when you have a perfectly wonderful one right in front of you? Your baby will have enough mess and "stuff" already, so let's at least make their name nice and simple.

Continuing this theme is that parents are choosing names they've heard for so long that they feel safe and familiar. Just take a look at the Top 10 (the first five spots for baby girls end in -a), or the highest climbers (six of the ten biggest climbers for baby girls end in either -a, -ie, -y, or a similar sound—see page 12). Most names ending in -a or -ie/-y are immensely popular for little girls right now, and that's because we simply love the sound they make.

All of this is to say, that there's a comfortable pattern to the way large numbers of us name our children that has prevailed for over 20 years now, and other old-fashioned names, such as Eleanor, Henry, James, and Josephine, have climbed the popularity ranks in the Top 100 lists, along with their alternate spellings of Ellie, Harry, Jack, and Josie.

Reason number two: Americans also love to buck tradition and do their own thing (looking at you, Revolution of 1776).

Despite our oh-so-traditional leanings when it comes to the names coasting at the top of the charts, research shows we are actually seeing more variation than ever before in the rest of the list. In the 1950s, the Top 25 boys' names and the Top 50 girls' names were given to half of all

A little inertia

Ryan Gosling helped actor Saoirse Ronan with her major PR problem when promoting a movie—namely, that nobody knows how to pronounce her name! Gosling helpfully provided an explanation that it was "Ser-sha … like inertia," and the memo seems to have worked. A cinema in Minnesota reportedly wanted to help its patrons remember this tip, and even listed the explanation next to the Irish actor's name on their billboard.

babies born in that decade. Think about that for a moment: half of all babies born in the 1950s were given one of either 25 boys' names or 50 girls' names. That's astonishing.

To reach the same figure now, you would have to include the Top 149 boys' names and the Top 196 girls'. That's everything from Liam (1st) to Amir (149th), and Emma (1st) to Everleigh (196th). In fact, if you look over the last decade, the percentage of babies given names in the Top 1,000 gets smaller every year: ten years ago 73.08% of registered births appeared in the Top 1,000 names, but in 2019 it was only 72.72%. This means there is a far greater variety of names, spellings, and pronunciations than ever before, even though the names at the very top of the charts remain traditional and stable.

> Some of the US's quirkiest baby names over the last year have included Eagle, Iton, Solar, and Trail for boys; and Canon, Fairy, Foreign, and Purpose for girls.

One explanation for this is that parents have begun to give their children names more unusual than their own. A parent who was one of a dozen Jennifers in their class in the 1980s or '90s might not want the same experience for their children. Alternatively, a parent who has a slightly unusual name and enjoyed that experience growing up might feel confident about giving their offspring an even more unique name.

There's also a massive trend for taking a name that sounds pretty traditional, but adding a creative twist with the spelling to make it more modern. Examples of this include Kinsley, Madelyn, Jaxon, and Kayden. In fact, substituting letters is probably the biggest trend of all in 2019, but because it results in such unique spellings, all the names in this trend get buried near the bottom of the charts. Collectively however, there are thousands of names where a C has been substituted for a K, or an I for a Y, and they make up a huge proportion of the data set. For more on how to get creative with spelling but not make it look like you're a toddler playing with letter fridge magnets, see page 52.

Statistical stuff

	Boys	Girls
Individual names registered	14,004	18,029
Total registrations	1,800,392	1,513,104
Top names	Liam (19,837 babies)	Emma (18,688 babies)
Babies with names in Top 10	143,173	138,766
Top 10 names as percentage	7.9% of all names	9.2% of all names
Highest climbers	Genesis (up 608 places)	Meghan (up 701 places)
Biggest fallers	Aaden (down 232 places)	Audrina (down 322 places)

Every year, the SSA releases a report on the biggest climbers and fallers, and most years these names tend to be the quirkiest. The names at the top of these lists have the greatest jumps in popularity, although it doesn't necessarily mean they are widely used across the USA. In fact, it's the opposite. The biggest climbers are always those further down the charts—if ten families chose a name last year, but then 20 families choose it this year, that's an increase of 100%. The same percentage increase for Liam would need an additional 19,800 families to choose the name. So a rarely-used name can jump several hundred spots in a single year, despite only having a handful of families choosing it for their little ones. Here's a short breakdown of the Top 10 game-changers:

Biggest winners		Biggest losers	
Boys	**Girls**	**Boys**	**Girls**
Genesis	Meghan	Aaden	Audrina
Saint	Dior	Dilan	Courtney
Baker	Adalee	Craig	Angelique
Kairo	Palmer	Mike	Annabelle
Watson	Oaklynn	Harper	Marjorie
Kenzo	Haisley	Darrell	Marissa
Jaxtyn	Kelly	Ayan	Elsa
Kylo	Novah	Maxton	Jessa
Dakari	Yara	Trent	Kenley
Karsyn	Ensley	Jessie	Kadence

So why do names increase or decrease so dramatically in a single year? I mean, look at what happened to Kylo, which was the second biggest loser on the charts last year and now finds itself as the eighth-highest climber. Well, this is probably down to the release of the final installment of the Star Wars franchise in late 2019. There wasn't a *Star Wars* movie released in 2018 (aside from *Solo*), so Kylo wasn't really part of pop culture that year. However, once *The Rise of Skywalker* was promoted in 2019, the name started picking up again. The Force will keep this trend going in 2020, I'm sure.

There's also an interesting new pattern on the boys' list of religious names, looking at Genesis and Saint. Granted this may be to do with Kim Kardashian-West's children Saint and Psalm, or it may speak to a bigger trend. For years we've been used to seeing Biblical names dominating the charts, but now that we're also embracing creativity, this might be a sign that parents want to stick with religious names but also do something a little more modern. Genesis and Saint therefore fit the bill perfectly.

> KFC gave an impressive $11,000 to the first baby born on 9 September 2018 who received the name Harland. The gimmick,which claimed to celebrate Colonel Harland Sander's 128th birthday, also promoted the 11 herbs and spices in its famous seasoning blend.

So, just like everything else, names fall in and out of fashion. The popularity of names tends to ebb and flow, and in the case of Elsa it may be that *Frozen 2* was released too late in the year to make an impact, or that because it was *so* popular in 2013 and 2014, parents have been turned off it entirely. Regardless, it will be interesting to see what happens in 2020, after the sequel has been out a full year again.

Trendy or tired?

One recurrent theme that's lasted for a few years now, and indeed will probably continue to last for another few more, is to use names that were considered deeply unfashionable a generation or so ago. Think names like Esther, Mae, Benedict, and August, all of which are stoically climbing the charts again.

The reason for this is pretty simple: rather like the fashion of clothing that comes in waves or cycles, names drop in and out of popularity. The names of our parents' generation have been used (or overused) so often, so recently, that they are all but disappearing, while the names of our

Harry's-son ... Archie Harrison

The most influential Royal baby name of recent years was that chosen by Prince Harry and Meghan, the Duke and Duchess of Sussex for their new baby boy. Two days after his birth, it was announced that Harry and Meghan's son would be called Archie Harrison. It's a great choice, and bang on trend with current baby names in the UK where nicknames-as-names is very much en vogue. The middle name was a nice nod to Meghan's American heritage too, as although Archie only just scoots in to the Top 1,000, Harrison is predicted to be in the Top 100 next year. Also, did you know Harrison literally means son of Henry/son of Harry? Ah, those modern royals: they love a good gag as much as the rest of us.

grandparents are suddenly unique and cool again. Even the names of more contemporary decades like the 1990s and early 2000s are fading away, to be replaced by Theodore, Lucas, Helena, and Ann.

> In 2018 a Swedish mom made the drastic decision to change her child's name after a tattoo artist incorrectly inked Kelvin instead of Kevin on her arm. Apparently both mom and son prefer it after the change though, which is a relief. Let's all be thankful it wasn't spelled with a random Q.

Another trend that's been on the rise for a few years and will only continue to develop, is the use of nicknames as full names. This started long before the birth of new royal baby Archie, but he can certainly be credited with continuing the fashion. And in 2019 the hottest nicknames-as-names were somewhat surprising: how about Wells, as a nickname for Maxwell? This was the fastest-rising nickname of last year, jumping 200 spots. Other trendy options included Sunny, Gus, Sylvie, and Dani.

This trend isn't exactly new though. Over in the UK it's been one of the most popular ways to pick a baby name for close to a decade. In fact, it's one of the few ways culture shifts across the Atlantic in this direction; usually pop culture blasts its way from west to east thanks to Hollywood and the music industry, but when it comes to names we've all agreed that the Brits seem to know what they're doing. Other trends happening across the pond right now include gender-neutral choices (Alex, Max, Charlie), 'sweet-sounding' names (Freya, Maisie, Zara), and using hyphens (Lily-Mae, Alfie-James, Ella-Rose). Watch out for these fashions to catch on here too.

Entertain us, baby

Everything, from films and TV to books and blogs, shapes the world of baby names.

The biggest influences to hit screens in recent years were the *Star Wars* franchise, *Game of Thrones*, and anything produced by Disney, but also some unexpected ones. Read on to discover if your love of binge watching Netflix during bouts of pregnancy-induced insomnia can technically be classified as research.

There were two major events in Hollywood history in 2019, and surprise surprise they were from the minds at Marvel and Lucasfilm. Back in the spring we had *Avengers: Endgame*, which broke box office records but had exactly zero impact on baby names (at least, at the time of writing). The only name to nudge even a little was Peter (Parker/Quill), but frankly I was expecting more from Carol, Natasha, and even Tony. I mean, even Fallout Boy singer Pete Wentz named his infant daughter Marvel in 2018. Ho hum.

The biggest movie to hit screens after that was the newest and final instalment in the *Star Wars* series. *Star Wars: The Rise of Skywalker*, which concluded the original trilogy storylines, brought to our screens familiar character names as well as some new ones. The name Luke has seen a small spike in popularity after the release of Episodes VIII and IX, and ended up in 29th place last year. Rey, however, has seen huge growth since Episode VII, appearing on the girls' lists for the first time ever, and leaping up the charts at an impressive rate for both boys and girls. Incidentally, Rey is also an inspiration for parents seeking out middle names, or names that are in keeping with a certain trend for Freya-Audrey-Aubrey names. Also, the name Finn has been in the Top 100 for several years in a row now. Clearly the Force is still strong.

Other big movies in 2019 included the live-action remake of Disney's *Aladdin*. In the 1990s the name Jasmine was hugely popular thanks to the original cartoon, and it ranked highest at position 23. However, it slumped a little in the years following, and fell to 136th. Last year though saw renewed interest in the name and it's starting to recover. In addition, stars Naomi Scott and Mena Massoud saw theirs names more than double in popularity … but only for baby girls. Unfortunately not a single baby boy was given the name Mena in 2019!

Small-screen style

Tell me you didn't fall in love with the gorgeous costuming and acting in *The Crown*? And now tell me you're not seriously considering the names George, Elizabeth, Philip, Margaret, or Charles for your new baby. No one could blame you for being sucked into such a feast for the eyes.

But the real story from 2019 is the astonishing final season of *Game of Thrones*, and the impact the entire series has had on our collective baby-naming psyche. Excluding the more mundane names of Jon and Jaime, more than 4,500 babies were given Westeros-inspired names in 2019, which is up from the 3,800 or so from the previous year. The most popular name by far is Arya/Aria, which was catapulted into last year's Top 20 for the spelling of Aria and 119th for Arya. Considering these names weren't even in the Top 1,000 before the year 2000, this is quite an achievement. Khaleesi was given to 560 children, but I'm presuming most of them were born before Daenerys did … what she did (shh no spoilers) … and that we'll see a slump in 2020.

> When *Unbreakable Kimmy Schmidt* star Ellie Kemper had her baby in 2016 she reportedly forgot to publicly announce her son's name. When quizzed about it several months later, she said, "Oh no, he has a name! That's so funny; it's James! What if we were so mortified by his name we were like, 'Don't tell anyone!'?"

Other big TV shows included *The Handmaid's Tale*, *This Is Us*, *The Marvelous Mrs Maisel*, and *Sneaky Pete*. Heart-wrenching NBC drama *This is Us* may be partially responsible for the recent popularity of the names Milo and Sterling, after actors Milo Ventimiglia and Sterling K. Brown; and the name Abe has popped up following Amazon Prime's surprise hit *The Marvelous Mrs Maisel*. *Sneaky Pete*, another Amazon Prime success, could be held accountable for the recent burst of interest in the name Otto, with the name entering the top 500 for the first time in 2018 and climbing to position 430 last year. While there aren't exactly many parents selecting Offred as an appropriate choice of name for their infant daughters, *The Handmaid's Tale* has helped actor Elisabeth Moss's name sneak ahead in the charts. Her particular spelling jumped 100 places since Season One was released, while the more traditional Elizabeth is steadfast in 13th place.

The sporting year

Names of sporting heroes are often an inspiration for new parents, particularly those with moving stories. When figure skater Adam Rippon took home his Winter Olympics bronze medal (and then won a far more important victory on *Dancing With the Stars* …) he saw his name pop up again in the charts. His backstory of a successful reversal of hearing loss is incredibly inspiring, and it seems there are a lot of parents who agree.

> Did you know the USA invented over 1,100 new names last year? That's right: 1,100 brand new spellings appeared on the SSA's data lists, proving that American parents have quite the imagination.

Stars of the NFL always make an impression, and the New England Patriots' Julian Endelman, MVP winner of Super Bowl 53, proved that once again. The name Julian showed a slight uptick in babies with that name in 2019. Football legend Peyton Manning has seen literally thousands of babies be given his name; there were almost 1,000 baby boys and a whopping 2,800 baby girls called Peyton in the most recent SSA list.

There is a long history of successful athletes creating baby name trends: Jackie Robinson, the first African-American baseball player to play professionally, and one of the great legends of the sport, increased the popularity of both the name Jack (for boys) and Jackie (for girls) during the peak of his fame in the US. He can be credited, in large part, for the continuous popularity of these names even in the 21st century— particularly after the film based on his life, *42: The True Story of an American Legend*, came out a few years ago and brought new attention to his story.

Celebrity power

Celebrities are, apparently, fickle creatures, and last year they once again enjoyed a mixture of traditional and completely outlandish baby name trends—which is what we've all come to love and expect from them. Our old favorites Kim Kardashian-West and Kanye West kick-started the bizarre choices with Psalm, which was given to their newest son. Impressively, little Psalm wasn't alone in 2019: seven other baby boys and 11 baby girls shared his moniker, and it appeared on our list of quirky US names in last year's edition of this book. Maybe Kim K read it and got inspired? As always though, the Kardashians are true trendsetters, and it will be interesting to see how this name—and all the other Krazy Kardashian names from the past—change in the rankings in the years to come.

> When matriarch Kris Jenner was interviewed about Kim's choice of name for new baby Psalm, she said, "The inspiration was the Book of Psalms in the Bible. I think it's just a wonderful way to celebrate how they feel. And he's such a blessing, so it's perfect."

Elsewhere, other celebrities took a more sedate approach. Chef Gordon Ramsay chose the simple and old-fashioned Oscar for his baby boy, and singer Ricky Martin went with Lucia. Actor Jeremy Jordan selected Clara Eloise for his little girl, and singer Robin Thicke opted for sweet Lola. Some other celebrities went with Biblical choices, like rapper Trey Songz's baby boy Noah, and presenter Tamron Hall's choice of Moses; while others went for multi-syllable names, such as Alexander (Richard Gere's son) or Genevieve (Kate Upton's daughter).

Other celebrities opted for nature-themed names, such as Ivy Jane, the daughter of reality TV star Jessa Duggar; Violet, the choice of singer Rachel Platten for her little girl; and Forrest, the son of British actor Tom Hardy. And finally, there's also Birdie Mae, from American singer and reality TV star Jessica Simpson. (I'm quite disappointed she didn't go more ridiculous really, because Birdie's actually kind of cute once you let it fly around a little in the air.)

> Both Beyoncé and Jay Z, and Kim Kardashian-West and Kanye West, have trademarked all their children's names. Gotta build your brand early these days, I guess!

Recent celebrity babies

Alexander (Richard Gere and Alejandra Silva)

Archie Harrison (Prince Harry and Meghan Markle)

Birdie Mae (Jessica Simpson and Eric Johnson)

Clara Eloise (Jeremy Jordan and Ashley Spencer)

Forrest (Tom Hardy and Charlotte Riley)

Gene Attell (Amy Schumer and Chris Fischer)

Genevieve (Kate Upton and Justin Verlander)

Ivy Jane (Jessa Dugger and Ben Seewald)

Lola (Robin Thicke and April Love Geary)

Lucia (Ricky Martin and Jwan Yosef)

Moses (Tamron Hall and Steven Hall)

Noah (Trey Songz and unknown girlfriend)

Oscar James (Gordon and Tana Ramsay)

Psalm (Kim Kardashian-West and Kanye West)

Violet (Rachel Platten and Kevin Lazan)

State differences

What's interesting about US baby name statistics is that there is such variety in the popularity of names across different states and territories. Olivia was a favorite name for baby girls in almost every state, and only the good people of Vermont chose not to honor it.

However, only 20 states chose Liam for their top spot and a mere eight picked Noah. This is in contrast to the national lists, in which Liam appears in first place and Noah in second. Also, looking at the other top-spot winners at state level can be a helpful predictor of which names might be the national favorites in years to come, so it's possible that either Oliver or William will be at the top of the charts in 2021 or 2022.

It seems as though geography can have a major impact on baby-naming decisions, and population density can certainly change the rankings. States with smaller populations, such as Wyoming or Vermont, usually have slightly different names making up their Top 5 each year. Nebraska, for example, has Jack for baby boys, which isn't found in any of the other states listed, and Minnesota has Theodore. The reasoning for this is simple: fewer babies born means each baby name chosen carries greater weight. For Aurora to make the number one spot in Alaska it needed only 45 parents to choose it; to have the same impact and overtake Emma in New York, it would need over 1,100. Likewise, only 45 babies were called Easton in North Dakota, but it still claimed fifth place.

There are some surprising entries here too. In the south-west, particularly those states along the Mexican border, Sebastian has appeared in an unusually high proportion of lists. It ranks only 18th nationwide, but sits in the Top 5 for Arizona, California, Nevada, and Texas. Definitely watch out for this one to appear in the national Top 10 in the next few years.

The most popular baby girl name given in any mainland US state was Emma in California, with over 2,700 registrations. Likewise for boys it was Noah, also in California, with some 2,500 registrations. The names with the fewest picks but still able to claim a top spot were Oliver and Amelia in Wyoming, with only 33 and 26 registrations apiece. So find your state in the following lists—and make sure your baby won't have another ten Emmas or Liams in their class!

Top 5 baby girl names by state

State	Rank 1	Rank 2	Rank 3	Rank 4	Rank 5
Alabama	Ava	Olivia	Harper	Emma	Amelia
Alaska	Aurora	Amelia	Charlotte	Olivia	Sophia
Arizona	Emma	Olivia	Mia	Isabella	Sophia
Arkansas	Ava	Olivia	Emma	Amelia	Harper
California	Emma	Mia	Olivia	Isabella	Sophia
Colorado	Olivia	Emma	Charlotte	Evelyn	Isabella
Connecticut	Olivia	Emma	Isabella	Charlotte	Ava
Delaware	Ava	Isabella	Charlotte	Olivia	Sophia
Dist. of Columbia	Ava	Olivia	Elizabeth	Emma	Charlotte
Florida	Isabella	Emma	Olivia	Sophia	Mia
Georgia	Ava	Olivia	Emma	Amelia	Isabella
Hawaii	Emma	Isabella	Aria	Mila	Olivia
Idaho	Olivia	Emma	Evelyn	Harper	Charlotte
Illinois	Olivia	Emma	Ava	Isabella	Sophia
Indiana	Emma	Olivia	Amelia	Charlotte	Ava
Iowa	Harper	Evelyn	Emma	Charlotte	Olivia
Kansas	Olivia	Emma	Charlotte	Evelyn	Ava
Kentucky	Emma	Olivia	Ava	Harper	Amelia
Louisiana	Ava	Olivia	Emma	Amelia	Harper
Maine	Charlotte	Amelia	Emma	Harper	Olivia
Maryland	Ava	Olivia	Charlotte	Emma	Sophia
Massachusetts	Emma	Olivia	Charlotte	Sophia	Isabella
Michigan	Olivia	Ava	Emma	Charlotte	Amelia
Minnesota	Evelyn	Olivia	Charlotte	Emma	Harper
Mississippi	Ava	Olivia	Emma	Amelia	Skylar
Missouri	Olivia	Emma	Charlotte	Harper	Ava
Montana	Harper	Olivia	Emma	Charlotte	Abigail

State	Rank 1	Rank 2	Rank 3	Rank 4	Rank 5
Nebraska	Olivia	Emma	Evelyn	Charlotte	Harper
Nevada	Emma	Isabella	Olivia	Sophia	Ava
New Hampshire	Olivia	Charlotte	Emma	Ava	Amelia
New Jersey	Emma	Isabella	Olivia	Mia	Ava
New Mexico	Isabella	Sophia	Mia	Emma	Olivia
New York	Emma	Olivia	Isabella	Sophia	Mia
North Carolina	Ava	Emma	Olivia	Charlotte	Harper
North Dakota	Olivia	Emma	Harper	Charlotte	Amelia
Ohio	Ava	Emma	Olivia	Amelia	Harper
Oklahoma	Emma	Olivia	Ava	Isabella	Harper
Oregon	Emma	Olivia	Evelyn	Charlotte	Amelia
Pennsylvania	Emma	Olivia	Ava	Charlotte	Sophia
Rhode Island	Amelia	Olivia	Emma	Sophia	Mia
South Carolina	Ava	Emma	Olivia	Charlotte	Harper
South Dakota	Harper	Emma	Olivia	Charlotte	Ava
Tennessee	Emma	Ava	Olivia	Harper	Amelia
Texas	Emma	Isabella	Olivia	Mia	Sophia
Utah	Olivia	Charlotte	Emma	Evelyn	Lucy
Vermont	Harper	Charlotte	Evelyn	Emma	Nora
Virginia	Ava	Olivia	Emma	Charlotte	Sophia
Washington	Olivia	Emma	Evelyn	Amelia	Charlotte
West Virginia	Emma	Olivia	Ava	Harper	Amelia
Wisconsin	Evelyn	Emma	Olivia	Harper	Charlotte
Wyoming	Amelia	Emma	Elizabeth	Harper	Olivia

Top 5 baby boy names by state

State	Rank 1	Rank 2	Rank 3	Rank 4	Rank 5
Alabama	William	James	John	Elijah	Noah
Alaska	Oliver	Logan	Liam	Benjamin	Michael
Arizona	Liam	Noah	Sebastian	Benjamin	Oliver
Arkansas	Noah	Elijah	William	Liam	Oliver
California	Noah	Liam	Sebastian	Mateo	Ethan
Colorado	Liam	Oliver	William	Noah	Benjamin
Connecticut	Noah	Liam	Benjamin	Logan	Lucas
Delaware	Liam	Noah	Mason	Logan	James
Dist. of Columbia	William	James	Henry	Alexander	Benjamin
Florida	Liam	Noah	Lucas	Elijah	Logan
Georgia	William	Noah	Liam	Elijah	James
Hawaii	Liam	Noah	Elijah	Logan	Ethan
Idaho	Liam	Oliver	Henry	William	James
Illinois	Noah	Liam	Oliver	Benjamin	Alexander
Indiana	Oliver	Liam	Noah	Elijah	William
Iowa	Oliver	Liam	Henry	William	Owen
Kansas	Liam	Oliver	Henry	William	Mason
Kentucky	William	Liam	Elijah	Noah	Grayson
Louisiana	Noah	Liam	Elijah	James	William
Maine	Oliver	Liam	Owen	Wyatt	Henry
Maryland	Liam	Noah	William	Dylan	Ethan
Massachusetts	Benjamin	Liam	James	Lucas	William
Michigan	Noah	Oliver	Liam	Benjamin	William
Minnesota	Henry	Oliver	William	Liam	Theodore
Mississippi	John	William	Noah	Elijah	James
Missouri	Liam	Oliver	William	Henry	Noah
Montana	Liam	William	Noah	Oliver	Henry
Nebraska	Liam	Henry	Oliver	William	Jack

State	Rank 1	Rank 2	Rank 3	Rank 4	Rank 5
Nevada	Liam	Noah	Sebastian	Elijah	Daniel
New Hampshire	Oliver	Jackson	Mason	Liam	Henry
New Jersey	Liam	Noah	Jacob	Michael	Matthew
New Mexico	Noah	Liam	Elijah	Mateo	Logan
New York	Liam	Noah	Jacob	Lucas	Ethan
North Carolina	Noah	William	Liam	James	Elijah
North Dakota	Oliver	Henry	Owen	Hudson	Easton
Ohio	Liam	Noah	William	Oliver	Owen
Oklahoma	Liam	Noah	William	Oliver	Elijah
Oregon	Oliver	William	Benjamin	Henry	Liam
Pennsylvania	Liam	Noah	Benjamin	Mason	Michael
Rhode Island	Liam	Noah	Benjamin	Alexander	Oliver
South Carolina	William	James	Noah	Elijah	Liam
South Dakota	Grayson	Henry	Liam	Owen	Oliver
Tennessee	William	James	Liam	Noah	Elijah
Texas	Liam	Noah	Sebastian	Mateo	Elijah
Utah	Oliver	William	Liam	James	Henry
Vermont	Oliver	Liam	Owen	Levi	Benjamin
Virginia	William	Liam	Noah	James	Alexander
Washington	Liam	Oliver	William	Noah	Henry
West Virginia	Mason	Liam	Elijah	Grayson	Owen
Wisconsin	Oliver	Liam	Henry	William	Logan
Wyoming	Oliver	Logan	Jackson	Lincoln	Wyatt

Canada's choices

Canada doesn't have a central database that tracks all baby name statistics across the country. Instead, each Canadian province issues its own data every year, and because some provinces are less populous than others, the information can get very specific. Alberta publishes every name given to every single baby. In 2019 their most popular name was Liam, with 225 registrations, but there were only 6,240 names in total; that's less than half of *all* the children called Liam in the United States last year!

However, even though Canada (very politely) declines to publish a central list of all baby names registered each year, there were still some identifiable national trends in 2019. For girls, Olivia and Emma were clear winners, with Charlotte and Amelia appearing next. And for boys, Liam and William took the top spots most often, while Oliver, Benjamin, and Noah weren't far behind.

Girls

Province	Rank 1	Rank 2	Rank 3	Rank 4	Rank 5
Alberta	Olivia	Emma	Charlotte	Emily	Ava
British Columbia	Olivia	Emma	Amelia	Charlotte	Chloe
Manitoba	Olivia	Emily	Charlotte	Amelia	Sophia
New Brunswick	Emma	Olivia	Charlotte	Amelia	Avery
Newfoundland and Labrador	Charlotte	Lily	Emma	Olivia	Layla
Nova Scotia	Olivia	Sophia	Charlotte	Emma	Amelia
Ontario	Olivia	Emma	Charlotte	Ava	Amelia
Price Edward Island	Charlotte	Evelyn	Isla	Nora	Sophia/Amelia
Quebec	Emma	Alica	Olivia	Lea	Charlie
Sasktachewan	Olivia	Emma	Harper	Ava	Sophia

Boys

Province	Rank 1	Rank 2	Rank 3	Rank 4	Rank 5
Alberta	Liam	Oliver	Noah	Ethan	Logan
British Columbia	Liam	Lucas	Oliver	Benjamin	Logan
Manitoba	Lucas	Liam	Noah	William	Benjamin
New Brunswick	William	Liam	Noah	Oliver	Jack
Newfoundland and Labrador	Jack	William	Liam	Greyson	Jackson
Nova Scotia	William	Benjamin	Hunter	Lincoln	Jack
Ontario	Noah	Liam	Benjamin	William	Logan
Price Edward Island	William	Lincoln	Landon	Benjamin	Jack
Quebec	William	Logan	Liam	Thomas	Noah
Sasktachewan	Liam	Oliver	Benjamin	Noah	Jacob

Perfect prophecies

Before we get into how next year's names are stacking up, let's revisit a few of the trends we predicted from last year and see whether we were right!

- More ethnically diverse names: This is a trend that started in late 2018 and continued well into 2019. As the USA becomes increasingly diverse, we have started seeing more names like Muhammad and Zuri, both of which climbed the charts and now appear in the Top 500.

- Names from around the world (particularly names from the UK, Australia, and New Zealand.) What's fascinating about most cultural influences is that the shift moves from the USA to the UK, Europe, and beyond. However, when it comes to baby names, it often goes the opposite way. Current trends in the UK especially are to use nicknames as names, and also more traditional names. It's having an impact here in the USA too, with numerous nicknames appearing such as Cali, Elsie, and Leo, as well as the longer traditional ones like Theodore, Joshua, and Penelope.

- Names from the Roaring Twenties: Oh yes, this is definitely a predicted trend we got right. Names such as Violet, Clara, Jack, and Arthur still climbing. This is one fashion that won't be going away any time soon.

The worst baby names ever

Every year Reddit users vote on their most hated or bizarre baby names. Does the one you love to hate the most make the list?

- Amyllion (pronounced A Million)
- Anita, with the last name Ball
- Felony
- Isaac, with the last name Cox
- Perfection
- Raindrop Iceflower
- Randy, with the last name Slutz
- Reaper
- Ya'Magesty

Other entries included the family that went the whole hog, naming their children Jaytyn, Arlyngtyn, Mykaylah, Jynsyn, and Rayvyn. Nothing like a healthy sprinkling of the letter Y to create a bond between siblings!

2 Predictions for the coming year

Future trends

What trends are coming up in 2020 and how do we know they're coming? Well, looking forward, we predict the Top 10 names will probably go largely unchanged for both boys and girls, but based on trends from previous years, we can make some other predictions.

Last year we predicted more global and ethnically diverse names, and in 2020 we're going one step further. Watch out for names from Europe and Africa making a grand entrance, particularly those with deeper meanings. We're talking about names such as Acacius, Cyrene, Lior, and Sena, or anything inspired by overseas mythology and folklore.

Along the same theme, we will continue to see a pattern of the US adopting trends from other countries—particularly the UK. Trends in Great Britain have been moving steadily towards shorter, cuter names such as Ellie, Bobby, Jamie, and Max, and the US has been slowly following suit for a couple of years now. You only have to look at royal baby Archie Harrison to see the trend in action!

Baby Names 2020

The USA might also see some very old names coming back into style—perhaps even inspired by the Puritans or the Founding Fathers. Look out for some virtuous names such as Mercy, Temperance, and Gideon, or even Alexander (Hamilton), Benjamin (Franklin), and of course George (Washington). We will also see the continuation of the trend from last year of using names from the Roaring Twenties. Names that were popular 100 years ago will continue to climb the charts, and names that were given to our own parents 50 years ago will keep falling. Watch for names such as William, James, Anna, and Charlotte to bump up, and Lisa, Brian, and Tammy to slide down.

> According to ABC News, the smashhit musical Hamilton, based on the life of US Founding Father Alexander Hamilton, gave rise to an increase in the number of babies given the name. This follows the trend of naming babies after US historical figures, such as Lincoln and Madison.

Predicted 2020 baby names

Boys		Girls	
1. Liam	6. Benjamin	1. Emma	6. Isabella
2. Noah	7. Elijah	2. Olivia	7. Mia
3. James	8. Lucas	3. Ava	8. Harper
4. William	9. Mason	4. Sophia	9. Amelia
5. Oliver	10. Alexander	5. Charlotte	10. Evelyn

For girls' names, it's certain that those ending in -a/-er will continue to dominate the Top 20 for at least a while longer. There are currently 13 names in that group that end in -a/-er, and of those 13, six moved up places from the year before (Aria, Camila, Ella, Harper, Mia, and Mila); six stayed put (Amelia, Ava, Emma, Isabella, Olivia, and Sophia), and only one moved down (Sofia). Other similar-sounding names in the Top 20 include Avery and Emily, which presumably means that names ending in -y or -ie sounds will also stick around for a few more years. To top it all off, two of the Top 20 names are so similar they're essentially the same name with a different spelling: Sophia and Sofia. In fact, there are only five names that don't fit into one of the -a or -y/-ie molds—Abigail, Charlotte, Elizabeth, Evelyn, and Scarlett—and all of those are such "classics" that they, too, have grown considerably in popularity over the last ten years.

With boys' names, trends are a little harder to predict. However, there are definitely names that sound very similar in the Top 20, such as Aiden, Benjamin, Ethan, Jackson, Liam, Logan, Mason and William, so expect to see names ending in -n/-m sounds also to be big in 2020. Also, names beginning with J or M are pretty big right now (Jackson, Jacob, and James; Mason, Matthew, and Michael), and if you really want to dig deep, a great many of the names in the boys' list are straight from the Bible: Alexander, Benjamin, Daniel, Elijah, Ethan, Jacob, James, Lucas, Matthew, Michael, and, of course, Noah. There is a great deal more shuffling in the ranks going on in the boys' names list, with huge differences over the last ten years—especially in names listed outside the Top 10. Therefore, it's probable that parents expecting baby boys in 2020 will be following trends such as traditional or religious names instead.

> According to the Huffington Post, trainer names will be big in 2020. Yes, you read that right: they predict that kids called Chuck, Taylor (other names for Converse), Van(s), Jordan and even Falcon will be big. I think they're crazy for even suggesting it, but prove me wrong, HuffPo! Prove me wrong!

Finally, gender-neutral names are going to be big in 2020. Already popular across the pond, names like Madison, Alex, Robin, and Laken are going to take off. Parents are searching for names that allow their children to express themselves no matter their identity, and a gender-neutral name is the perfect place to start.

Most popular biblical names

According to data from the SSA, these are the most popular names taken from the Bible for the last 100 years:

1. James	6. Joseph
2. John	7. Thomas
3. Michael	8. Christopher
4. David	9. Daniel
5. Mary	10. Matthew

In general, US parents prefer to give their children full-length names rather than shortened versions or nicknames, although, as mentioned previously, this trend may start to decline in the coming years. Elizabeth (13th) appears higher up the charts than Ellie (37th), but the gap is closing compared to last year, as Ellie has climbed several spots but Elizabeth has stayed put. We do see this over and over again: Jacob (ranked 13th) is more popular than Jake (262nd); Abigail (11th) is higher than Abby (475th); and Eve (442nd) is much further down the charts than Evelyn (10th).

However, in some cases, a short version or a nickname actually now ranks higher than the traditional name it's taken from. The name Ella (15th last year), for example, is a shortened version of Eleanor (32nd), while Leo (50th) is a shortened version of either Leon (238th) or Leonardo (92nd); both of these shorter names are certainly more widespread than the longer ones. In parts of Europe this is particularly fashionable right now, so perhaps in 2019 we will see more of a European flair to our baby-naming game.

Goings-on in 2020

2020 is predicted to be a bit of a stonker of a year. Between the Summer Olympics, a massive Presidential election here at home, and goodness

Liberal Lena or conservative Kim?

What about the theory that you can tell the political leanings of a family by the name a parent gives their child? Well, in a study conducted at the University of Chicago, researchers noticed that parents with more liberal leanings tended to give names that contained softer sounds, like -a and -l. Examples included Ella, Sophia, Liam, and Lena. Parents with more conservative views chose names with harder or stronger sounds, like -d, -b, -t, and -k. Examples of those names were Kurt, Kim, Donald, and Bryce. However, the researchers also noted that the level of education each parent obtained had as much of an impact as their political viewpoint: well-educated parents chose unusual names, but with traditional spellings (such as Atticus or Finnegan), and less educated parents chose traditional names with more unusual spellings (such as Andruw instead of Andrew). So, while it's true that politicians and political stances definitely affect baby name trends, it might have quite a lot to do with levels of education as well.

knows what else in Europe's political landscape, 2020 is going to be busy. And the fallout from all of these goings on will naturally affect baby names, because let's face it: pretty much everything else does.

In 2020 there will be a number of major sporting events, and athletes who perform well at them will no doubt become inspiration for new parents. The Summer Olympic and Paralympic Games will take place in Tokyo, Euro 2020 is being held in a cool dozen different European cities, and of course there's the usual smattering of annual events such as the Superbowl, World Series, and tennis at Wimbledon. Watch out for at least some sports-star names to pop up in 2020 if history is anything to go by.

There is a chance that not only sport stars themselves, but also the names they choose for their own children might prove influential. It wouldn't be the first time: Dallas Cowboys defensive end Datone Jones chose the name Laila for his baby girl, citing a great admiration for boxer Muhammad Ali and Ali's daughter Laila Ali; and Arizona Cardinals cornerback Patrick Peterson chose the name Paityn for his little girl, after NFL quarterback legend Peyton Manning. Watch out for athletes that perform well at the Olympics and Superbowl, and possibly even what they name their children!

> Word of caution when considering the name of your second or third child. If your first child is called Sam, don't do what one family almost did and name your daughter Ella. Sam-and-Ella sounds a little too close to Salmonella for comfort!

So what of politics? If nothing else, you can't say that 2019 wasn't an eventful year for our country, and if the trend continues, 2020 will follow suit with the election in November. But the question is, how will political events and headlines affect the names we give our babies? Well, one thing is for certain: few parents are turned on to the name Donald (it's currently at its lowest rank since records started to be kept), and even though the name Melania jumped up a massive 720 spots in 2018, it actually fell completely out of the Top 1,000 in 2019. Whether you like the divisive President or not, it's almost definite that you don't like his – or the First Lady's – name.

The idea that we don't name our children after our politicians isn't new, mind you. Neither Barack nor Obama appeared in the Top 1,000 at any point during the former president's two terms, and despite the name Hillary scoring high in the years preceding the election, it hasn't appeared there again since. However, Barack Obama's daughters are named Malia and Sasha, and the name Malia jumped a whopping 350 places the year Obama was first elected and has continued to grow in popularity ever since. Sasha, which was already fairly common, also jumped a further 100, although it's been steadily falling since the Obamas left the White House.

When Pope Francis I was elected a few years ago, there was a flurry of parents choosing to honor him. The name Francis jumped nearly 20 places last year alone and Frances (for baby girls) also moved up to almost hit the Top 40. In fact, Francesco is now the most popular name for baby boys in Italy.

There's always the chance of a regal influence, particularly with celebrities such as the Kardashians and Lil' Kim choosing names like Reign and Duke. Queen Elizabeth II is Britain's longest-reigning monarch, since she has been on the throne longer than the 63 years and seven months Queen Victoria reigned. It's possible, although extremely unlikely, that she will choose to step down for her eldest son Prince Charles, sparking renewed interest in both her name and his. The name Elizabeth is in 13th place in the US right now, and has held firm in the Top 20 for over 50 years. Victoria is in 21st place, and it too has been in about the same place for over decades. Both are considered such classic names that it's hard to imagine them disappearing entirely.

Banned names around the world

@—China

Akuma (meaning "devil")—Japan

Anus—Denmark

Chow Tow (meaning "smelly head")—Malaysia

Dalmata (meaning "Dalmatian")—Italy

Gesher (meaning "bridge")—Norway

Monkey—Denmark

Ovnis (meaning "UFO")—Portugal

Q—Sweden

Sor Chai (meaning "insane")—Malaysia

Stompy—German

A law in Sonora, Mexico, states parents cannot give their babies names that are defined by authorities as "derogatory, pejorative, discriminatory or lacking in meaning." Names on the published list include Twitter, Burger King, Hitler, Facebook, Harry Potter, Escroto (Spanish for scrotum), and Batman.

America's strange choices

According to the website BabyCenter.com, parents are choosing some pretty imaginative names. Users recently registered the following names for their children:

Boys	Girls
Beau	Alayna
Jossen	Eliana
Kyrie	Journee
Legend	Nur
Messiah	Quiera

Showbiz babies

As always, pop culture will probably be the most prominent influence on baby names in the coming year. Celebrities with new arrivals include Ryan Reynolds and Blake Lively, Michael Phelps and Nicole Phelps, and Keira Knightley and James Righton. If history is anything to go by, the names these couples pick will be highly scrutinised and influential on the rest of us.

Frankly, I'm expecting big things from the names on this list. Come on Ryan Reynolds and Blake Lively … you gave us Inez and James for your daughters (yes, James is a girl), so the next one just can't be called something simple like Sam. Or how about Panthers quarterback

Cam Newton and girlfriend Kia Proctor? Their older children are called Chosen Sebastian, Camidas Swain, and Sovereign Dior Cambella. Fingers crossed for something equally crazy this time around.

The year 2020 will be a massive year for action flick sequels. Let's see … we've got *Bad Boys For Life*, the third in the *Bad Boys* series featuring Will Smith and Martin Lawrence; the 25th James Bond film, starring Daniel Craig; *Top Gun: Maverick*, with the insatiable Tom Cruise; and a spin-off/prequel type thing called *Kingsmen: The Great Game*. In the sci-fi world we've got a sequel to *Avatar*, *Godzilla vs. Kong*, and possibly the most anticipated film for nerds since the last Avengers movie: *Dune*. There's also a sprinkling of fun films for families, such as *The Croods 2* and something rather exciting from Disney/Pixar called *Onward*. So get down to the cinema before your baby arrives to catch them all!

Names that are featured in these films stand a good chance of influencing baby names if past trends are repeated. *Avatar 2*, for example, will almost definitely spike interest in the names Zoe and Zoey again, after lead

Most popular names of all time

Boys	Girls
1. James	1. Mary
2. John	2. Patricia
3. Robert	3. Jennifer
4. Michael	4. Linda
5. William	5. Elizabeth
6. David	6. Barbara
7. Richard	7. Susan
8. Joseph	8. Jessica
9. Thomas	9. Sarah
10. Charles	10. Karen

actress Zoe Saldana. Both of these names have been on the rise since the release of the original Avatar movie in 2009, and Zoey now stands in 29th place, so it could easily climb even higher. It's also entirely possible the sequel will introduce a new generation to names such as Neytiri and Jake, although a Na'vi name is perhaps a bit of stretch.

As for the influence the small screen could wield on our collective baby-naming psyche, zombies is a good place to start … right? Well, according to newest data about popular zombie series *The Walking Dead*, we at least love naming our babies after them. Walker, Abraham, and Maggie have all been big climbers since the show was first broadcast, and a new spin-off series in 2020 will have a similar impact. In fact, British actor Andrew Lincoln has seen his own name move up the charts recently – Lincoln is now in 40 place and has jumped over 150 spots in ten years.

The big news for other shows is the first full year of Disney+, the Disney streaming service launched in late 2019. Much like how Netflix, Hulu, and Amazon Prime have dominated the industry in making ground-breaking programming, Disney+ is predicted to do the same. Flexing its muscles (and dollars) on new family shows will bring us *Diary of a Female President*, a new *Muppets* series, and something rather fun for us 'parents-of-a-certain-generation': a series based on *The Sandlot*. Programs coming to an end in 2020 include *Modern Family*, *Empire*, and *Vikings*.

As some of you may be heavily pregnant, putting your feet up and watching some TV, you may be influenced by some of these shows.

Big and small screen baby names

Boys	Girls
Daniel	Aria
Finn	Arya
James	Elizabeth
Kylo	Khaleesi
Peter	Neytiri
Philip	Piper
Ted	Rey
Tom	Trixie
Will	Zoe

What about Kermit (*The Muppets*), Scotty (*The Sandlot*), Ragnar (*Vikings*), Cameron (*Modern Family*) … or even Cookie (*Empire*)?

Reality series will continue to influence our decisions—especially after Kim Kardashian-West named her son Psalm last year and seven parents promptly followed suit. Kim and singer/rapper Kanye West named their other son Saint and their daughters North (also known as Nori, which is a lot cuter) and Chicago, although Kim confessed last year that she wishes she had used a single-syllable name for Chicago so all four children's names match. Apparently Chicago is often called Chi at home instead. The names North and Saint both picked up steam last year, with 16 babies called North and an impressed 262 called Saint (that's a 75% increase for that name), and even Chicago was given to 11 kids! Other Kardashian Kid names include Dream, Stormi, True, Mason, Penelope, and Reign.

Fictional characters with hidden meanings in their names

Bran Stark (*Game of Thrones*)—bran is an old Welsh name from the word for "raven".

Darth Vader (*Star Wars*)—darth is related to "dark" or "death"; vader is Dutch for "father".

Frodo Baggins (*The Lord of the Rings*)—from fród, meaning "wise by experience" in Old English.

Katniss Everdeen (*The Hunger Games*)—from the katniss plant, meaning "archer" in Latin.

Nyota Uhura (*Star Trek*)—from the Swahili term for "star freedom".

Remus Lupin (*Harry Potter*)—Remus was an ancient Roman orphan raised by wolves; lupinus is the Latin word for "wolfish".

3 How to choose a name

Your baby-naming checklist

- Fall in love with the name(s) you've chosen. Pick a name that makes you smile because, if you love it, hopefully your child will too.

- Don't listen to other people. Sometimes grandparents and friends will offer you baby-naming "advice," which may not always be welcome. If you've got your heart set on a name, keep it a secret until after the birth. Trust your own instincts: they will come in handy later.

  > Norwegian baby-naming law is so strict that Norwegians are only allowed to use names that appear on an approved list. Parents who break this law have been fined and even jailed! Banned names include Gesher (meaning bridge), and anything that could be mistaken for a last name.

- Find a name with meaning. Having a name that has a backstory helps your child understand their significance in the world, so whether you name them after a religious saint or prophet, an important political figure, or a hero in a Greek tragedy, ensure they know where their name came from. They may just be inspired to be as great as their namesake.

- Have fun. Picking out names should be fun. Laughing at the ones you'd never dream of choosing can really help you narrow it down to the ones you would. You can also experiment with different spellings, pronunciations, or variations of names you like, or go to places where you might feel inspired.

- Expand your mind. Don't rule out the weird ones just yet! As a teenager I went to school with a girl named Siam. Her parents had conceived her on a honeymoon trip to Thailand and gave her the country's former name. She loved growing up and having an unusual name, as I'm sure Penelope Scotland (Kourtney Kardashian and Scott Disick's daughter) and Winnie Fallon do too. (Jimmy Fallon's daughter is named after the New Hampshire lake where he proposed to his wife.)

  > The shortest baby names are only two letters long (Al, Ed, Jo, and Ty), but the longest could be any length imaginable. Popular 11-letter-long names include Bartholomew, Christopher, Constantine, and Maximillian.

- Try it out. While you're pregnant, talk to your baby and address it using a variety of your favorite names to see if it responds. There are numerous stories of names being chosen because the baby kicked when it was called Charlie or Aisha, but was suspiciously silent when it was called Dexter or Mildred, so see if it has a preference! Try writing names down and sticking them to your fridge, practicing a few signatures, or saying one out loud enough times to see if you ever get sick of it.

- Do *not* pick the name of an ex. No matter how lovely you think your ex's name is, it would take a very understanding partner to allow you to pick it for your baby. Just steer clear of any names you know will cause problems to other people, paying particular attention to your partner and loved ones.

- What if you can't agree? This is probably the trickiest problem to solve in the baby-naming process. It's wise to research a number of names you and your partner are both interested in and make a point of discussing your reasons for liking or disliking them long before the baby is due to be born. The labor and delivery room is probably not the best place to argue as you'll both be tired, emotional, and at least one of you will be in pain. Avoid sticking to your guns on a name one of you really isn't happy with because it might lead to your baby being caught in the middle.

- Compromise is the name of the game. You could try compromising and picking two middle names so you both have a name in there that you love; or you could each have five names you're allowed to "veto," but no more. Whichever way you go about it, it is important that you both eventually agree on the name you are giving your baby, even if it means losing out on the one you've had your heart set on.

Think to the future

One important aspect of naming your child is thinking ahead to their future. Will the name you've chosen stand the test of time? Will names popular in 2020 remain well-liked in 2060? Will they be able to confidently enter a room and give a crucial business presentation with an awkward or unpronounceable name? Will they be able to hand their business card over to a potential client without that client looking bemused? Even sooner, can they survive the potential minefields of elementary school and junior high with a name that could easily be shortened to something embarrassing? Would you want to try catching criminals as Sheriff Apple Blossom or have other politicians take you seriously with a name like Senator Fortune Scarlett? You don't want to give your child a name they just cannot live with for the rest of their life, so make your choice based on what's appropriate for an adult as well as a child. To make this easier you might want to choose a longer name that can be shortened or extended as your child desires.

If your child doesn't like the name you've given them because their first and last names make a funny combination, they may choose to use just their first name professionally as an adult. An old colleague of mine goes by "Shiney" only—omitting her last name on business cards and emails because it's a euphemism for male genitalia.

Popular names from the past

Boys	Girls
Abraham	Agatha
Arthur	Bertha
Edmund	Clara
Emmett	Edith
Franklin	Gladys
Gilbert	Mabel
Jasper	Pearl
Neville	Theodora
Percival	Wilhelmina
Vincent	Winifred

Buzzfeed.com once ran an article on people with funny names who were caught on camera. Living among us are Dr Whet Fartz, horse riding judge Willie Stroker, and store district manager Rick Roll … which is probably only funny if you've ever been "rickrolled" online. At the same time another article appeared, listing all the reasons why having an unusual name is a hassle—examples given were not ever being able to find your name on novelty souvenirs, coffee shop baristas not knowing how to spell or pronounce your name for your order, and other people giving you "fun, new" nicknames because they can't be bothered with your given name.

> Another Buzzfeed article in 2018 asked users to submit the strangest names they'd ever come across. The accuracy of the submissions cannot be verified for accuracy, but did include the glorious Guitar, Gamble, Peachy, Random, and twins Nikola and Tesla. There's an idea: give your baby a name so obscure they appear in future pop news articles 20 years from now!

Stereotypes—true or false?

Will the name you choose actually affect your child's life? Will names that seem clever make your child brainier? Will names with positive meanings make your child a happier person? The answer is … possibly.

One thing you should consider is how your child's name will be perceived by the outside world. Typically, judgments are passed on a person before they are met, and made purely based on their name, such as at job interviews or in school. A survey of 3,000 teachers found that 49% of them make assumptions about their pupils based on their names alone. Topping the "naughty" charts were Callum, Connor, and Jack for boys; and Chelsea, Courtney, and Chardonnay for girls. On the other hand, the names in the "clever" category were Alexander, Adam, and Christopher for boys; and Charlotte, Elizabeth, and Emma for girls.

Research has also indicated that certain names are more likely to provoke strong responses in people. A study analyzed the number of stickers given to children as rewards for good behavior. Children named Abigail and Jacob are more likely to be praised for being well-behaved than children named Beth and Josh; and children who do not shorten their name or go by nicknames are more likely to be better behaved, too.

Along the same lines, a study conducted by the Hebrew University of Jerusalem in 2017 found that we subconsciously act like stereotypes of our names, and that other people can pick up on it. They asked students to guess the names of faces they were shown, and the students were able to correctly match them twice as often as expected. So think carefully about the names on your

Ivy League names

Alcott	Graydon
Arthur	Katherine
Beatrice	Martha
Caroline	Robert
Charles	Victoria

favorites list, and consider what types of personalities tend to have these names. If you don't like the answers, it might be time to reconsider. (But you can probably relax: Herbert was the name suggested to be most associated with an idiot and only 80 baby boys were given that last year, so you're probably safe.)

And finally, a recent university study suggests that names are particularly important for language development in early childhood. Apparently, a child's name is one of the first words they can identify (probably from all that cooing into the cot that goes on when they're born), and they use it to learn how to construct and deconstruct sentences. Their name anchors the sentence spoken to them, enabling them to pick out other familiar words and sounds, and put them all together to identify the meaning of the entire thing. Brainy stuff!

Inspirational names		Aspirational names	
Destiny	Joy	Armani	Ferrari
Happy	Peace	Aston	Jaguar
Heaven	Serenity	Bugatti	Mercedes
Hope	Unique	Chanel	Porsche
Innocence	Unity	Dolce	Prada

Eccentric names

There are lots of advantages to having an eccentric name. For one thing, people will never forget your child's name, and if they do something influential with their life their name could become an inspiration for other parents. On the other hand, a quirky name often requires a quirky personality. If you don't think your genes could stand up to a name like Satchel or Zizi, perhaps it's time to think of one a little more run-of-the-mill.

Baby Names 2020

An eccentric name often says more about the parents than the child, and their own personalities may affect the personality of their child in a significant way. A conventional family that names its baby John will probably find he becomes a conventional child, whereas a quirky family that names its baby Zanzibar will find he develops a quirky personality. The name itself is not the leading factor; it's the eccentric or conventional behavior encouraged by the parents who chose the name that's important.

Children who are told they have inherited an ancestor's name or are named after an influential character from history might be more driven and focused than children who are told disappointingly, "We just liked the sound of it." As a parent, therefore, it seems it's okay to pick an unusual name if you have a story or reason behind it. So naming your child Atticus (after Atticus Finch from Harper Lee's *To Kill a Mockingbird*, known for being a strong and moral character), or even Harper (which is now the ninth most popular name in the country), may not be a bad idea …

However, be warned: there is also new research from baby website Bounty.com which says that as many as one in five parents regret their choice of baby name. Of the 1,300 parents interviewed, 11% said they no longer thought the unusual choice of spelling or pronunciation was appropriate. Around 8% said they were tired of people mispronouncing their child's name, and a staggering 25% thought their child's name was too commonly used to be enjoyable. Sadly, a further 20% said they felt like they had been pressured into using a name they didn't like, which has to be the most upsetting way to choose such an important thing. However, they also said they would now pick a new name that had not occurred to them or been an option before.

One possible way to avoid potential regret or humiliation is to download the SSA's hard data on the most recent baby-name choices, and scour

Controversial names adopted by real people

Adolf Hitler	Himmler	Mussolini
Beelzebub	Jezebel	Stalin
Hannibal Lecter	Lucifer	Voldemort

the names down at the bottom of the lists for inspiration. You are likely to find a wealth of unusual and currently unpopular names there, but it's comforting to know that your child won't be the only one in the world with that name. Suggestions from last year's data include Hurley, Luxley, Sayeda, and Yanxi for girls; and Endrick, Jenner, and Wylen for boys.

While avoiding any kind of possible connection to a fictional character is nigh on impossible, you can help make things easier for your child by educating them about their namesake and encouraging them to read more about them. Stay up to date with new cartoons and children's characters to prepare both yourself and your child for preschool and childhood. That way they can be proud of their name and have ammunition if things get rough in the schoolyard.

Masculine or feminine?

How do we define what makes a name masculine or feminine? Well, it may be to do with the sounds the letters create, either when written down or spoken aloud. Harder-sounding combinations (-ter, -it, -ld) tend to be found in masculine names, and softer-sounding combinations (-ie, -ay, -la) are more associated with feminine names. You therefore end up with Sophia, Joanie, and Bella; or Harold, Walter, David, and Oscar. If you're planning on choosing a feminine-sounding name, approach with caution: recent research suggests that girls who are given particularly "girly" names—think Tiana, Kayla, or Isabella—are much more likely to misbehave when they reach school age. These "feminine" girls were also far less likely to choose subjects at school such as math and science, while their sisters with more masculine names—such as Morgan, Alexis, and Ashley—were encouraged to excel in these courses.

Nowadays, names are becoming more androgynous and loads of names appear in both boys' and girls' lists: Madison, Riley, Hayden, and, of course, Alex—some form of which appears in the Top 100 for both boys and girls every year. Therefore, if you want a more gender-neutral name for your new arrival, you won't be alone.

But what about your own gender? Does the fact you're a man or woman mean you're more likely to pick certain names for your child? Well, it looks like this isn't the case, but there might be an element of truth to it. Apparently, mothers are prone to picking names that are similar to, or exactly the same as, their maiden name, if they got rid of it when they got married. This system allows a mother to pass on a part of her own lineage, as well as the father's. A lot of celebrities do this, too, allowing a child to either use their middle name as an additional last name, or to ignore it altogether. Either way, it ensures the famous mom's name gets to stick around a bit longer!

Another recent study found that mothers tend to win the argument over who gets to pick the final name of a newborn, with four in ten moms ignoring the choices selected by dads, and one in ten dads just simply backing down. However, four in ten couples don't make the final decision until after the baby is born, and a third will argue about it before settling—but hey, at least they're talking about it! Now, I'm not saying that the person who grows the baby and goes through the process of removing said baby from her own body should get final say … but really that's exactly what I'm saying.

Nicknames

Nicknames are unavoidable. They can range from the common—Mike from Michael, Sam from Samantha—to the trendy, funny, or downright insulting. Don't be put off if the name you love has an unfortunate nickname associated with it, though—if you don't encourage the use of nicknames, chances are they won't stick. Another way to avoid embarrassing nicknames is to select one for your child that you actually like so that others don't even get a mention. Call your daughter Elizabeth by the name Liz, Lizzie, or Libby if you don't like Betty or Beth, and no one will even consider the alternatives. You can pre-empt possible nicknames to some extent by saying the name you've chosen out loud and trying to find rhymes for it. This is a clever way to avoid children's chants and nursery rhyme-type insults, such as Dora the Explorer or Georgie Porgie. But don't be too concerned about schoolyard chants—most children are subjected to them at some point and emerge unscathed.

> Pronunciation matters: A Swedish couple was once banned from naming their child "Brfxxccxxmnpccccllllmmnprxvclmnck-ssqlbb11116," which they claimed was pronounced "Albin."

Your last name

Try to avoid first names that might lead to unfortunate phrases when combined with your surname, to prevent a lifetime of embarrassment for your child. The best way to work out if this might happen is to write down all the names you like alongside your child's surname and have someone else read them out loud. This second pair of eyes and ears might just spot something you didn't. The age of the internet has given parents a wonderful new weapon in their baby-naming arsenal: the search engine. Before you settle on anything final, try searching for any examples of the complete first, middle, and last name of your new baby.

You may find out that your baby has an ax-murderer namesake—or, as with one of my colleagues, the same name as a well-known porn star.

> One California family changed their daughter's name when she was three months old, from Ottilie to Margot. Their reason? Ottilie is a German name, and when it's pronounced in Europe it comes with hard T sounds (Ott-ti-lee). But due to the slacker T sounds of many regional accents in the USA, their poor daughter's name ended up sounding like Oddly ... oddly enough.

Initials

What last name will your baby have? Will it lend itself easily to amusing acronyms when coupled with certain first and middle names? My brother-in-law was going to be called Andrew Steven Schmitt before he was born, until his parents realized at the last minute what his initials would spell ...

It's also worth taking the time to think about how credit cards display names or how your child's name would look written out on a form. Nobody should have to go through life known as S. Lugg because their parents didn't think that far ahead.

Using family names

Some families have a strong tradition of using names for babies that come from the family tree. There are families where naming your son Augustine VIII is simply not an option—it's a rule. Another way families do this is to give children the name of their parent of the same sex and add "Junior" (Jr.) to the end. This could only create a problem if that child then decides to carry on the tradition and name their child after themselves—after all, who wants to be known as Frederick Jr. Jr.?

There are pros and cons to using family names.

- **Pros:** Your child will feel part of a strong tradition, which will create a sense of security for them and help make them feel a complete member of the family. If you're having a problem selecting a name you and your partner both agree on, this is a very simple solution and will make your new child's family very happy.

- **Cons:** You might not actually like the name that's being passed down. Naming your child the 12th Thumbelina in a row might not actually hold the same attraction for you as for the generation before. Another drawback could be if the cultural associations with a name have changed over time and it is no longer appropriate.

One way to include a family name is to compromise. You could use the name as a middle name, or refer to your baby by a nickname instead. Another possible solution is to use monikers—if your family is insisting your daughter be called Jade, maybe you could choose Giada instead. Or if your partner is determined the next child be called Michael after himself, and it turns out to be a girl, choose Michaela in its place. In many Jewish families the tradition is to take the name of a deceased relative and give it to a new baby. If this thought fills you with dread, you could opt for a possible solution a lot of families adopt, which is to use the first initial instead. If you're not keen on Solomon, pick Samuel; if you don't like Ruth, choose Rebecca.

Bizarre baby names from around the country

Boys	Girls
Aero	Ace
Burger	Kaixin
Donathan	Leeloo
Espn	Monalisa
Haven'T	Rogue
Kix	Sesame
Pawk	Thinn
Rysk	Yoga
Zaniel	Zealand

Spellings and pronunciation

Once you've finally agreed on a name, it's time to consider how you wish it to be spelled and pronounced. Some parents love experimenting with unusual variations of traditional names, while others prefer names to be instantly recognizable. Try to avoid making a common name too long or too unusual in its spelling as this will be the first thing your child learns how to write. They will also have to spell it out constantly during their lifetime, as other people misspell or mispronounce their name. Substituting the odd "i" for a "y" isn't too bad, but turning the name Jonathan into Jonnaythanne doesn't do anyone any favors.

> A palindrome name is a name that is spelt the same backwards and forwards, as with Bob, Elle, Eve, and Hannah.

According to the journal *Scientific American*, participants in one particular study were more likely to believe statements made by people with names they could pronounce, and distrust statements from those they could not. The study only used names from countries outside of the USA, to adjust for pre-existing prejudices, and found that the harder to pronounce the name, the less trustworthy the statement coming from the person seemed to be. Interesting stuff, and worth thinking about if you're debating whether to add that extra "xyz" to your baby's name.

Middle names

Giving your child a middle name is generally acknowledged to be standard practice these days. In fact, it has become fairly uncommon to name a child without a middle name, although the use of second and third names only became popular around the turn of the 20th century. Before then, giving a child a middle name was seen as a status symbol; it was only really used when a man married a higher-class woman and they wanted to keep the woman's maiden name as a reminder of the child's heritage. Once the fashion caught on, it became popular to give more than one middle name to children of status, but it's only been since the 1900s that it has become standard for everyone.

Regardless of your status, a middle name can have just as much of an impact as a first name, so your choice for your own baby should be made as carefully as the decision about their first name.

> New Zealand has a law that baby names, including first, middle and last names, cannot exceed 100 characters, be offensive, be an official rank or title (such as King or Royal), or spelled with numbers or symbols.

Here are some common trends to help you choose.

• Opposite-length names. It has become popular to give a child either a long first name and short middle name (e.g. Jennifer Ruth, Nicholas John), or vice versa.

• Name from the family tree. Honoring your ancestors is another current trend. Parents are looking back to their own lineage for interesting, unusual, or influential names.

• Unusual names. Parents who aren't brave enough to give their child an out-there name as a first name are using it as a middle name.

• Maiden name or other parent name. It is becoming increasingly common to use a parent's first name, or mother's maiden name, as a middle name for a baby.

You may have already decided what middle name to give your child due to tradition or culture, in which case the following advice may be moot. In some Hispanic cultures, for example, middle names are often the mother's last name or another name to promote the matriarchal lineage. Similarly, parents who have not taken each other's last names or are not married

"Text speak" spellings

Camron

Conna

Ema

Esta

Flicity

Jayk

Lora

Patryk

Samiul

Summa

Wilym

may choose to give their child one last name as a middle name and one as a last name so both parents are represented. Other traditions use an old family name, passed down to each first-born son or daughter, to encourage a sense of family pride and history. A decision about what middle name to pass on may have therefore already been made for you, even before your own birth.

Many people actually choose to go by their middle name instead of their first name, so it could be seen as a safety net if you're worried your child won't like their name.

Sweden has a pretty strict naming law, enacted in 1982, which says: "First names shall not be approved if they can cause offense or can be supposed to cause discomfort for the one using it, or names which for some obvious reason are not suitable as a first name." However, the Swedish government did recently approve the use of "Google" as a middle name, so there's that.

Even the British Royal family likes to give many middle names. Prince Charles's full name is Charles Philip Arthur George Mountbatten-Windsor, and Prince William is William Arthur Philip Louis Mountbatten-Windsor. The newest direct-line heir to the throne is, of course, Prince Louis Arthur Charles, named after Lord Louis Mountbatten, his great-great-grandfather Albert Frederick Arthur George Windsor (King George VI), and of course his grandfather Prince Charles. Big sister Princess Charlotte Elizabeth Diana was named after the current queen and her late grandmother, Diana Spencer; and then there's her elder brother,

Prince George Alexander Louis, also named after King George VI and Lord Louis Mountbatten. Deliciously, Prince Harry and Meghan Markle's son Archie, born in 2019, has only one middle name, Harrison.

Celebrities who go by their middle name

Antonio Banderas (José Antonio Domínguez Banderas)

Ashton Kutcher (Christopher Ashton Kutcher)

Bob Marley (Nesta Robert Marley)

Brad Pitt (William Bradley Pitt)

Kelsey Grammer (Allen Kelsey Grammer)

Reese Witherspoon (Laura Jeanne Reese Witherspoon)

Rihanna (Robyn Rihanna Fenty)

Will Ferrell (John William Ferrell)

Naming twins, triplets, and more

If you have discovered you are expecting multiples, congratulations! Naming multiples needn't be any different to naming a single child … unless you want it to be. You could stick to the same process everyone else does, by picking an individual name for each individual child. Even "Octomom" Nadya Suleman chose eight different names for her octuplets, although they do all sound reasonably similar and biblical: Isaiah, Jeremiah, Jonah, Josiah, Maliyah, Makai, Nariyah, and Noah. All eight children also share the middle name Angel.

Of course, when all's said and done you can just stick to giving each child a name unique to them. For triplets, quads, and more, this is probably an easier choice than twisting your head around three names with the same meaning, or trying to create four anagrams you like for all of your

Twin names with the same meaning

Bernard and Brian (strong)

Daphne and Laura (laurel)

Deborah and Melissa (bee)

Dorcas and Tabitha (gazelle)

Elijah and Joel (God)

Eve and Zoe (life)

Irene and Salome (peace)

Lucius and Uri (light)

Lucy and Helen (light)

Sarah and Almira (princess)

babies. Some parents do like to use a theme, though, such as going down the alphabet (think Alastair, Benjamin, Christopher, and David), or doing what the famous acting Phoenix clan did and giving each child a name to do with nature: River, Rain, Leaf (now Joaquin), Liberty, and Summer.

Others choose matching initials (Cash and Cainen; Stella and Sophia), or names that mean the same. You could use two Roman deities, such as Jupiter and Juno, or monarchs of England, like Elizabeth and Victoria—or Henry and Arthur. Heck, choose your favourite characters from a children's book, like Roald Dahl's Matilda and Charlie, or even name your twins after a secret pregnancy craving. No, not Bacon and Cheeseburger, but maybe Olive and Rosemary or Basil and Brie.

The possibilities for triplets go even further. Think of the fun you could have! You could have a row of beautiful flowers, such as Daisy, Violet, and Lily; or a collection of Shakespearean heroes: Beatrice, Helena, and Antonio. Be bold with a set of House Stark kids from *Game of Thrones* (Brandon, Robb, and Arya), or fabulous with some baby girls from *Clueless* (Cher, Tai, and Dionne). As if! The point is, expecting multiples can be scary—make naming them stress-free and fun by getting really creative.

There are a few things to keep in mind when naming twins or multiples, but they are at least pretty simple ones.

Celebrity twin names of the past few years

Alexander and Ella (George and Amal Clooney)

Esther and Stella (Madonna)

Eva and Mateo (Cristiano Ronaldo and Georgina Rodriguez)

Hayes Taj and India Moss (Jonathan and Tara Tucker)

John and Gus (Julie Bowen and Scott Phillips)

Myla Rose and Charlene Riva, and Leo and Lenny (two sets for Roger and Mirka Federer!)

Poppy and Charlie (Anna Paquin and Stephen Moyer)

Rumi and Sir (Beyoncé and Jay Z)

Tristan and Sasha (Chris Hemsworth and Elsa Pataky)

Victoria and Ysabel (Michael Jordan and Yvette Jordan)

- Don't use very long names. You will often find yourself needing to write both names down, so use shorter versions of the names you like, such as Max for Maximilian, or Eve for Evangeline.

- Don't get too complicated. Stick with traditional spellings if possible, like Cameron instead of Kammeryn and Elizabeth instead of Alyzybeth.

- Don't forget that your babies are still individuals. If you use names that sound so similar you often mix them up, your children may get frustrated as they get older and other people confuse them. Instead, keep those nearly identical names you love as middle names and explore more individual first names to match your babies' unique personalities.

> The official Guinness World Record for the most siblings baptized with the same initial is held by a Canadian family, who had ten sons and six daughters named with the letter E. However the unofficial challenger to this would be the notorious Duggar family, whose 19 children all have names starting with J.

Around the world in popular baby names

Country	Girls	Boys
England	Olivia, Amelia, Emily	Oliver, George, Harry
Wales	Olivia, Amelia, Ella	Oliver, Jacob, Noah
Scotland	Olivia, Emily, Isla	Jack, Oliver, James
Northern Ireland	Emily, Grace, Olivia	James, Jack, Oliver
Republic of Ireland	Emily, Emma, Amelia	Jack, James, Daniel
Netherlands	Emma, Tess, Sophie	Noah, Sem, Lucas
Germany	Emma, Hannah, Mia	Ben, Jonas, Leon
Sweden	Alice, Alicia, Olivia	William, Oscar, Liam
Norway	Sofie, Nora, Emma	Jakob, Lucas, Emil
Iceland	Emilã, Emma, Elisabet	Alexander, Aron, Mikael
Portugal	Maria, Matilda, Leonor	João, Rodrigo, Francisco
Spain	Maria, Lucia, Paula	Alejandro, Daniel, David
New Zealand	Charlotte, Harper, Isla	Oliver, Jack, Noah
Australia	Charlotte, Olivia, Mia	Oliver, William, Jack
South Africa	Precious, Princess, Amahle	Junior, Blessing, Gift

Part Two

Boys' names
A–Z

Baby names vary widely in spelling and pronunciation. To simplify things, this book usually lists each name only once: under the most common initial and spelling. If a name has a common alternate spelling with a different initial, it may also be listed under that letter.

A

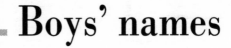

Boys' names

Aaron

Hebrew, meaning "mountain of strength." In the Bible, Aaron was the older brother of Moses and the first high priest of Israel.

Abasi

Egyptian Arabic, meaning "male"; Swahili, meaning "stern."

Abdiel

Hebrew, meaning "servant of God." Also the name of an important seraph in Milton's *Paradise Lost*.

Abdul
(alt. Abdullah)

Arabic, meaning "servant of God." Often followed with a suffix indicating who Abdul is the servant of (e.g. Abdul-Basit, servant of the creator).

Abel

Hebrew, meaning "breath" or "breathing spirit." The biblical son of Adam and Eve who was killed by his brother Cain.

Abelard

German, meaning "resolute."

Aberforth

Gaelic, meaning "mouth of the river Forth." Name of Dumbledore's brother in the *Harry Potter* series.

Abner

Hebrew, meaning "father of light." Abner was the commander of Saul's army in the Bible.

Abraham
(alt. Abram; abbrev. Abe)

Hebrew, meaning "exalted father." Famous Abrahams include President Abraham Lincoln and Abraham Van Helsing—the vampire hunter and doctor in Bram Stoker's *Dracula*.

Absalom
(alt. Absalon)

Hebrew, meaning "father/leader of peace." The name of King David's favorite son in the Bible, and one of Chaucer's curly-haired characters in *The Canterbury Tales*.

Acacio

Greek origin, meaning "thorny tree." Now widely used in Spain.

Ace

Latin, meaning "unit." Also used to mean "number one" or "the best."

Achebe

Yoruba, meaning "may the earth protect us."

Achilles

Greek, mythological hero of the Trojan War, whose heel was his only weak spot.

Achim

Hebrew, meaning "God will establish"; Polish, meaning "The Lord exalts." Also a shortened form of Joachim.

Ackerley

Old English, meaning "oak meadow."

Adam
(alt. Adome, Admon)

Hebrew, meaning "man" or "earth." The biblical creation story names Adam as the first man on Earth.

Adão

Portuguese variant of Adam, meaning "earth."

Addison

Old English, meaning "son of Adam." Also used as a female name.

Ade

Yoruba, meaning "peak" or "royal." A common name in Nigeria.

Adelard

French or German, meaning "brave" or "noble." Became popular in Canada during the 19th century.

Adin

Hebrew, meaning "slender" or "voluptuous"; Swahili, meaning "ornamental."

Aditya

Sanskrit, meaning "belonging to the sun." Refers to the offspring of Aditi—the mother of the gods.

Adlai

Hebrew, meaning "God is just," or sometimes "ornamental."

Adler

Old German, meaning "eagle."

Adley

English, meaning "son of Adam." Also used as a girls' name.

Adolf
(alt. Adolfo, Adolph)

Old German, meaning "noble majestic wolf." Popularity of the name plummeted after World War II, for obvious reasons.

Adonis

Phoenician, meaning "Lord." Adonis was the god of beauty and desire in ancient Greek mythology.

Adrian
(abbrev. Ade)

Latin origin, meaning "from Hadria," a town in northern Italy.

Adriel

Hebrew, meaning "of God's flock." Adriel was one of Saul's sons-in-law in the Bible.

Aeneas

Greek/Latin origin, meaning "to praise." Name of the hero who founded Rome in Virgil's *Aeneid*.

Aero

Greek, meaning "air."

Aeson

Greek, after the father of Jason in ancient Greek mythology.

Afonso

Portuguese, meaning "eager noble warrior." King Afonso of Portugal was nicknamed "The Conqueror" during the Middle Ages.

Agamemnon

Greek, meaning "leader of the assembly." Figure in mythology who commanded the Greeks at the siege of Troy.

Agathon

Greek, meaning "good" or "superior." The name of a tragic poet in ancient Greece.

Agustin

Latin/Spanish, meaning "venerated."

Ahab

Hebrew, meaning "father's brother." Name of the obsessed captain in Herman Melville's *Moby-Dick*.

Ahijah

Hebrew, meaning "brother of God" or "friend of God." Common name in the Bible.

Ahmed

Arabic/Turkish, meaning "worthy of praise." Also one of the prophet Muhammad's many given names.

Aidan
(alt. Aden, Aiden)

Gaelic, meaning "little fire." Derives from Aodh, the name of a Celtic sun god.

Aidric

Old English, meaning "oaken."

Airyck

Old Norse, from Eric, meaning "eternal ruler."

Ajani

Yoruba, meaning "he fights for what he is"; Sanskrit, meaning "of noble birth."

Ajax

Greek, meaning "mourner of the Earth." A Greek hero from the siege of Troy.

Ajay

Hindi, meaning "unconquerable." One of the most popular names in India.

Ajit

Sanskrit, meaning "invincible." Another name for Shiva or Vishnu in Hindu mythology.

Akeem

Arabic, meaning "wise or insightful." Popular name in Nigeria.

Akio

Japanese, meaning "bright man." Akio Morita was one of the founders of Sony.

Akira

Japanese, meaning "intelligent." Also the name of one of the most successful Japanese anime films of all time.

Akiva

Hebrew, meaning "to protect" or "to shelter." Rabbi Akiva is an important figure in the Jewish faith.

Akon

American English, meaning "flower." Made popular after rapper Akon.

Aksel

Hebrew/Danish, meaning "father of peace."

Aladdin

Arabic, meaning "servant of Allah." Character in *The Arabian Nights*, made popular by Disney.

Alan
(alt. Allan, Allen, Allyn, Alun)

Gaelic or Old French, meaning "rock." One of the oldest names still widely used in Western countries, dating back to the 11th century.

Alaric

Old German, meaning "noble regal ruler." Also the name of a king who helped bring about the fall of the Roman Empire.

Alastair
(alt. Alasdair, Alastor, Allister; abbrev. Al, Ali)

Greek/Gaelic, meaning "defending men." Also the name of a demon in the horror series *Supernatural*.

Alban

Latin, meaning "from Alba"; Welsh and Scottish Gaelic for "Scotland."

Alberic

Germanic, meaning "Elfin king."

Albert

(alt. Adalberto, Adelbert, Alberto, Elbert)

Old German, meaning "noble, bright, famous." Prince Albert was the husband of Queen Victoria.

Albus

(alt. Albin)

Latin, meaning "white." Albus Dumbledore is headmaster of Hogwarts School in the *Harry Potter* series.

Alcaeus

Greek, meaning "strength." The name of an ancient Greek poet.

Alden

Old English, meaning "old friend."

Aldis

Latvian, meaning "from the old house."

Aldo

Latin, meaning "the tall one." Also the name of the main gorilla character in *Planet of the Apes*.

Aldric

English, meaning "old king."

Aled

Welsh, meaning "child" or "offspring."

Aleph

Hebrew, meaning "first letter of the alphabet," or "leader." The aleph is the first character of many Middle Eastern alphabets.

Alessio

Italian, meaning "defender."

Alexander

(alt. Alexandro, Alessandro, Alejandro; abbrev. Al, Alec, Alek, Alex, Alexei, Sandro, Sandy, Xander, Zander)

Greek, meaning "defending men." Alexander the Great was an undefeated fourth-century king whose empire stretched from Greece to modern Pakistan. The abbreviation Alexei is enduringly popular in Russia.

Alfonso

Germanic/Spanish, meaning "noble and prompt, ready to struggle." Alfonso Cuarón is the director of the film *Gravity* and *Roma*, among others. Actor Alfonso Ribeiro is known for *Fresh Prince of Bel Air* and *America's Funniest Home Videos*.

Alford
Old English, meaning "old river/ford."

Alfred
(alt. Alfredo; abbrev. Alf, Alfi, Alfie)
English, meaning "elf" or "magical counsel." Name of legendary English king Alfred the Great.

Algernon
(abbrev. Algie)
French, meaning "with a moustache." A popular name for the nobility in 18th- and 19th-century England. *Flowers for Algernon* is a novel by Daniel Keyes.

Ali
(alt. Allie)
Arabic, meaning "noble, sublime."

Alijah
Hebrew, meaning "the Lord is my God."

Alois
German, meaning "famous warrior." Also the name of Adolf Hitler's father.

Alok
Sanskrit, meaning "cry of triumph."

Alon
Hebrew, meaning "oak tree." A popular name in Jewish communities.

Alonso
(alt. Alonzo)
Germanic, meaning "noble and ready."

Aloysius
Italian saint's name, meaning "fame and war."

Alpha
First letter of the Greek alphabet and synonymous with "beginning."

Alphaeus
Hebrew, meaning "changing." Father of two of the Apostles in the Bible.

Alpin
Gaelic, meaning "related to the Alps." The House of Alpin was a dynasty of Scottish kings.

Altair
Arabic, meaning "flying" or "bird." Altair is one of the brightest stars seen in the night sky.

Alter
Yiddish, meaning "old man."

Alton
Old English, meaning "old town."

Alvin
(alt. Alvie)
English, meaning "friend of elves." Often associated with *Alvin and the Chipmunks*.

Alwyn
(alt. Alwen)
Welsh, meaning "wise friend."

Amachi
African, meaning "who knows what God has brought us through this child."

Amadeus
Latin, meaning "God's love." One of composer Wolfgang Amadeus Mozart's many given names.

Amadi
Igbo, meaning "appeared destined to die at birth." Often given to babies who survive against the odds.

Amado
Spanish, meaning "God's love."

Amador
Spanish, meaning "one who loves." Two towns in California were named after rancher José María Amador.

Amari
Hebrew, meaning "given by God." Used for both boys and girls.

Amarion
(alt. Omarion)
Arabic, meaning "populous, flushing." Made popular after R&B singer Omarion.

Amasa
Hebrew, meaning "burden." Found in the Bible.

Ambrose
Greek, meaning "undying, immortal." St. Ambrose of Milan was one of the four original doctors of the Church.

Americo
Germanic, meaning "ever powerful in battle."

Amias
Latin, meaning "loved."

Amir
(alt. Emir)
Arabic, meaning "chieftain" or "commander." Amir or Emir is a title for a high-ranking sheikh in many Muslim communities.

Amit
Hindi, meaning "infinite." One of the many name of the Hindu god Shri Ganesha.

Ammon
Hebrew, meaning "the hidden one." The Ammonites were an ancient group of people named in the Bible.

Amory
German/English, meaning "work" and "power."

Amos

Hebrew, meaning "encumbered" or "burdened."

Anacletus

Latin, meaning "called back" or "invoked." Also the name of the third Pope.

Anakin

American English, meaning "warrior." Made famous by Anakin Skywalker in the *Star Wars* films.

Ananias

Greek/Italian, meaning "answered by the Lord." Ananias Dare was the first baby born to English parents in the New World, making him the first ever "modern" American.

Anastasius
(alt. Anastasios)

Greek, meaning "resurrection." A very popular name for popes, emperors, and saints.

Anatole

French, meaning "sunrise."

Anders

Greek, meaning "lion man." A very popular name in Sweden.

Anderson

English, meaning "male." Anderson Cooper is a TV host.

Andrew
(alt. Andreas, Andre; abbrev. Andy)

Greek, meaning "man" or "warrior." Andrew Lincoln is known for his role in *The Walking Dead*.

Androcles

Greek, meaning "glory of a warrior." *Androcles and the Lion* was a well-known folktale in the second century, and influenced Aesop's *Fables*.

Angel

Greek, meaning "messenger." A very popular name in Hispanic communities. Used for both boys and girls.

Angelo

Italian, meaning "angel."

Angus
(abbrev. Gus)

Scottish, meaning "one choice." Name of Merida's horse in *Brave*.

Anil

Sanskrit, meaning "air" or "wind."

Anselm

German, meaning "helmet of God." St. Anselm was an influential figure in the formation of Christianity.

Anson

English, meaning "son of Agnes." Anson Jones was the last independent President of Texas, before it became incorporated into the USA.

Anthony
(alt. Antony; abbrev. Ant, Tony)
English, from the old Roman family name. *Antony and Cleopatra* is a Shakespearean play about the romance between Roman general Mark Antony and Cleopatra of Egypt.

Antipas
Hebrew, meaning "for all or against all." Herod Antipas is acknowledged as being responsible for the executions of John the Baptist and Jesus Christ in the Bible.

Antwan
(alt. Antoine)
Old English, meaning "flower."

Apollo
Greek, meaning "to destroy." Greek god of poetry, music, and the sun.

Apostolos
Greek, meaning "apostle." The Apostolos is a text believed to have been written by one of the Apostles.

Ara
Armenian, from the legendary king of the same name.

Aragorn
Literary, used by Tolkien in *The Lord of the Rings* trilogy.

Aram
Hebrew, meaning "Royal Highness." Also the name of an ancient region in modern-day Syria.

Aramis
Latin, meaning "swordsman." One of the three musketeers in Alexandre Dumas's novel.

Arcadio
Greek/Spanish, meaning "paradise."

Archibald
(alt. Archie, Archy)
Old German, meaning "genuine/bold/brave." Archie is the son of Prince Harry and Meghan Markle.

Ardell
Latin, meaning "eager, burning with enthusiasm."

Arden
Celtic, meaning "high."

Ares
Greek, meaning "ruin." Son of Zeus and Hera, and the Greek god of war.

Ari
Hebrew, meaning "lion" or "eagle." Also used to refer to an important man in Hebrew.

Arias
Germanic, meaning "lion."

Ariel

Hebrew, meaning "lion of God."
One of the archangels, the angel of
healing and new beginnings.

Arild

Old Norse, meaning "battle
commander."

Aris

Greek, meaning "best figure."
Popular name in Greece.

Ariston

Greek, meaning "the best." Also the
name of Plato's father.

Aristotle

Greek, meaning "best." Also an
ancient Greek philosopher.

Arjun

Sanskrit, meaning "bright and
shining." Taken from Arjuna, an
ancient and legendary archer.

Arkady

Greek, region of central Greece.
Popular throughout Eastern Europe.

Arlan

Gaelic, meaning "pledge" or "oath."

Arlie

Old English place name, meaning
"eagle wood."

Arliss

(alt. Arlis)

Hebrew, meaning "pledge." A 1990s
sitcom.

Arlo

Spanish, meaning "barberry tree."

Armani

(alt. Armand)

Old German, meaning "soldier."
A well-known Italian fashion house.

Arnaldo

Spanish, meaning "eagle power."

Arnav

Indian, meaning "the sea."

Arnold

(abbrev. Arnie)

Old German, meaning "eagle ruler."
Arnold Schwarzenegger is an actor,
former bodybuilder, and former
governor of California.

Arrow

English, from the common word
denoting weaponry.

Art

Irish, from the name of a warrior in
Irish mythology, Art Oenfer (Art the
Lonely). Also used as a shortened
form of Arthur.

Arthur
(abbrev. Art, Artie, Artis)
Celtic, probably from "artos," meaning "bear." Made famous by the tales of King Arthur and the Knights of the Round Table.

Arturo
Celtic or Italian, meaning "strong as a bear."

Arvel
From the Welsh "Arwel," meaning "wept over." Arvel Crynyd appears in *Star Wars*.

Arvid
English, meaning "eagle in the woods." Popular name in Scandinavia.

Arvind
Sanskrit, meaning "red lotus." Also derived from the word for "white lotus," upon which the Hindu goddess Lakshmi sits.

Arvo
Finnish, meaning "value" or "worth."

Asa
Hebrew, meaning "doctor" or "healer." Popular with Puritans in the 17th century.

Asante
African, meaning "thank you." Also the language of the Ashanti people.

Asher
Hebrew, meaning "fortunate" or "lucky." One of the 12 sons of Jacob in the Bible.

Ashley
Old English, meaning "ash meadow." Used for both boys and girls.

Ashok
Sanskrit, meaning "not causing sorrow." Popular in India and Sri Lanka.

Ashton
English, meaning "settlement in the ash-tree grove." The middle but chosen name of actor Ashton Kutcher.

Aslan
Turkish, meaning "lion." The name of the lion from C. S. Lewis's *The Lion, The Witch and The Wardrobe*.

Asriel
(alt. Azriel)
Hebrew, meaning "God is my help." Lord Asriel is an important character in the *His Dark Materials* trilogy. Azriel is the name of the angel of death in Christianity and Judaism.

Astrophel
Latin, meaning "star lover."

Athanasios
Greek, meaning "eternal life." Extremely popular in ancient and modern Greece.

Atílio

Portuguese, meaning "father."

Atlas

Greek, meaning "to carry." In ancient Greek mythology Atlas was a Titan forced to carry the weight of the heavens.

Atlee

Hebrew, meaning "God is just."

Atticus

Latin, meaning "from Athens." Atticus Finch is a central character in Harper Lee's *To Kill A Mockingbird*.

Auberon
(alt. Oberon)

Old German, meaning "royal bear." Oberon is the Fairy King in Shakespeare's *A Midsummer Night's Dream*.

Aubrey

Old German, meaning "power." Used for both boys and girls.

Auden

Old English, meaning "old friend." W. H. Auden is considered one of the most influential 20th-century poets.

Audie

Old English, meaning "noble strength." Audie L. Murphy was one of the most decorated US soldiers during World War II.

August

Latin, meaning "magnificent."

Augustus
(alt. Augastas; abbrev. Gus)

Latin, meaning "venerated." Also the name of a spoiled child in *Charlie and the Chocolate Factory*.

Aurelien

French, meaning "golden." An ancient Roman emperor.

Austin

Latin, meaning "venerated." Also the city in Texas.

Avi

Hebrew, meaning "father of a multitude of nations."

Awnan

Irish, meaning "little Adam."

Axel
(alt. Aksel, Axl)

Hebrew, meaning "father is peace." Made famous by Guns 'n' Roses frontman Axl Rose.

Azarel
(alt. Azaryah)

Hebrew, meaning "helped by God." Also an evil spirit in the Bible.

Azuko

African, meaning "past glory." Popular in Japan.

Boys' names

Babe

American English, meaning "baby." George Herman "Babe" Ruth was a legendary baseball player.

Baden

German, meaning "battle." Also the name of a city in Switzerland known for its hot springs.

Bailey

English, meaning "bailiff." Baileys is a popular Irish crème liqueur.

Baird

Scottish, meaning "poet" or "one who sings ballads."

Bakari

Swahili, meaning "hope" or "promise."

Baker

English, from the word "baker."

Baldwin

Old French, meaning "bold, brave friend."

Balin

Old English, meaning "powerful and strong." Balin was one of the Knights of the Round Table.

Balthazar

Babylonian, meaning "protect the king." Also the name of one of the Three Wise Men in the Nativity story.

Balwinder
(alt. Balvinder)

Hindi, meaning "merciful, compassionate."

Bannon

Irish, meaning "descendant of O'Banain."

Barack

African, meaning "blessed." Made popular by the 44th President of the United States Barack Obama.

Barclay

Old English, meaning "birch tree meadow"; Persian, meaning "messenger."

Barker

Old English, meaning "shepherd."

Barnaby
(abbrev. Barney)

Greek, meaning "son of consolation." *Barnaby Rudge* is one of Charles Dickens's less well-known novels.

Barnard

English, meaning "strong as a bear."

Baron

Old English, meaning "young warrior." A title given to certain men of nobility in Europe. The name of Donald and Melania Trump's son.

Barrett

English, meaning "strong as a bear."

Barron

Old German, meaning "old clearing."

Barry
(abbrev. Baz)

Irish Gaelic, meaning "fair haired." *Great Gatsby* film director Baz Luhrman's real name is Mark.

Bartholomew
(abbrev. Bart, Barty)

Hebrew, meaning "son of the farmer." Bartholomew "Bart" Simpson appears in *The Simpsons*.

Barton

Old English, meaning "barley settlement." The name of several towns in the UK.

Baruch

Hebrew, meaning "blessed." Also the name of a Jewish blessing ceremony.

Bascom

Old English, meaning "from Bascombe."

Bashir

Arabic, meaning "well educated" and "wise." British journalist Martin Bashir is known for his infamous interviews with Diana, Princess of Wales, and Michael Jackson.

Basil

Greek, meaning "royal, kingly." Also the name of the herb.

Basim

Arabic, meaning "smile."

Bastien

Greek, meaning "revered."

Baxter

Old English, meaning "baker." One of the most popular names for towns across the USA.

Bayard

French, meaning "auburn haired." Bayard Rustin was one of Martin Luther King Jr.'s mentors and advisors during the Civil Rights Movement.

Bayo

Yoruba, meaning "to find joy."

Beau

French, meaning "handsome." Actor Beau Bridges' real name is Lloyd Vernet Bridges.

Beck

Old Norse, meaning "stream." Singer Beck Hansen is usually known as just "Beck."

Beckett

Old English, meaning "beehive" or "bee cottage."

Beckham

English, meaning "homestead by the stream." Finding popularity as a given name due to English soccer star David Beckham.

Belarius

Shakespearean, meaning "a banished lord"; from the play *Cymbeline*.

Benedict

Latin, meaning "blessed." Made popular by British actor Benedict Cumberbatch.

Benjamin
(abbrev. Ben, Benny)

Hebrew, meaning "son of the south." Benjamin Franklin was one of the Founding Fathers of the USA.

Bennett

French/Latin vernacular form of Benedict, meaning "blessed."

Benoit

French form of Benedict, meaning "blessed."

Benson

English, meaning "son of Ben."

Bentley

Old English, meaning "bent grass meadow." Popularity has increased since the shows *16 and Pregnant* and *Teen Mom* first aired.

Benton

Old English, meaning "town in the bent grass."

Beriah

Hebrew, meaning "in fellowship" or "in envy." The son of Asher in the Bible.

Bernard
(abbrev. Bernie)
Germanic, meaning "strong, brave bear."

Berry
Old English, meaning "berry." Also used as a shortened form of Bernard.

Berton
Old English, meaning "bright settlement." Berton Averre is the guitarist from The Knack.

Bertrand
(alt. Bertram; abbrev. Bert, Bertie)
Old English, meaning "illustrious." The name of a *Sesame Street* muppet. Bertram (Bertie) Wooster was one of P. G. Wodehouse's most beloved characters. Bert is also a shortened form of Albert.

Bevan
Welsh, meaning "son of Evan."

Bicknell
Old English, meaning "from Bicknell."

Bilal
Arabic, meaning "wetting, refreshing." Popular in many Muslim communities.

Birch
Old English, meaning "bright" or "shining." Also a type of tree.

Birger
Norwegian, meaning "rescue."

Bishop
Old English, meaning "bishop." Bishops are members of the Church who oversee several parishes and jurisdictions.

Bjorn
Old Norse, meaning "bear." Bjorn Ulvaeus was one of the founding members of ABBA.

Bladen
Hebrew, meaning "hero."

Blaine
(alt. Blayne)
Irish Gaelic, meaning "yellow." Has risen in profile due to entertainer David Blaine, known for his magic, illusions, and extreme stunts.

Blair
English, meaning "plain."

Blaise
French, meaning "lisp" or "stutter."

Blake
Old English, meaning "dark, black."

Blaze
(alt. Blas)
German, meaning "firebrand." Also the name of a mountain in the Alps.

Bo

Scandinavian, from Robert, meaning "bright fame." Also the name of the Obamas' pet dog.

Boaz

Hebrew, meaning "swiftness" or "strength." Found in the Bible.

Boden
(alt. Bodie)

Scandinavian, meaning "shelter" or "messenger."

Bogumil

Slavic, meaning "God's favor."

Bond

Old English, meaning "peasant farmer." Often associated with the fictional character James Bond.

Boris

Slavic, meaning "battle glory." Boris Yeltsin was the president of Russia during the 1990s. Boris Johnson is a British politician.

Boston
(alt. Bosten)

English, meaning "town by the woods."

Bowen

Welsh, meaning "son of Owen." The Bowen knot is a common sight in heraldic symbolism.

Boyd

Scottish Gaelic, meaning "yellow."

Bradley
(abbrev. Brad)

Old English, meaning "broad" or "wide." Actor Brad Pitt's full name is William Bradley Pitt.

Brady

Irish, meaning "large-chested." Made famous by *The Brady Bunch*.

Bradyn
(alt. Braden, Bradan)

Gaelic, meaning "descendant of Bradan."

Bram

Gaelic, meaning "raven." Bram Stoker was the author of *Dracula*.

Brando

Old Norse, meaning "sword" or "flaming torch." Name of the movie star Marlon Brando.

Brandon
(abbrev. Bran)

Old English, meaning "gorse." Bran Stark is a main character in *Game of Thrones*.

Brandt

Old English, meaning "beacon."

Brannon

Gaelic, meaning "raven."

Branson

English, meaning "son of Brand."

Brant

Old English, meaning "hill."

Braulio

Greek, meaning "shining."

Braxton

English, meaning "Brock's town." Associated with Braxton Hicks contractions during pregnancy.

Brayden

Irish, meaning "broad meadow."

Brendan

Gaelic, meaning "prince." Actor Brendan Fraser is known for his role in *The Mummy* film series.

Brennan

Gaelic, meaning "teardrop."

Brent

English, meaning "hill." Ice hockey star Brent Seabrook currently plays for the Chicago Blackhawks.

Brenton

English, meaning "hill town."

Brett
(alt. Bret)

English, meaning "a Breton." Made popular by Poison lead vocalist Bret Michaels.

Brian
(alt. Bryan, Bryant)

Gaelic, meaning "high" or "noble." Singer songwriter Brian Wilson was a founding member of The Beach Boys. Actor Bryan Cranston is best known for *Breaking Bad*.

Brice

Latin, meaning "speckled."

Brier

French, meaning "heather." Also the name of a type of thorny plant.

Brock

Old English, meaning "badger." One of the more popular characters in the Pokémon franchise.

Broderick

English, meaning "ruler."

Brody

Gaelic, meaning both "ditch" and "brother." Brody Jenner is known for being part of the Jenner/Kardashian clan.

Brogan

Irish, meaning "sturdy shoe."

Bronwyn
(alt. Bronwen)

Welsh, meaning "fair breast." The spelling of Bronwyn is more common for boys, and Bronwen for girls.

Brooklyn

American English, from the New York City borough of the same name. Brooklyn Beckham is the eldest son of David and Victoria Beckham.

Bruce

Scottish, meaning "high" or "noble." The former name of Olympian decathlete and Jenner/Kardashian clan member Caitlyn Jenner.

Bruno

Germanic, meaning "brown." Bruno Tonioli is a judge on *Dancing With The Stars*.

Bryce

Scottish, meaning "of Britain."

Bryden

Irish, meaning "strong one."

Bryson
(alt. Brycen)

Welsh, meaning "descendant of Brice." Bryson was the name of an ancient Greek philosopher and also a mathematician from the same time.

Bubba

American English, meaning "boy." The restaurant chain Bubba Gump Shrimp Co. takes its name from the characters of Benjamin Buford "Bubba" Blue and Forrest Gump in the movie *Forrest Gump*.

Buck

American English, meaning "goat" or "deer," specifically a male deer.

Buddy
(alt. Bud)

American English, meaning "friend." Buddy has been used as a stage name by a number of musicians including Buddy Holly and Buddy Guy.

Burdett

Middle English, meaning "bird."

Burke

French, meaning "fortified settlement."

Burl

French, meaning "knotty wood."

Buzz

American English, from Busby, meaning "village in the thicket." Buzz Aldrin was the second man on the moon and Buzz Lightyear appears in Disney's *Toy Story* film series.

Byron

Old English, meaning "barn." Famous Byrons include the Romantic poet Lord Byron.

Boys' names

Cabot
Old English, meaning "to sail."

Cade
(alt. Caden, Caiden, Kayden)
English, meaning "round, lumpy."
A character in the novel *Gone With The Wind*.

Cadence
Latin, meaning "with rhythm."
Poetry, music, and marching all have some type of cadence.

Cadogan
Welsh, meaning "battle glory and honor." Sir Cadogan is a knight in a painting in the *Harry Potter* series.

Caedmon
Celtic, meaning "wise warrior." An early English poet.

Caelan
Gaelic, meaning "slender."

Caerwyn
(alt. Carwyn, Gerwyn)
Welsh, meaning "white fort" or "settlement."

Caesar
(alt. Cesar)
Latin, meaning "head of hair." Made famous by the first Roman emperor, Julius Caesar.

Caetano
Portuguese, meaning "from Gaeta, Italy."

Caillou
French, meaning "pebble." Name of a children's cartoon character.

Cain
Hebrew, meaning "full of beauty." Brother of Abel in the Bible.

Cainan
Hebrew, meaning "possessor" or "purchaser."

Cairo
Egyptian city near Giza. Also home of the Great Pyramids.

Calder
Scottish, meaning "rough waters."

Caleb
(alt. Cal, Calen)
Hebrew, meaning "dog." Found in the Bible.

Calix
Greek, meaning "very handsome."

Callahan
Irish, meaning "contention" or "strife."

Callum
(alt. Calum)
Gaelic, meaning "dove." Very popular name in Ireland.

Calvin
(alt. Kalvin)
French, meaning "little bald one." Associated with the comic strip *Calvin and Hobbes* and fashion line Calvin Klein.

Camden
(alt. Kamden)
Gaelic, meaning "winding valley." A district in north London, UK, known for its market.

Cameron
Scottish Gaelic, meaning "crooked nose." Used for boys and girls.

Camillo
Latin, meaning "free born" or "noble."

Campbell
Scottish Gaelic, meaning "crooked mouth." The name of a famous brand of soup.

Canaan
Hebrew, meaning "to be humbled." A region heavily referenced in the Bible.

Candido
Latin, meaning "candid" or "honest." Candido Jacuzzi was the inventor of the Jacuzzi tub.

Canon
(alt. Cannon)
French, meaning "of the church." Originally given to members of a certain order in the Church.

Canton
French, meaning "dweller of corner." Also the name given to provinces of Switzerland.

Cappy
Italian, meaning "lucky." Can also be a nickname for Captain.

Carden

Old English, meaning "wool carder"—which refers to someone who would "card" wool to remove impurities from it.

Carey

Gaelic, meaning "love." Used for both boys and girls.

Carl
(alt. Carlo, Carlos, Karl)

Old Norse, meaning "free man." Carl Jung was a famous psychologist.

Carlton

Old English, meaning "free peasant settlement." Carlton is a character in the sitcom *The Fresh Prince of Bel Air*.

Carmelo

Latin, meaning "garden" or "orchard."

Carmen

Latin/Spanish, meaning "song." The title of an opera by French composer Georges Bizet. Used for boys and girls.

Carmine

Latin, meaning "song." Also the name of a bright-red pigment used in the production of red fruit juices.

Carnell

English, meaning "defender of the castle."

Carson
(alt. Carsten)

Scottish, meaning "marshdwellers." Carson Daly is a late night TV host.

Carter

Old English, meaning "transporter of goods." Jimmy Carter was the 39th President of the United States and Carter Camper is an American professional ice hockey player.

Cary

Celtic, meaning "love." Old Celtic river name. Cary Elwes is a current actor and Cary Grant was the stage name of the dashing English-American actor of the 1930s–1950s.

Case
(alt. Casey, Kace, Kacey, Kasey)

Irish Gaelic, meaning "alert" or "watchful."

Cash

Latin, shortened form of Cassius, meaning "empty, hollow." Associated with musician Johnny Cash.

Casimer

Slavic, meaning "famous destroyer of peace."

Cason

Latin, from Cassius, meaning "empty, hollow."

Casper
(alt. Caspar, Kaspar, Kasper)
Persian, meaning "treasurer." The ghost character in *Casper the Friendly Ghost*.

Caspian
English, meaning "of the Caspy people." Taken from the children's novel *Prince Caspian*.

Cassidy
Gaelic, meaning "curly haired." Originated from the last name Caiside.

Cassius
(alt. Cassio)
Latin, meaning "empty, hollow." Legendary boxer Muhammad Ali's birth name was Cassius Clay.

Cathal
Celtic, meaning "battle rule." Variation of Charles.

Cato
Latin, meaning "all-knowing." Also the name of a character in *The Hunger Games*.

Cecil
Latin, meaning "blind." Cecil B. DeMille was a legendary film director.

Cedar
English, name of an evergreen tree.

Cedric
Welsh, meaning "spectacular bounty." Taken from Sir Walter Scott's novel *Ivanhoe*.

Celestino
Spanish/Italian meaning "heavenly."

Chad
(alt. Chadrick)
Old English, meaning "warlike, warrior." Also the name of an African country.

Chaim
(alt. Chayyim)
Hebrew, meaning "life."

Champion
English, from the word "warrior."

Chance
English, meaning "good fortune."

Chandler
Old English, meaning "candle maker and seller." Made famous by Chandler Bing from 1990s sitcom *Friends*.

Charles
(alt. Charley, Charlie; abbrev. Chas)
Old German, meaning "free man." Charles, Prince of Wales, is heir to the British throne.

Chase
(alt. Chace)

Old French, meaning "huntermen." Actor Chace Crawford is known for his role on TV series *Gossip Girl*.

Chaska

Native American name usually given to first son.

Che

Spanish, shortened form of José. Made famous by Che Guevara.

Chesley

Old English, meaning "camp on the meadow."

Chesney

English, meaning "place to camp." Also used as a girls' name.

Chester

Latin, meaning "camp of soldiers." Chester Arthur was the 21st President of the United States and Chester Bennington was the lead singer of rock band Linkin Park.

Chima

Old English, meaning "hilly land."

Christian
(abbrev. Chris)

English, from the word "Christian." Actor Christian Slater is known for his roles in *Heathers* and *Breaking In*.

Christopher
(alt. Christophe, Kristopher; abbrev. Chris, Kris)

Greek, meaning "bearing Christ inside." Christopher Columbus is credited with discovering America.

Cian

Irish, meaning "ancient." Father of Lug in Gaelic mythology.

Ciaran

Irish, meaning "black." Actor Ciaran Hinds is known for, among others, *Justice League* and his voice work as Gree in *Rio 2*, and the Troll King in *Frozen*.

Cicero

Latin, meaning "chickpea." Also the Roman philosopher and orator.

Cimarron

City in western Kansas.

Ciprian

Latin, meaning "from Cyprus." Popular in ancient Rome.

Ciro

Spanish, meaning "sun." Also the title of a 17th-century opera.

Clancy

Old Irish, meaning "red warrior." Clancy has been a popular name for US actors, writers and sports stars. Also a character in *The Simpsons*.

Clarence

Latin, meaning "one who lives near the river Clare." Clarence Thomas is one of the current Associate Justices of the Supreme Court.

Clark

Latin, meaning "clerk." Superman's human name is Clark Kent.

Claude
(alt. Claudie, Claudio, Claudius)

Latin, meaning "lame."

Claus

Variant of Nicholas, meaning "people of victory." Associated with Santa Claus.

Clay

English, from the word "clay." Singer Clay Aiken is known for his appearances on *American Idol*.

Clement
(alt. Clem)

Latin, meaning "merciful." Also the taken name for 14 different popes.

Cletus

Greek, meaning "illustrious." Cletus Spuckler is a hillbilly character in *The Simpsons*.

Clifford
(alt. Clifton; abbrev. Cliff)

English, meaning "ford by a cliff." Associated with children's character Clifford the Big Red Dog.

Clinton
(alt. Clint)

Old English, meaning "fenced settlement." Actor Clint Eastwood is known for dozens of movie roles, both as an actor and as a director.

Clive

Old English, meaning "cliff" or "slope." Clive Owen is an actor and Clive Davis is a record producer and record label executive.

Clyde

Scottish, from the river that passes through Glasgow. Also the name of one half of the bank robber duo Bonnie and Clyde.

Coby
(alt. Koby, Kobe)

Diminutive of Jacob, meaning "he who supplants." Also used as a girls' name.

Colden

Old English, meaning "dark valley."

Cole
(alt. Coley)

Old French, meaning "coal black." Composer Cole Porter is known for dozens of popular songs and musicals.

Colin

Gaelic, meaning "young creature." Actor Colin Firth is known for his roles in *Pride and Prejudice* and *Kingsman*. Colin Powell was a US secretary of state and is a retired army general.

Colson

Old English, meaning "coal black."

Colton

English, meaning "swarthy." Actor Colton Haynes is known for his role in *Arrow*.

Columbus

Latin, meaning "dove."

Colwyn

Welsh, from the river in Wales.

Conan

Gaelic, meaning "wolf." Comedian Conan O'Brien is known for his work as a late-night TV host.

Conley

Gaelic, meaning "sensible."

Connell
(alt. Connolly)

Irish, meaning "high" or "mighty."

Connor
(alt. Conrad, Conroy)

Irish, meaning "lover of hounds." Very popular name in Ireland.

Constant
(alt. Constantine)

English, from the word "constant." Popular with Puritans during the 17th century.

Cooper

Old English, meaning "barrel maker."

Corban
(alt. Corbin, Corby)

Hebrew, meaning "dedicated and belonging to God."

Corbett
(alt. Corby)

Norman French, meaning "young crow."

Cordell

Old English, meaning "cord maker." An old term for people who made or sold cords.

Corey

Gaelic, meaning "hill hollow." Corey Hart is a Canadian singer who rose to fame in the 1980s.

Corin

Latin, meaning "spear."

Cormac

Gaelic, meaning "impure son." American writer Cormac McCarthy is the author of modern classics *No Country for Old Men* and *The Road*.

Cornelius
(alt. Cornell)

Latin, meaning "horn." Cornelius Fudge is the Minister for Magic in the *Harry Potter* series.

Cortez
Spanish, meaning "courteous."

Corwin
Old English, meaning "heart's friend" or "companion."

Cosimo
(alt. Cosme, Cosmo)
Italian, meaning "order" or "beauty." Masculine form of Cosima.

Coty
French, meaning "riverbank." Refers to people who live on the French coast.

Coulter
(alt. Colt)
English, meaning "young horse."

Courtney
Old English, meaning "domain of Curtis." Used for both boys and girls.

Covey
English, meaning "flock of birds."

Cowan
Gaelic, meaning "hollow in the hill."

Craig
Welsh, meaning "rock." Comedian Craig Ferguson is known for his work as a late night TV host.

Crispin
Latin, meaning "curly haired." A patron saint of shoemakers.

Croix
French, meaning "cross."

Cruz
Spanish, meaning "cross." Made famous after David and Victoria Beckham chose it for their third son.

Curran
Gaelic, meaning "dagger" or "hero."

Curtis
(alt. Curt)
Old French, meaning "courteous." Curtis Mayfield was a soul and R&B singer and Curtis LeMay was a general in the US Air Force during World War II.

Cutler
Old English, meaning "knife maker."

Cyprian
English, meaning "from Cyprus." Also the name of an early Christian bishop and writer.

Cyril
Greek, meaning "master" or "Lord." Associated with St. Cyril.

Cyrus
Persian, meaning "Lord." Cyrus the Great was a ruler of Persia in ancient times.

Boys' names

Dai

Welsh, meaning "darling." Sometimes used as a girls' name.

Daichi

Japanese, meaning "great wisdom."

Daisuke

Japanese, meaning "lionhearted."

Dakari

African, meaning "happy."

Dakota

Native American, meaning "friend" or "ally." Both North and South Dakota take their names from the Native American tribe of the same name.

Dale

Old English, meaning "valley." Dale Earnhardt Jr. is one of the best-known NASCAR drivers.

Dallin

English, meaning "dweller in the valley."

Dalton

English, meaning "town in the valley."

Daly

Gaelic, meaning "assembly."

Damarion

Greek, meaning "gentle."

Damian
(alt. Damon)

Greek, meaning "to tame, subdue." Actor Damian Lewis is known for his role in *Homeland*.

Dane

Old English, meaning "from Denmark." Dane Cook is known for his stand-up comedy.

Daniel
(abbrev. Dan, Danny)
Hebrew, meaning "God is my judge."
Found in the Bible.

Dante
Latin, meaning "lasting." Name of
the Italian 13th-century poet Dante
Alighieri.

Darby
Irish, meaning "without envy."

Darcy
(alt. Darcey)
Gaelic, meaning "dark." Mr. Darcy
is a main character in Jane Austen's
Pride and Prejudice.

Dario
(alt. Darius)
Greek, meaning "kingly." Dario
Argento is an Italian film director
known for his horror fims.

Darnell
Old English, meaning "the hidden
spot."

Darragh
Irish, meaning "dark oak."

Darren
(alt. Darrian)
Gaelic, meaning "great." Darren
Aronofsky is a film director and
producer.

Darrick
Old German, meaning "power of the
tribe."

Darryl
(alt. Darrell, Daryl)
Old English, meaning "open."
Comedian Darrell Hammond was
known for his roles on *Saturday
Night Live*. The spelling Daryl is more
commonly used as a girls' name.

Darshan
Hindi, meaning "vision."

Darwin
Old English, meaning "dear friend."
Often associated with naturalist and
author Charles Darwin.

Dash
(alt. Dashawn)
American English, meaning
"enlightened one." Dash is a
character in Disney Pixar's *The
Incredibles*.

Dashiell
French, meaning "page boy." Author
Dashiell Hammett was known for his
detective novels.

David
*(alt. Daffyd, Davian; abbrev. Dave,
Davey, Davie)*
Hebrew, meaning "beloved." David
was a king of Israel who killed the
giant Goliath in the Bible.

Davis

Old English, meaning "son of David."

Dawson

Old English, meaning "son of David." Associated with 1990s teen drama *Dawson's Creek*.

Dax

(alt. Daxton)

French, from the town in southwestern France. Actor Dax Shepard is known for his role in *Parenthood*.

Dayal

Indian, meaning "kind."

Dayton

Old English, meaning "David's place." Also the name of a city in Ohio.

Dean

(alt. Dino)

Old English, meaning "valley." Actor and reality TV star Dean McDermott is married to Tori Spelling.

Declan

Irish, meaning "full of goodness." Declan Porter was a character on the soap opera *Revenge*.

Dedric

Old English, meaning "gifted ruler."

Deegan

(alt. Deagon, Daegan)

Irish, meaning "black-haired."

Deepak

(alt. Deepan)

Indian, meaning "illumination." Deepak Chopra is known for his work as a doctor and author.

Del

(alt. Delano, Delbert, Dell)

Old English, meaning "bright shining one."

Demetrius

Greek, meaning "harvest lover." One of the star-crossed lovers in Shakespeare's *A Midsummer Night's Dream*.

Dempsey

Irish, meaning "proud."

Denham

(alt. Denholm)

Old English, meaning "valley settlement."

Dennis

(alt. Denny, Denton)

English, meaning "follower of Dionysius." The main character in comic strip *Dennis the Menace*.

Denver

Old English, meaning "green valley." City in Colorado.

Denzel
(alt. Denzil)

English, meaning "fort." Actor Denzel Washington is known for his roles in *Malcolm X* and *Philadelphia*.

Deon

Greek, meaning "of Zeus." The male version of Dionne.

Derek

English, meaning "power of the tribe." Dancer and choreographer Derek Hough is known for his work on *Dancing With The Stars*.

Dermot

Irish, meaning "free man." Actor Dermot Mulroney is known for his roles in *My Best Friend's Wedding* and *New Girl*.

Desmond
(abbrev. Des)

Irish, meaning "from south Munster." Former Archbishop Desmond Tutu is a high-profile South African social activist.

Destin

French, meaning "destiny."

Devyn
(alt. Devin, Devon)

Irish, meaning "poet."

Long names

Alexander	Bartholomew
Christopher	Demetrius
Giovanni	Maximillian
Montgomery	Nathaniel
Sebastian	Zachariah

Dewey
(alt. Dewi)

Welsh, meaning "beloved." One of Donald Duck's three nephews.

Dexter
(alt. Dex)

Latin, meaning "right-handed." Became more popular since the massive success of TV drama *Dexter*.

Didier

French, meaning "much desired."

Diego

Spanish, meaning "supplanter." A character in children's cartoon *Dora the Explorer*.

Dietrich

Old German, meaning "power of the tribe."

Diggory

English, meaning "dyke." Cedric Diggory is a character in the *Harry Potter* series.

Dilbert

English, meaning "day-bright." Main character in the comic strip of the same name.

Dimitri

(alt. Dimitrios, Dimitris)

Greek, meaning "prince." Popular name for boys in Russia.

Dion

Greek, short form of Dionysius.

Dirk

Variant of Derek, meaning "power of the tribe." Famous Dirks include actors Dirk Bogarde and Dirk Benedict.

Dominic

Latin, meaning "Lord." Actor Dominic Monaghan is known for his roles in *Lost* and *The Lord of the Rings*.

Donald

(alt. Donal, Donaldo; abbrev. Don, Donnie)

Gaelic, meaning "great chief." Famous Donalds include the 45th US President Donald Trump, actor Donald Sutherland, and Donald Duck.

Donato

Italian, meaning "gift." Given name of the Italian sculptor Donatello.

Short names	
Al	Ben
Dai	Ed
Jay	Jon
Max	Rio
Sam	Ty

Donnell

(alt. Donnie, Donny)

Gaelic, meaning "world fighter."

Donovan

Gaelic, meaning "dark-haired chief."

Doran

Gaelic, meaning "exile."

Dorian

Greek, meaning "descendant of Doris." The title character of Oscar Wilde's *The Picture of Dorian Gray*.

Douglas

(alt. Dougal, Dougie)

Scottish, meaning "black river." Author Douglas Adams wrote *The Hitchhiker's Guide to the Galaxy*.

Draco

Latin, meaning "dragon." Draco Malfoy is a main character in the *Harry Potter* series.

Drake

Greek, meaning "dragon." Canadian rapper and actor Drake's full name is Aubrey Drake Bell.

Drew

Greek, from Andrew, meaning "man" or "warrior." Drew Carey is known for his work in comedy and as a TV host.

Dudley

Old English, meaning "people's field." The name of Harry's cousin in the *Harry Potter* series.

Duff

Gaelic, meaning "swarthy."

Duke

Latin, meaning "leader." Became popular as a first name after the birth of Giuliana and Bill Rancic's son Duke.

Duncan

Scottish, meaning "dark warrior." King Duncan is a character in Shakespeare's *Macbeth*.

Dustin
(alt. Dusty)

French, meaning "brave warrior." Actor Dustin Hoffman is known for his roles in *Rain Man* and *Tootsie*.

Dwayne

Irish Gaelic, meaning "swarthy." Actor Dwayne Johnson was known as "The Rock" during his professional wrestling career.

Dwight

Flemish, meaning "blond." Dwight D. Eisenhower was the 34th President of the United States.

Dwyer

Gaelic, meaning "dark wise one."

Dylan
(alt. Delyn, Dillon)

Welsh, meaning "son of the sea." Dylan Thomas was a famous Welsh poet.

 Boys' names

Eamon
(alt. Eames, Eamonn)

Irish, meaning "wealthy protector."
Eamonn Walker is known for his role
in TV series *Oz*.

Earl
(alt. Earle, Errol)

English, meaning "nobleman,
warrior." Became popular after the
sitcom *My Name is Earl*.

Ebenezer
(abbrev. Ebb)

Hebrew, meaning "stone of help."
The main character in Charles
Dickens's *A Christmas Carol* is
Ebenezer Scrooge.

Edgar
(alt. Elgar)

Old English, meaning "wealthy
spear." Gothic author Edgar Allen
Poe wrote "The Raven," among other
poems.

Edison

English, meaning "son of Edward."
Thomas Edison was one of the most
influential American inventors.

Edmund

English, meaning "wealthy protector."
Sir Edmund Hillary became the first
Westerner to reach the summit of
Mount Everest, in 1953.

Edric

Old English, meaning "rich and
powerful."

Edsel

Old German, meaning "noble." Car
pioneer Henry Ford named his son
Edsel.

Edward
*(alt. Eduard; abbrev. Ed, Eddie, Eddy,
Ned, Ted)*

Old English, meaning "wealthy guard."
A character in the *Twilight* series.

Edwin

English, meaning "wealthy friend."

Efrain

Hebrew, meaning "fruitful."

Egan

Irish, meaning "fire."

Einar

Old Norse, meaning "battle leader." A popular name for boys in Iceland.

Eladio

Greek, meaning "Greek."

Elam

Hebrew, meaning "eternal." The son of Shem and of Noah in the Bible.

Eldon

Old English, meaning "Ella's hill."

Eldred
(alt. Eldridge)

Old English, meaning "old venerable counsel."

Elgin

Old English, meaning "high minded." Also the name of a town in Scotland.

Eli
(alt. Eliah)

Hebrew, meaning "high." Eli Whitney is credited with inventing the cotton gin.

Elijah
(alt. Elias, Elio, Ellis; abbrev. Eli)

Hebrew, meaning "the Lord is my God." Elias is the Greek form of the same name, Elio is the Spanish version and Ellis the Welsh version. Actor Elijah Wood played Frodo in *The Lord of the Rings*.

Ellery

Old English, meaning "elder tree."

Elliott

Variant of Elio, meaning "the Lord is my God." Elliot was the little boy in the classic film *E.T.*

Ellison

English, meaning "son of Ellis."

Elmer
(alt. Elmo)

Old English, meaning "noble"; Arabic, meaning "aristocratic." Associated with the children's characters Elmer the Elephant and Elmo from *Sesame Street*.

Elon

Hebrew, meaning "oak tree."

Elroy

French, meaning "king." A cartoon character in *The Jetsons*.

Elton

Old English, meaning "Ella's town." Sir Elton John is one of the most successful recording artists of all time.

Elvin

English, meaning "elf-like." Elvin Bale was a huge circus performer known for cannonball stunts.

Elvis

Figure in Norse mythology. Made famous by the singer Elvis Presley.

Emanuel
(alt. Immanuel, Imanol)

Hebrew, meaning "God is with us."

Emeric

German, meaning "work rule." St. Emeric was known for living a pure and pious life.

Emile
(alt. Emiliano, Emilio)

Latin, meaning "eager." Emile is Remy the rat's older brother in Disney's *Ratatouille*.

Emlyn

Welsh, from the UK town of Newcastle Emlyn.

Emmett

English, meaning "universal." Emmett Kelly was known for his role as Weary Willie, the Depression-era clown.

Emrys

Welsh, meaning "immortal." Said to be the birth name of the magician Merlin.

Enoch

Hebrew, meaning "dedicated." Enoch is an ancestor of Noah in the Bible.

Enrico
(alt. Enrique)

Italian form of Henry, meaning "home ruler."

Enzo

Italian, short for Lorenzo, meaning "laurel." Enzo Ferrari was the founder of the Ferrari car company.

Ephron
(alt. Effron, Efron)

Hebrew, meaning "dust."

Erasmo
(alt. Erasmus)

Greek, meaning "to love."

Eric

Old Norse, meaning "ruler." Famous Erics include legendary guitarist Eric Clapton.

Ernest
(alt. Ernesto, Ernie, Ernst)

Old German, meaning "serious." Author Ernest Hemingway wrote the novel *The Old Man and the Sea*, among others.

Erskine

Scottish, meaning "high cliff."

Erwin

Old English, meaning "boar friend."

Ethan

(alt. Etienne)

Hebrew, meaning "long lived." Ethan Hawke is an actor. Ethan Coen and his brother Joel are award-winning film producers and directors.

Eugene

Greek, meaning "well born." Eugene Allen was a butler at the White House for 34 years and the inspiration for the film *The Butler*.

Evan

Welsh, meaning "God is good." Evan Williams founded Twitter.

Everard

Old English, meaning "strong boar."

Everett

English, meaning "strong boar."

Ewan

(alt. Ewald, Ewell)

Old English, from Owen, meaning "well born" or "noble." Actor Ewan McGregor is known for his roles in *Moulin Rouge* and the *Star Wars* series.

Exton

English, meaning "on the river Exe."

Ezra

Hebrew, meaning "helper." Name of the poet Ezra Pound.

Boys' names

Fabian
(alt. Fabien, Fabio)
Latin, meaning "one who grows beans."

Fabrice
(alt. Fabrizio)
Latin, meaning "works with his hands."

Faisal
(alt. Faison)
Arabic, meaning "resolute."

Faron
Spanish, meaning "pharaoh," and Gaelic for "thunder."

Farrell
Gaelic, meaning "hero."

Faulkner
Latin, from "falcon."

Faustino
Latin, meaning "fortunate."

Felipe
(alt. Filippo)
Spanish, meaning "lover of horses."

Felix
(alt. Felice)
Italian/Latin, meaning "happy." Felix the Cat was first developed as a cartoon during the silent movie era.

Fennel
Latin, name of a herb.

Ferdinand
(alt. Fernando)
Old German, meaning "bold voyager." Ferdinand was a popular name for Roman emperors and kings of Spain.

Fergus
(alt. Ferguson)

Gaelic, meaning "supreme man." King Fergus is Merida's father in Disney's *Brave*.

Ferris

Gaelic, meaning "rock." The lead character from 1980s cult film *Ferris Bueller's Day Off*.

Fidel

Latin, meaning "faithful." Fidel Castro was president of Cuba from 1976 to 2008.

Finbarr

Gaelic, meaning "fair head."

Finian

Gaelic, meaning "fair." St. Finnian is an important Irish saint.

Finlay
(alt. Finley)

Gaelic, meaning "fair-haired courageous one." Actor Finlay Robertson is known for his role in TV series *Doctor Who*.

Finn
(alt. Fynn)

Irish Gaelic, meaning "fair." Associated with the novel *Huckleberry Finn* and the *Star Wars* series.

Finnegan

Gaelic, meaning "fair." *Finnegans Wake* is a work by James Joyce.

Fintan

Gaelic, meaning "little fair one." Fintan supposedly saved one of Noah's granddaughters from the flood.

Flavio

Latin, meaning "yellow hair." *Flavio* is the name of an opera by Handel.

Florencio
(alt. Florentino)

Latin, meaning "from Florence."

Florian
(alt. Florin)

Slavic/Latin, meaning "flower," though it is a masculine name. Popular in Germany and Switzerland and the name of the patron saint of Poland.

Floyd

Welsh, meaning "gray haired." Floyd is the given name of two title-winning American professional boxers.

Flynn

Gaelic, meaning "with a ruddy complexion." Flynn Rider is Rapunzel's unlikely love interest in Disney's *Tangled*.

Fortunato

Italian, meaning "lucky."

Forrest

(alt. Forest)

Old French, meaning "woodsman." Made popular by the movie *Forrest Gump*.

Foster

Old English, meaning "woodsman."

Fotini

(alt. Fotis)

Greek, meaning "light."

Famous male guitarists

Brian (May)

Carlos (Santana)

Chuck (Berry)

Eddie (Van Halen)

Eric (Clapton)

Frank (Zappa)

Jeff (Beck)

Jimi/Jimmy (Hendrix/Page)

Joe (Satriani)

Keith (Richards)

Prince (Rogers Nelson)

Francesco

(alt. Francis, Francisco, Franco, François)

Latin, meaning "from France." After the election of Pope Francis, Francesco has become the most popular name for baby boys in Italy.

Frank

(alt. Frankie, Franklin, Franz)

Middle English, meaning "free landholder." Famous Franks include singers Frank Sinatra and Frank Zappa, and 32nd US President Franklin D. Roosevelt.

Fraser

(alt. Frasier)

Scottish, meaning "of the forest men." *Frasier* was a 1990s sitcom revolving around main character, Dr. Frasier Crane.

Frederick

(alt. Fred, Freddie, Freddy)

Old German, meaning "peaceful ruler." There is a spelling or pronunciation variation of Frederick in virtually every Western language.

Furman

Old German, meaning "ferryman."

G

Boys' names

Gabino
Latin, meaning "God is my strength."

Gabriel
(alt. Gale)
Hebrew, meaning "hero of God."
An archangel of God.

Gael
(alt. Gale)
English, old reference to the Celts.
Gale has increased in popularity since
The Hunger Games series.

Gage
(alt. Gaige)
Old French, meaning "pledge."

Galen
Greek, meaning "healer." Name of
an ancient Roman philosopher.

Galileo
Italian, meaning "from Galilee."
Galileo Galilei was an important
physicist during the Scientific
Revolution.

Ganesh
Hindi, meaning "Lord of the
throngs." One of the Hindu deities.

Gannon
Irish, meaning "fair skinned."

Gareth
(alt. Garth)
Welsh, meaning "gentle." Also the
name of one of the Knights of the
Round Table.

Garfield
Old English, meaning "spear field."
Also the name of the cartoon cat.

Garland

English, as in "garland of flowers."

Garrett

(alt. Garet, Gared, Garratt, Garrod)

Derived in the Middle Ages from Gerald or Gerard. Garret the Great was a political powerhouse in 15th-century Ireland.

Gary

(alt. Garry, Geary)

Germanic, meaning "spear." The name peaked in popularity in the 1950s, when actor Gary Cooper won an Oscar. Modern Garys include actor Gary Oldman.

Gaspar

(alt. Gaspard)

Persian, meaning "treasurer." A children's cartoon character from *Gaspar and Lisa*.

Gaston

From the region in the south of France.

Gavin

(alt. Gawain)

Scottish/Welsh, meaning "little falcon." Gavin DeGraw and Gavin Christopher are both singers.

Gene

Greek, shortened form of Eugene, meaning "well born." Made popular by actor and dancer Gene Kelly.

Gennaro

Italian, meaning "of Janus."

Geoffrey

(abbrev. Geoff)

Old German, meaning "peace." Actor Geoffrey Rush appeared in *Shine* and the *Pirates of the Caribbean* series.

George

(alt. Giorgio)

Greek, meaning "farmer." Queen Elizabeth's great-grandson Prince George is third in line to the British throne.

Gerald

(alt. Geraldo, Gerard, Gerardo, Gerhard)

Old German, meaning "spear ruler." Former President of the United States Gerald Ford is the only person to have served as both president and vice president without being elected to either position, thanks to two infamous resignations before him.

Geronimo

Italian, meaning "sacred name." Geronimo led the Apache Indians against the Spanish in the 19th century.

Gerry

English, meaning "independent." Famous Gerrys include singer Gerry Rafferty.

Gert

Old German, meaning "strong spear."

Gervase

Old German, meaning "with honor." Gervase Peterson is a long-time *Survivor* contestant.

Giacomo

Italian, meaning "God's son." Legendary womanizer Casanova's full name was actually Giacomo Girolame Casanova.

Gibson

English, meaning "son of Gilbert." The name of a legendary guitar company.

Gideon

Hebrew, meaning "tree cutter." Found in the Bible.

Gilbert
(alt. *Gilberto*)

French, meaning "bright promise." One half of the famous comedy opera duo Gilbert and Sullivan.

Giles

Greek, meaning "small goat."

Gino

Italian, meaning "well born."

Giovanni

Italian form of John, meaning "God is gracious." Actor Giovanni Ribisi is known for his roles in *Friends* and *Avatar*.

Giulio

Italian, meaning "youthful."

Giuseppe

Italian form of Joseph, meaning "Jehovah increases."

Glen
(alt. *Glenn, Glyn*)

English, from the word "glen." Glenn Miller was a world-renowned big band director and composer.

Godfrey

German, meaning "peace of God." Now associated woith the comedian Godfrey.

Gordon

Gaelic, meaning "large fortification." Gordon Ramsay is a chef and reality TV star.

Gottlieb

German, meaning "good love." Also one of composer Mozart's birth names.

Graeme
(alt. *Graham*)

English, meaning "gravelled area."

Grant

English, from the word "grant."

Granville

English, meaning "gravelly town." Granville Woods was the first African-American electrical engineer after the Civil War.

Gray
(alt. Grey)

English, from the word "gray."

Grayson

English, meaning "son of gray."

Green

English, from the word "green." The Green Lantern is a superhero from DC Comics.

Gregory
(alt. Gregorio, Grieg; abbrev. Greg)

English, meaning "watcher." Actor Gregory Peck was known for his role in *To Kill A Mockingbird*.

Griffin

English, from the word "griffin." A mythological creature.

Guido

Italian, meaning "guide." Popularized after the show *Jersey Shore*.

Guillaume

French form of William, meaning "strong protector."

Gulliver

English, meaning "glutton." Made popular after the publication of *Gulliver's Travels* by Jonathan Swift.

Gunther

German, meaning "warrior." Gunther von Hagans is the *Body Works* artist.

Gurpreet

Indian, meaning "love of the teacher."

Gustave
(abbrev. Gus)

Scandinavian, meaning "royal staff."

Guy

Englishform of Guido, meaning "guide." Chef Guy Fieri regularly appears on the Food Network.

 Boys' names

Habib

Arabic, meaning "beloved one."

Haden
(alt. Haiden, Hayden, Haydn)

English, meaning "hedged valley."

Hades

Greek, meaning "sightless." Name of the underworld in Greek mythology.

Hadrian

From Hadria, a north Italian city. The name of an influential Roman emperor.

Hadwin

Old English, meaning "friend in war."

Hakeem

Arabic, meaning "wise and insightful." Actor Hakeem Kae-Kazim is known for his role in *Hotel Rwanda*.

Hamid

Arabic, meaning "praiseworthy." Hamid Karzai was the president of Afghanistan 2004–14.

Hamilton

Old English, meaning "flat-topped hill." Alexander Hamilton was one of the nation's Founding Fathers.

Hamish

Scottish form of James, meaning "he who supplants."

Hampus

Swedish form of Homer, meaning "pledge." Hampus Lindholm currently plays for the Anaheim Ducks.

Hamza

Arabic, meaning "lamb." Also a letter in the Arabic alphabet.

Han
(alt. Hannes, Hans)
Scandinavian, meaning "the Lord is gracious." Han Solo is a central character in the *Star Wars* films.

Hank
German, form of Henry, meaning "home ruler." Singer Hank Williams was a country superstar.

Hansel
German, meaning "the Lord is gracious." *Hansel and Gretel* is a children's fairy tale by the Brothers Grimm.

Hardy
English, meaning "tough."

Harlan
English, meaning "dweller by the boundary wood."

Harland
Old English, meaning "army land." KFC was founded by Colonel Harland David Sanders.

Harley
Old English, meaning "hare meadow." Associated with the Harley Davidson motorcycle company.

Harmon
Old German, meaning "soldier."

Harold
Scandinavian, meaning "army ruler." Actor Harold Ramis was known for his roles in *Ghostbusters* and *Stripes*.

Harrison
(alt. Harison)
Old English, meaning "son of Harry." Famous Harrisons include actor Harrison Ford, and it is the middle name of the son of Prince Harry and Megan Markle.

Harry
Old German, form of Henry, meaning "home ruler." Famous Harrys include fictional character Harry Potter and singer Harry Styles.

Hart
Old English, meaning "stag."

Harvey
Old English, meaning "strong and worthy." The title character of the film *Harvey*, starring James Stewart.

Haskell
Hebrew, meaning "intellect."

Hassan
Arabic, meaning "handsome." Hassan Rouhani is the current president of Iran.

Heart
English, from the word "heart."

Heath

English, meaning "heath" or "moor." Actor Heath Ledger was known for his roles in *Brokeback Mountain* and *The Dark Knight*.

Heathcliff

English, meaning "cliff near a heath." Also the main male character in Emily Bronte's novel *Wuthering Heights*.

Heber

Hebrew, meaning "partner."

Hector

Greek, meaning "steadfast."

Henry
(alt. Hal, Hale, Henri, Hendrik, Hendrix)

Old German, meaning "home ruler." Eight kings of England were called Henry. Harry is often used as a name by boys given the name Henry, as with Prince Harry, who is officially Prince Henry of Wales.

Henson

English, meaning "son of Henry."

Herbert
(alt., Herb, Heriberto; abbrev. Bert, Herbie)

Old German, meaning "illustrious warrior." Herbert Hoover was the 31st President of the United States.

Herman
(alt. Herminio, Hermon)

Old German, meaning "soldier." Herman Melville was the author of *Moby-Dick*.

Hermes

Greek, meaning "messenger." Hermes was the messenger of the gods in Greek mythology.

Herschel

Yiddish, meaning "deer."

Hezekiah

Hebrew, meaning "God gives strength."

Hideki

Japanese, meaning "excellent trees." The prime minister of Japan during World War II was Hideki Tojo.

Hideo

Japanese, meaning "excellent name."

Hilario

Latin, meaning "cheerful, happy."

Hilary
(alt. Hillary)

English, meaning "cheerful." Sir Edmund Hillary became the first Westerner to reach the summit of Mount Everest, in 1953.

Hillel

Hebrew, meaning "greatly praised."

Hilliard

Old German, meaning "battle guard."

Hilton

Old English, meaning "hill settlement." The name of a large hotel chain.

Hiram
(alt. Hyrum)

Hebrew, meaning "exalted brother."

Hiro

Spanish, meaning "sacred name." Hiro is a character on *Heroes*.

Hiroshi

Japanese, meaning "generous."

Hirsch

Yiddish, meaning "deer."

Hobart

English, meaning "bright and shining intellect."

Hodge

English, meaning "son of Roger."

Hogan

Gaelic, meaning "youth." Became well known after the success of sitcom *Hogan's Heroes* in the 1960s. Also made famous by wrestler Hulk Hogan.

Holden

English, meaning "deep valley." Holden Caulfield is the teenage protagonist of *The Catcher in the Rye*.

Hollis

Old English, meaning "holly tree."

Homer

Greek, meaning "pledge." Famous Homers include the ancient Greek poet, and Homer Simpson from *The Simpsons*.

Honorius

Latin, meaning "honorable."

Horace

Latin, common name of the Roman poet Quintus Horatius Flaccus.

Houston

Old English, meaning "Hugh's town."

Howard

Old English, meaning "noble watchman." Famous Howards include Howard Carter, who discovered the tomb of King Tut, and Howard Hughes, the aviator and movie maker.

Howell

Welsh, meaning "eminent and remarkable."

Hoyt

Norse, meaning "spirit" or "soul," or Old English meaning "hill inhabitant." Hoyt Fortenberry is a character in *True Blood*.

Hristo

From Christo, meaning "follower of Christ."

Hubert

German, meaning "bright and shining intellect." Givenchy's founder was Count Hubert de Givenchy.

Hudson

Old English, meaning "son of Hugh." Associated with the Hudson River.

Hugh

(alt. Hugo, Huw, Ugo)
Old German, meaning "soul, mind, and intellect." Famous Hughs include actors Hugh Jackman, Hugh Laurie, and Hugh Grant.

Humbert

Old German, meaning "famous giant." Became well known due to the paedophile protagonist of Vladimir Nabokov's *Lolita*.

Humphrey

Old German, meaning "peaceful warrior." Actor Humphrey Bogart is best known for his role in *Casablanca*.

Hunter

English, from the word "hunter." Name of singer Hunter Hayes.

Hurley

Gaelic, meaning "sea tide."

Huxley

Old English, meaning "Hugh's meadow."

I Boys' names

Iago

Spanish, meaning "he who supplants." Also the name of the villain in Shakespeare's *Othello*.

Ian
(alt. Iain, Ion)

Gaelic, variant of John, meaning "God is gracious." Novelist Ian Fleming wrote the "James Bond" novels.

Ianto

Welsh, meaning "gift of God."

Ibrahim

Arabic, meaning "father of many." An Arabic name for the father of Islam, Abraham.

Ichabod

Hebrew, meaning "glory is good." Also the name of the protagonist in *The Legend of Sleepy Hollow*.

Ichiro

Japanese, meaning "firstborn son."

Idris

Welsh, meaning "fiery leader." Actor Idris Elba is known for his roles in *Luther* and *Mandela: Long Walk to Freedom*.

Ifan

Welsh variant of John, meaning "God is gracious."

Ignacio

Latin, meaning "ardent" or "burning."

Ignatz

German, meaning "fiery."

Igor

Russian, meaning "Ing's soldier."

Ikaika

Hawaiian, meaning "strong."

Ike

Hebrew, short for Isaac, meaning "laughter." Famous Ikes include singer Ike Turner and former US President Dwight D. Eisenhower (known as Ike).

Ilan

Hebrew, meaning "tree."

Ilias

Greek variant of Elijah, Hebrew, meaning "the Lord is my God."

Indiana

Latin, meaning "from India." Also the name of a US state.

Indigo

English, describing a deep blue color derived from a plant.

Indio

Spanish, meaning "indigenous people."

Ingo

Danish, meaning "meadow."

Inigo

Spanish, meaning "fiery." Inigo Montoya is a character in *The Princess Bride*.

Ioannis

Greek, meaning "the Lord is gracious."

Ira

Hebrew, meaning "full grown and watchful."

Irvin
(alt. Irving, Irwin)

Gaelic, meaning "green and fresh water." Composer Irving Berlin is known for songs such as "White Christmas."

Isaac
(alt. Isaak)

Hebrew, meaning "laughter." Isaac was the son of Abraham and Sarah in the Bible and the Qur'an.

Isadore
(alt. Isidore, Isidro)

Greek, meaning "gift of Isis."

Isai
(alt. Isaiah, Isaias, Izaiah)

Arabic, meaning "protection and security."

Iser

Yiddish, meaning "God wrestler."

Ishmael
(alt. Ismael)

Hebrew, meaning "God listens." The narrator and protagonist of *Moby-Dick*, by Herman Melville.

Israel

Hebrew, meaning "God perseveres."
Also the name of the country.

Istvan

Hungarian variant of Stephen,
meaning "crowned."

Itai

Hebrew, meaning "the Lord is with
me."

Ivan

A Slavic version of John, meaning
"God is gracious." Several Russian
tsars bore the name, including the
infamous Ivan the Terrible. Ivan
Rodriguez was a Major League
Baseball player for many years.

Ivanhoe

Russian, meaning "God is gracious."
Also title of the novel by Walter
Scott.

Ivey

English, variant of Ivy.

Ivo

French, from the word "yves,"
meaning "yew tree."

Ivor

Scandinavian, meaning "yew."
Associated with the Ivor Novello
songwriting awards.

Ivory

English, from the word "ivory."

J

Boys' names

Jabari

Swahili, meaning "valiant."

Jabez

Hebrew, meaning "borne in pain."

Jace
(alt. Jaece, Jase, Jayce)

Hebrew, meaning "healer."

Jacek
(alt. Jacirto)

Polish, meaning "hyacinth." Derived from the Greek name Hyakinthos, which comes from a myth about a beautiful boy.

Jack
(alt. Jackie, Jacky, Jacques, Jaquez)

From the Hebrew John, meaning "God is gracious." Famous Jacks include actors Jack Black, Jack Nicholson, and Jack Lemmon.

Jackson
(alt. Jaxon)

English, meaning "son of Jack." Artist Jackson Pollock is known for his large, paint-splashed paintings.

Jacob
(alt. Jaco, Jacobo, Jago)

Hebrew, meaning "he who supplants." A main character in the *Twilight* series.

Jaden
(alt. Jadyn, Jaeden, Jaiden, Jaidyn, Jayden, Jaydin)

Hebrew, meaning "Jehovah has heard." Will Smith and Jada Pinkett Smith's son is Jaden.

Jafar

Arabic, meaning "stream." The villain in Disney's *Aladdin*.

Jagger

Old English, meaning "one who cuts." Made famous by Rolling Stones singer Mick Jagger.

Jaheem
(alt. Jaheim)

Hebrew, meaning "raised up."

Jahir

Hindi, meaning "jewel."

Jaime
(alt. Jamie))

Variant for James, meaning "he who supplants." "J'aime" is also French for "I love."

Jair
(alt. Jairo)

Hebrew, meaning "God enlightens."

Jake

Shortened form of Jacob, meaning "he who supplants." Famous Jakes include actor Jake Gyllenhaal and pitcher Jake Peavy.

Jalen

American English, meaning "healer" or "tranquil." Derives from the Greek Galen.

Jali

Gujarati, meaning "latticed screen."

Jalon

Greek, meaning "healer" or "tranquil."

Jamaal
(alt. Jamal, Jamar, Jamarcus, Jamari, Jamarion, Jamir)

Arabic, meaning "handsome." Jamar is a modern variant of the name.

James
(abbrev. Jamie, Jaimie, Jim, Jimmy)

English, meaning "he who supplants." Famous Jameses include actors James Franco, James Coburn, and Jim Carey, and fictional characters James Bond and James T. Kirk.

Jameson
(alt. Jamison)

English, meaning "son of James." Associated with Jameson Irish Whiskey.

Jamil

Arabic, meaning "handsome."

Jamin

Hebrew, meaning "son of the right hand."

Jan
(alt. Janko, János)

Slavic, from John, meaning "the Lord is gracious." Also a term of endearment in Arabic, meaning "dear."

Janus

Latin, meaning "gateway." Roman god of doors, beginnings and endings.

Japheth
(alt. Japhet)

Hebrew, meaning "comely." One of the sons of Noah.

Jared
(alt. Jarem, Jaren, Jaret, Jarod, Jarrod)

Hebrew, meaning "descending." Actor Jared Leto appeared in *Dallas Buyers' Club*.

Jarlath

Gaelic, from Iarlaith, from St. Iarlaithe mac Loga.

Jarom

Greek, meaning "to raise and exalt." One of the prophets in the Book of Mormon.

Jarrell

Variant of Gerald, meaning "spear ruler."

Jarrett

Old English, meaning "spearbrave."

Jarvis

Old German, meaning "with honor."

Jason
(alt. Jayce)

Greek, meaning "healer." Famous Jasons include actors Jason Sudeikis and Jason Bateman, and singer Jason Derulo.

Jasper

Greek, meaning "treasure holder" or "speckled stone." Jasper as a stone has been used for jewelry for thousands of years.

Javen

Arabic, meaning "youth." One of Noah's grandsons in the Bible.

Javier

Spanish, meaning "bright." Actor Javier Bardem appeared in *Skyfall*.

Jay

Latin, meaning "jaybird." Associated with rapper Jay-Z.

Jaylan
(alt. Jaylen, Jalon)

Greek, meaning "healer."

Jeevan

Indian, meaning "life."

Jefferson

English, meaning "son of Jeffrey." Thomas Jefferson was the third president of the United States.

Jeffrey
(abbrev. Jeff)

Old German, meaning "peace."
Famous Jeffs include actors Jeff
Bridges and Jeff Daniels.

Jensen
(alt. Jenson)

Scandinavian, meaning "son of Jan."
Famous Jensens include actor Jensen
Ackles and Formula 1 driver Jenson
Button.

Jeremy
(alt. Jem)

Hebrew, meaning "the Lord exalts."
Famous Jeremys include Jeremy
Renner and Jeremy Irons.

Jeriah

Hebrew, meaning "Jehovah has seen."

Jericho

Arabic, meaning "city of the moon."
Site of the epic biblical Battle of
Jericho.

Jermaine

Latin, meaning "brotherly." Jermaine
Jackson was one of the original
members of the Jackson Five.

Jerome

Greek, meaning "sacred name."

Jerry

English, from Gerald, meaning
"spear ruler." Famous Jerrys include
presenter Jerry Singer, comedian Jerry
Seinfeld, and the film *Jerry Maguire*.

Jesse

Hebrew, meaning "the Lord exists."
Famous Jesses include outlaw Jesse
James.

Jesus

Hebrew, meaning "the Lord is
Salvation" and the Son of God.

Jet
(alt. Jett)

English, meaning "black gemstone."

Jethro

Hebrew, meaning "eminent."
Famous Jethros include the band
Jethro Tull, and the father-in-law of
Moses in the Bible.

Jiri
(alt. Jiro)

Czech, meaning "farmer."

Joachim

Hebrew, meaning "established by
God." The name of the Virgin Mary's
father in the Bible.

Joah
(alt. João)

Hebrew, meaning "God is gracious."

Joaquin

Hebrew, meaning "established by God." Academy Award-winner Joaquin Phoenix changed his name to "Leaf" as a child to match his siblings River and Rain.

Joel

Hebrew, meaning "Jehovah is the Lord." Famous Joels include comedian Joel McHale and singer Joel Madden.

John

(alt. Jon, Johnny)

Hebrew, meaning "God is gracious." Famous Johns include musicians John Lennon and John Legend, and comedian Jon Stewart. Actor Johnny Depp and singer Johnny Cash are both also Johns by birth.

Jolyon

English, meaning "young."

Jonah

(alt. Jonas)

Hebrew, meaning "dove." A figure in the Bible who was swallowed by a whale.

Jonathan

(alt. Johnathan, Johnathon, Jonathon; abbrev. Jon, Johnny, Jonny, Jonty)

Hebrew, meaning "God is gracious." Famous Jonathans include actors Jonathan Taylor Thomas and Jonathan Rhys Meyers, and author Jonathan Swift.

Jordan

(alt. Jory, Judd)

Hebrew, meaning "downflowing." Michael Jordan is a legendary basketball player.

Jorge

From George, meaning "farmer." Actor Jorge Garcia is known for his role as Hurley in *Lost*.

José

Spanish variant of Joseph, meaning "God increases." Associated with Jose Cuervo tequila.

Joseph

(abbrev. Joe, Joey, Joss)

Hebrew, meaning "Jehovah increases." Famous Josephs include actor Joseph Gordon-Levitt and baseball legend Joe DiMaggio.

Joshua

(alt. Joshué; abbrev. Josh)

Hebrew, meaning "Jehovah is salvation." The leader of the Israelites after Moses' death in the Bible. Actor Josh Hutcherson is known for his role in *The Hunger Games* trilogy.

Josiah

Hebrew, meaning "God helps." One of the kings of Judah in the Bible.

Jovan

Latin, meaning "the supreme God."

Joweese

Native American, meaning "chirping bird." More commonly used for girls originally, it has now become a boys' name.

Joyce

Latin, meaning "joy." Used for boys and girls.

Juan

Spanish variant of John, meaning "God is gracious." Juan Pablo Galavis was a notorious contestant on the TV show *The Bachelor*.

Jubal

Hebrew, meaning "ram's horn."

Jude

Hebrew, meaning "praise" or "thanks." Associated with the Beatles' song "Hey Jude."

Judson

Variant of Jude, meaning "praise" or "thanks."

Julian

(alt. Julien, Julio; abbrev. Jules)

Greek, meaning "belonging to Julius." The original calendar in the Roman Empire was the Julian calendar.

Julius

Latin, meaning "youthful." Julius Caesar was a Roman emperor.

Junior

Latin, meaning "the younger one." Can also be used as a suffix to names to denote a name that has been passed down generations—for example James Earl Carter, Sr. was the father of US President James Earl Carter, Jr.

Junius

Latin, meaning "young."

Jupiter

Latin, meaning "the supreme God." Jupiter was king of the Roman gods and the god of thunder.

Juraj

Hebrew, meaning "God is my judge."

Jurgen

German form of George, meaning "farmer."

Justice

English, from the word "justice," meaning a set of moral values, ethics, and law.

Justin

(alt. Justus)

Latin, meaning "just and upright." Famous Justins include singers Justin Timberlake and Justin Bieber.

Juwan

Hebrew, meaning "the Lord is gracious."

K

Boys' names

Kabelo
African, meaning "gift."

Kade
Scottish, meaning "from the wetlands."

Kadeem
Arabic, meaning "one who serves." Actor Kadeem Hardison is known for his role in *A Different World*.

Kaden
(alt. Kadin, Kaeden, Kaedin, Kaiden)
Arabic, meaning "companion."

Kadir
Arabic, meaning "capable and competent."

Kafka
Czech, meaning "bird-like." Name of the influential author Franz Kafka.

Kahekili
Hawaiian, meaning "the thunder." Also the name of several kings of Maui.

Kai
Greek, meaning "keeper of the keys." Kai also means "dog" in Cornish, "ocean water" in Hawaiian, and "food" in Maori.

Kaito
Japanese, meaning "ocean and sake dipper." One of the most popular names for boys in Japan.

Kalani
Hawaiian, meaning "sky."

Kale
German, meaning "free man."

Kaleb
Hebrew, meaning "dog" or "aggressive." Also an alternate spelling for Caleb.

Kalen
(alt. Kaelen, Kalan)
Gaelic, meaning "uncertain."

Kaleo
Hawaiian, meaning "the voice." Kaleo Kanahele is a silver medal-winning paralympian in volleyball.

Kamari
Indian, meaning "the enemy of desire."

Kamil
Arabic, meaning "perfection"; Polish/Slovakian, meaning "religious service attender."

Kane
Gaelic, meaning "little battler." The title character of the film *Citizen Kane*.

Kani
Hawaiian, meaning "sound."

Kanye
Town in Botswana. Made popular by rapper Kanye West.

Kareem
(alt. Karim)
Arabic, meaning "generous." Kareem Abdul-Jabur is a legendary basketball player.

Karl
(alt. Karlson)
Old German, meaning "free man." Actor Karl Urban is known for his roles in *The Lord of the Rings* and *Star Trek*.

Kavon
Gaelic, meaning "handsome."

Kayden
Arabic, meaning "companion."

Kazimierz
Polish, meaning "declares peace."

Kazuki
Japanese, meaning "radiant hope."

Kazuo
Japanese, meaning "harmonious man." Depending on the characters/spellings used, Kazuo can also mean "first son" or "first in leadership."

Keagan
(alt. Keegan, Kegan)
Gaelic, meaning "small flame."

Keane
Gaelic, meaning "fighter."

Keanu
Hawaiian, meaning "breeze." Actor Keanu Reeves is known for his roles in *Speed* and *The Matrix* trilogy.

Keary

Gaelic, meaning "black-haired."

Keaton

English, meaning "place of hawks."

Keeler

Gaelic, meaning "beautiful and graceful."

Keenan
(alt. Kenan, Keenen)

Gaelic, meaning "little ancient one." Keenen Ivory Wayans is one of the Wayans comedy brothers.

Keiji

Japanese, meaning "govern with discretion."

Keir

Gaelic, meaning "dark-haired" or "dark-skinned."

Keith

Gaelic, meaning "woodland." Keith Richards is one of the legendary members of the Rolling Stones.

Kekoa
(alt. Koa)

Hawaiian, meaning "brave one" or "soldier."

Kelby

Old English, meaning "farmhouse near the stream."

Kell
(alt. Kellan, Kellen, Kelley, Kelly, Kiel)

Norse, meaning "spring." Associated with the ancient Book of Kells.

Kelsey

Old English, meaning "victorious ship." Actor Kelsey Grammer is known for his roles in *Cheers* and *Frasier*.

Kelton

Old English, meaning "town of the keels."

Kelvin

Old English, meaning "friend of ships." A kelvin is a unit of temperature measurement.

Kendal

Old English, meaning "the Kent river valley."

Kendon

Old English, meaning "brave guard."

Kendrick

Gaelic, meaning "royal ruler."

Kenelm

Old English, meaning "bold."

Kenji

Japanese, meaning "intelligent second son." Also the name of a period in Japanese history in the 13th century.

Kennedy

Gaelic, meaning "helmet head."
The Kennedy family is a prominent
American Catholic dynasty, whose
members included the 35th
President of the United States, John
F. Kennedy.

Kenneth
(alt. Kenne; abbrev. Ken)

Gaelic, meaning "born of fire." Sir
Kenneth Branagh is an acclaimed
actor of stage and screen.

Kennison

English, meaning "son of Kenneth."

Kent

English, meaning "rim or border."
Associated with Clark Kent, aka
Superman.

Kenton

English, meaning "town of Ken."

Kenya
(alt. Kenyatta, Kenyon)

From the country and mountain in
Africa.

Kenzo

Japanese, meaning "wise." Kenzo is
the name of a fashion brand.

Keola

Hawaiian, meaning "life."

Keon
(alt. Keoni)

Persian, meaning "King of Kings."
In Hawaiian, the name also means
"God is gracious."

Kepler

German, meaning "hat maker."

Kermit
(alt. Kerwin)

Gaelic, meaning "without envy."
Associated with Kermit the Frog.

Kerr

English, meaning "wetland." Kerr
Smith is an American actor.

Keshav

Indian, meaning "beautiful haired."
One of the names for Vishnu in the
Hindu religion.

Kevin

Gaelic, meaning "handsome
beloved." Famous Kevins include
actors Kevin Bacon and Kevin Kline.

Khalid
(alt. Khalif)

Arabic, meaning "immortal." Actor
Khalid Abdalla is known for his roles
in *United 93* and *The Kite Runner*.

Khalil

Arabic, meaning "friend." Khalil
Gibran is an influential poet, writer,
and philosopher.

Kian
(alt. Keyon, Kyan)

Persian, meaning "king or realm." In Ireland, the same spelling also means "ancient."

Kiefer

German, meaning "barrel maker." *24* star Kiefer Sutherland's full name is Kiefer William Frederick Dempsey George Rufus Sutherland.

Kieran
(alt. Kieron, Kyron)

Gaelic, meaning "black." Actor Kieran Culkin is known for his role in *Scott Pilgrim vs. the World*.

Kijana

Swahili, meaning "youth."

Kilby

English, from the town of the same name.

Kilian

Irish, meaning "bright-headed."

Kimani

African, meaning "beautiful and sweet."

King

English, meaning "male ruler of state."

Kingsley

English, meaning "the king's meadow." Kingsley Shacklebolt is a character in the *Harry Potter* series.

Kirby

German, meaning "settlement by a church." Also the name of a small, pink, bubble-like video game character.

Kirk

Old German, meaning "church." Famous Kirks include Kirk Douglas and Captain James T. Kirk from *Star Trek*.

Klaus

German, meaning "victorious."

Kobe
(alt. Koda, Kody)

Japanese, meaning "a Japanese city." Legendary player Kobe Bryant retired from professional basketball in 2016.

Kofi

Ghanaian, meaning "born on Friday." Kofi Annan was the secretary general of the UN until 2006.

Kohana

Japanese, meaning "little flower."

Kojo

Ghanaian, meaning "Monday."

Korben
(alt. Korbin)

Gaelic, meaning "a steep hill." Korben Dallas is a character in *The Fifth Element*.

Kramer

German, meaning "shopkeeper." Kramer is a character from *Seinfeld*.

Kurt

German, meaning "courageous advice." Famous Kurts include *Glee* character Kurt, actor Kurt Russell, and the late Nirvana singer Kurt Cobain.

Kurtis

French, meaning "courtier."

Names of poets

Alfred (Lord Tennyson)
Allen (Ginsberg)
Dylan (Thomas)
Geoffrey (Chaucer)
Langston (Hughes)
Ralph (Waldo Emerson)
Robert (Burns)
Seamus (Heaney)
Walt (Whitman)
William (Wordsworth)

Kwame

Ghanaian, meaning "born on Saturday."

Kyden

English, meaning "narrow little fire."

Kyle
(alt. Kylan, Kyleb, Kyler)

Gaelic, meaning "narrow and straight." Actor Kyle Massey is known for his roles on The Disney Channel.

Kyllion

Irish, meaning "war."

Kylo
(alt. Kyloh)

American English, from the Latin word for "sky." Kylo Ren is a main character in the modern *Star Wars* films.

Kyree

From Cree, a Canadian tribe.

Kyros

Greek, meaning "legitimate power."

L
Boys' names

Laban
Hebrew, meaning "white." Laban is the brother of Rebekah in the Bible.

Lachlan
Gaelic, meaning "from the land of lakes."

Lacy
Old French, after the place in France. Masculine form of Lacey.

Lalit
Hindi, meaning "beautiful."

Lamar
(alt. Lemar)
Old German, meaning "water." Lamar Odom is known for his marriage to Khloe Kardashian and his skills as a basketball player.

Lambert
Scandinavian, meaning "land brilliant."

Lambros
Greek, meaning "brilliant and radiant."

Lamont
Old Norse, meaning "law man."

Lance
French, meaning "land." Lance Armstrong is a disgraced former racing cyclist.

Lancelot
Variant of Lance, meaning "land." The name of one of the Knights of the Round Table.

Landen
(alt. Lando, Landon, Landyn, Langdon)
English, meaning "long hill."

Lane
(alt. Layne)
English, from the word "lane."

Lannie
(alt. Lanny)

German, meaning "precious." Also a nickname for Roland or Orlando.

Larkin

Gaelic, meaning "rough" or "fierce." Philip Larkin was a famous poet.

Laron

French, meaning "thief."

Lasse

Finnish, meaning "girl." (Still, ironically, a boy's name.) Lasse Holstrom is a film director and Lasse Viren one of the all-time great long distance runners.

Laszlo

Hungarian, meaning "glorious rule."

Lathyn

Latin, meaning "fighter."

Latif

Arabic, meaning "gentle."

Laurel

Latin, meaning "bay." One of the founders of Jamaican ska music was Laurel Aitken. More commonly a girls' name.

Laurent

French, from Laurence, meaning "man from Laurentum." The founder of fashion line YSL was Yves Saint Laurent.

Lawrence
(alt. Lars, Lawrence; abbrev. Larry)

Latin, meaning "man from Laurentum." Actor Laurence Olivier was a stage legend also known for his roles in dozens of Hollywood movies. Larry King is a longstanding live TV presenter.

Lawson

Old English, meaning "son of Lawrence."

Lazarus

Hebrew, meaning "God is my help."

Leandro

Latin, meaning "lion man."

Lear

German, meaning "of the meadow." The title character in Shakespeare's play *King Lear*.

Lee
(alt. Leigh)

Old English, meaning "meadow" or "valley." Famous Lees include actor Lee Marvin and JFK assassin Lee Harvey Oswald.

Leib

Yiddish, meaning "lion."

Leif
(alt. Leiv, Lief, Liev)

Scandinavian, meaning "heir." Actor Liev Schreiber is known for his roles in *X-Men Origins: Wolverine*, and the *Scream* trilogy.

Leith

From the Scottish town of the same name.

Lennox

(alt. Lenny)

Gaelic, meaning "with many elm trees." Famous Lennoxes include boxer Lennox Lewis.

Leo

Latin, meaning "lion." Also the name of the star sign.

Leon

Latin, meaning "lion." Associated with the band Kings of Leon.

Leonard

Old German, meaning "lion strength." Actor Leonard Nimoy was known for his role in *Star Trek*.

Leonardo

Italian, meaning "bold lion." Artist Leonardo da Vinci painted the *Mona Lisa*.

Leopold

German, meaning "brave people."

Leroy

French, meaning "king." The title character of the song "Bad Bad Leroy Brown."

Lesley

(alt. Leslie; abbrev. Les)

Scottish, meaning "holly garden." Used for boys and girls.

Lester

English, meaning "from Leicester."

Lewis

French, meaning "renowned fighter." Famous Lewises include comedian Lewis Black and author Lewis Carroll.

Lexar

(alt. Lex, Lexer)

Shortened form of Alexander, meaning "man's defender."

Liam

German, meaning "helmet." Famous Liams include actor Liam Neeson and One Direction member Liam Payne.

Lincoln

English, meaning "lake colony." Abraham Lincoln was the 16th President of the United States.

Lindsay

(alt. Lindsey)

Scottish, meaning "linden tree." Singer Lindsey Buckingham is a founding member of Fleetwood Mac. Used for boys and girls.

Linus

Latin, meaning "lion." A character in the *Peanuts* cartoon.

Lionel

English, meaning "lion." Famous Lionels include singer Lionel Richie, and composer Lionel Bart.

Llewellyn

Welsh, meaning "like a lion."

Lloyd

Welsh, meaning "gray-haired and sacred." Andrew Lloyd Webber is the composer of *Cats* and other musicals.

Logan

Gaelic, meaning "hollow." Increased in popularity after 2017's *Logan* Wolverine film.

Lonnie

English, meaning "lion strength."

Lorcan

Gaelic, meaning "little fierce one."

Louis
(alt. Lou, Louie, Luigi, Luis)

French, meaning "famous warrior." Famous Louises include fifth in line to the British throne Prince Louis and designer Louis Vuitton.

Lucas
(alt. Lukas, Luca)

English, meaning "man from Luciana." George Lucas is the legendary *Star Wars* producer.

Lucian
(alt. Lucio)

Latin, meaning "light."

Ludwig

German, meaning "famous fighter." Ludwig van Beethoven was a hugely influential composer.

Luke
(alt. Luc, Luka)

Latin, meaning "from Lucanus" (in southern Italy). Famous Lukes include the Gospel of Luke from the Bible, *Star Wars* character Luke Skywalker, and actor Luke Perry.

Lupe

Latin, meaning "wolf." Lupe Fiasco is a rapper.

Luther

German, meaning "soldier of the people." Superman's arch-enemy is supervillain Lex Luther.

Lyle

French, meaning "the island." Lyle Lovett is a country singer-songwriter and actor.

Lyn
(alt. Lyndon)

Spanish, meaning "pretty." Used for both boys and girls.

M Boys' names

Mac
(alt. Mack, Mackie)
Scottish, meaning "son of."

Macaulay
Scottish, meaning "son of the phantom." Actor Macaulay Culkin starred in the *Home Alone* films.

Mace
English, meaning "heavy staff" or "club." Also a shortened form of Mason.

Mackenzie
Scottish, meaning "the fair one." Actor Mackenzie Crook is known for his roles in *Pirates of the Caribbean* and *Game of Thrones*.

Mackland
Scottish, meaning "land of Mac."

Macon
French, from the name of towns in France and Georgia.

Macsen
Scottish, meaning "son of Mac."

Madden
(alt. Mads)
Irish, meaning "descendant of the hound." Associated with the Madden NFL gaming series.

Maddox
(alt. Maddux)
English, meaning "good" or "generous." Derived from Madoc, who was a legendary Welsh prince. Name chosen by Angelina Jolie for her first adopted child, now Maddox Jolie-Pitt.

Madison
(alt. Madsen)

Irish, meaning "son of Madden." James Madison was the fourth President of the United States.

Magnus
(alt. Manus)

Latin, meaning "great." Popular name in Scandinavia.

Maguire

Gaelic, meaning "son of the beige one." The title character of the movie *Jerry Maguire*.

Mahesh

Hindi, meaning "great ruler." One of the names for Lord Shiva in the Hindu faith.

Mahir

Arabic, meaning "skillful."

Mahlon

Hebrew, meaning "sickness."

Mahmoud

Arabic, meaning "praiseworthy." Mahmoud Ahmadinejad was the president of Iran until 2013.

Mahoney

Irish, meaning "bear."

Major

English, from the word "major."

Makal

From Michael, meaning "close to God."

Makani

Hawaiian, meaning "wind."

Makis

Hebrew, meaning "gift from God."

Mako

Hebrew, meaning "God is with us."

Malachi
(alt. Malachy)

Irish, meaning "messenger of God." The name of a Jewish prophet in the Bible.

Malcolm

English, meaning "Columba's servant." Well-known Malcolms include activist Malcolm X, and sitcom *Malcolm in the Middle*.

Mali

Arabic, meaning "full and rich." Also the name of a West African republic.

Manfred

Old German, meaning "man of peace." Associated with the band Manfred Mann.

Manish
(alt. Manesh)

English, meaning "manly."

Manley

English, meaning "manly and brave."

Mannix

Gaelic, meaning "little monk." Associated with the show *Mannix*.

Manoi
(alt. Manos)

Japanese, meaning "love springing from intellect."

Manuel

Hebrew, meaning "God is with us."

Manus

Gaelic, meaning "great." Popular during the Viking period.

Manzi

Italian, meaning "steer."

Marcel
(alt. Marcelino, Marcello)

French, meaning "little warrior." Marcel Marceau was perhaps the most famous mime of all time.

Mariano

Latin, meaning "from the god Mars." Also a tribute to the Virgin Mary.

Mario
(alt. Marius)

Latin, meaning "manly." Famous Marios include presenter Mario Lopez, and Nintendo character Mario.

Mark
(alt. Marc, Marco, Marcus, Marek, Markus)

English, meaning "from the god Mars." Famous Marks include the Gospel of Mark in the Bible, and actors Mark Hamill and Mark Wahlberg.

Marley
(alt. Marlin, Marlow)

Old English, meaning "meadow near the lake." Famous Marleys include singer Bob Marley, and the infamous Labrador dog Marley.

Marlon

English origin, meaning "little hawk." Actor Marlon Brando is a famous bearer of this name.

Marshall

Old French, meaning "caretaker of horses."

Martin
(alt. Marty)

Latin, meaning "dedicated to Mars." Famous Martins include actors Martin Freeman and Martin Sheen, and director Martin Scorsese.

Marvel

English, from the word "marvel." Associated with Marvel comic books.

Marvin

Welsh, meaning "sea friend."
Famous Marvins include singer
Marvin Gaye, composer Marvin
Hamlish, and character Marvin
the Martian.

Mason

English, from the word for someone
who works with either stone or brick.

Mathias

(alt. Matthias)

Hebrew, meaning "gift of God."
Matthias was the apostle chosen to
replace Judas in the Bible.

Matthew

(alt. Mathieu; abbrev. Matt)

Hebrew, meaning "gift of the Lord."
Famous Matthews include the Gospel
of Matthew from the Bible, and
actors Matthew McConaughey and
Matthew Perry.

Maurice

(alt. Mauricio)

Latin, meaning "dark skinned" or
"Moorish." Famous Maurices
include children's author Maurice
Sendak.

Maverick

American English, meaning
"nonconformist leader." Made
popular by the movie *Top Gun*.

Maximillian

(alt. Max, Maxie, Maxim, Maximilian)

Latin, meaning "greatest." Also the
name of several Roman emperors.
More common now in the
abbreviated form Max, as with actor
Max Greenfield.

Maximino

Latin, meaning "little Max."

Maxwell

Latin, meaning "Maccus' stream."
Actor Maxwell Caulfield is known for
his role in *Dynasty*.

Maynard

Old German, meaning "brave." A
character from *Desperate Housewives*.

McArthur

Scottish, meaning "son of Arthur."
Associated with General Douglas
MacArthur.

McCoy

Scottish, meaning "son of Coy."

Mckenna

(alt. Mackenna)

Irish Gaelic, meaning "son of the
handsome one." Also used as a girl's
name.

Mearl

English, meaning "my earl."

Mederic

French, meaning "doctor."

Mekhi

African, meaning "who is God?" Actor Mekhi Phifer is known for his roles in *ER* and *8 Mile*.

Mel

Gaelic, meaning "smooth brow." Famous Mels include actor Mel Gibson. Also an abbreviation for Melvin.

Melbourne

From the city in Victoria, Australia.

Melchior

Persian, meaning "king of the city." The name of one of the Three Kings in the Bible.

Melton

English, meaning "town of Mel."

Melva

Hawaiian, meaning "plumeria."

Melville

Scottish, meaning "town of Mel." Author Herman Melville wrote *Moby-Dick*.

Melvin

(alt. Melvyn; abbrev. Mel)

English, meaning "smooth brow." Actor Melvyn Douglas was known for his roles in *Hud* and *Being There*.

Memphis

Greek, meaning "established and beautiful." Also the name of the Tennessee city.

Mercer

English, from the word "mercer."

Merl

French, meaning "blackbird."

Merlin

Welsh, meaning "sea fortress." Merlin is perhaps the most famous wizard of all, appearing in stories from the medieval era.

Merrick

Welsh, meaning "Moorish."

Merrill

Gaelic, meaning "shining sea."

Merritt

English, from the word "merit."

Merton

Old English, meaning "town by the lake."

Meyer

Hebrew, meaning "bright farmer."

Michael

(alt. Michel, Michele, Miguel; abbrev. Mick, Mickey, Mike, Mikey)

Hebrew, meaning "resembles God." Famous Michaels include the archangel, singers Michael Jackson and Michael Bublé, and legendary basketball player Michael Jordan.

Michalis
(alt. Miklos)

Greek form of Michael, meaning "resembles God."

Michelangelo

Italian, meaning "Michael's angel." Name of the famous Italian artist who painted the Sistine Chapel.

Milan

From the name of the Italian city. Also the name of Shakira's oldest son.

Miles
(alt. Milo, Milos, Myles)

English, from the word "miles." Famous Mileses include trumpeter Miles Davies, singer Miles Kane, and *Star Trek: Next Generation* character Miles O'Brien.

Milton

English, meaning "miller's town." Poet John Milton was the author of *Paradise Lost*.

Miro

Slavic, meaning "peace."

Misha

Russian, meaning "who is like God."

Mitchell
(abbrev. Mitch)

English, meaning "who is like God."

Modesto

Italian, meaning "modest." Also the name of a Californian town.

Moe

Hebrew, meaning "God's helmet." Moe is a character from *The Simpsons*.

Mohamed
(alt. Mohammad, Mohamet, Mohammed, Muhammad)

Arabic, meaning "praiseworthy." Acknowledged as the prophet and founder of Islam.

Monroe

Gaelic, meaning "mouth of the river Rotha."

Monserrate

Latin, meaning "jagged mountain."

Montague
(abbrev. Monty)

French, meaning "pointed hill."

Montana

Latin, meaning "mountain." Also the name of the state.

Monte

Italian, meaning "mountain."

Montgomery
(abbrev. Monty)

Variant of Montague, meaning "pointed hill." Actor Montgomery Clift was known for his roles in *From Here to Eternity* and *A Place in the Sun*.

Moody

English, from the word "moody."

Mordecai

Hebrew, meaning "little man."

Morgan

Welsh, meaning "circling sea." Famous Morgans include actor Morgan Freeman and filmmaker Morgan Spurlock. Can be both a boys' and girls' name.

Moritz

Latin, meaning "dark skinned and Moorish." Also a German variation of Maurice.

Moroccan

Arabic, meaning "from Morocco." Popularized by Mariah Carey's choice for her son.

Morpheus

Greek, meaning "shape." The Roman god of dreams in the epic poem *Metamorphoses*.

Morris

Welsh, meaning "dark-skinned and Moorish."

Morrison

English, meaning "son of Morris." Associated with singer and guitarist Jim Morrison.

Mortimer

French, meaning "dead sea."

Morton

Old English, meaning "moor town."

Moses
(alt. Moshe, Moshon)

Hebrew, meaning "savior." A key figure in the Bible.

Moss

English, from the word "moss."

Mungo

Gaelic, meaning "most dear." Lake Mungo is in Australia.

Murphy

Irish, meaning "sea warrior." Murphy's Law states if something can go wrong, it will.

Murray

Gaelic, meaning "lord and master."

Mustafa

Arabic, meaning "chosen." Also a name for the prophet Muhammad in Islam.

Myron

Greek, meaning "myrrh."

Boys' names

Najee

Arabic, meaning "dear companion."
Also the name of an influential jazz
musician.

Nakia

Arabic, meaning "pure."

Nakul

Indian, meaning "mongoose."
Choreographer Nakul Dev
Mahajan has made a name for
himself as a mainstream Bollywood
choreographer.

Nana
(alt. Nanna)

Ghanaiian, meaning "Your Royal
Highness."

Naphtali

Hebrew, meaning "wrestling." One
of Joseph's brothers in the Bible.

Napoleon

Italian origin, meaning "man from
Naples." Name of the French general
who became Emperor of France.

Narciso

Latin, from the myth of Narcissus,
who drowned after gazing at his own
reflection.

Nash

English, meaning "at the ash tree."
Singer-songwriter Graham Nash
is known for his involvement with
Crosby, Stills & Nash.

Nasir

Arabic, meaning "helper."

Nathan
(alt. Nathaniel; abbrev. Nate)

Hebrew, meaning "God has given."
Found in the Bible.

Naveen

Indian, meaning "new." Actor Naveen Andrews is known for his roles in *Lost* and *The English Patient*.

Ned

Originally a nickname for Edward, meaning "wealthy guard." Ned Stark is a character from *Game of Thrones*.

Neftali

Hebrew, meaning "struggling."

Nehemiah

Hebrew, meaning "comforter."

Neil
(alt. Neal, Niall)

Irish, meaning "champion." Famous Neils include astrophysicist Neil deGrasse Tyson, actor Neil Patrick Harris, and singer Neil Young.

Neilson

Irish, meaning "son of Neil."

Nelson

Variant of Neil, meaning "champion." Famous Nelsons include Nelson Mandela and Lord Horatio Nelson.

Nemo

Latin, meaning "nobody." Made popular after the Disney/Pixar film *Finding Nemo*.

Neo

Latin, meaning "new." Neo is a character in "The Matrix" trilogy.

Nephi

Greek, meaning "cloud."

Nessim

Arabic, meaning "breeze."

Nestor

Greek, meaning "traveler." Also the name of a king in ancient Greek mythology.

Neville

Old French, meaning "new village." Neville Longbottom is a character in the *Harry Potter* series.

Newton

English, meaning "new town." Scientist Sir Isaac Newton is celebrated as the discoverer of gravity.

Nicholas
(alt. Nicklas, Nicolas, Niklas, Nikola; abbrev. Nick, Nicky, Nicoi)

Greek, meaning "victorious." Famous Nicholases include St. Nicholas (the original Santa Claus), actor Nicolas Cage, and alchemist Nicholas Flamel.

Nigel

Gaelic, meaning "champion."
Producer Nigel Lythgoe is known for
his work on *So You Think You Can
Dance*.

Nikhil

Sanskrit, meaning "whole" or
"entire."

Nikita

Greek, meaning "unconquered."
Used for both boys and girls.

Nimrod

Hebrew, meaning "we will rebel."
Found in the Bible.

Nissim

Hebrew, meaning "wonderful
things."

Noah

Hebrew, meaning "peaceful." Found
in the Bible.

Noel

French, meaning "Christmas."
Famous Noels include comedian and
actor Noel Coward.

Nolan

Gaelic, meaning "champion."

Norbert

Old German, meaning "northern
brightness."

Norman
(abbrev. Norm)

Old German, meaning "northerner."
The Norman people of the Middle
Ages originated from Normandy in
France.

Normand

French, meaning "from Normandy."

Norris

Old French, meaning "northerner."

Norton

English, meaning "northern town."

Norval

French, meaning "northern town."

Norwood

English, meaning "northern forest."

Nova

Latin, meaning "new." Also the name
of a vast nuclear explosion in a white
dwarf star.

Nuno

Latin, meaning "ninth."

Nunzio

Italian, meaning "messenger."

O

Boys' names

Oakley

English, meaning "from the oak meadow." The name of a brand of clothing.

Obadiah

Hebrew, meaning "God's worker." Used throughout the Bible to indicate a servant of God.

Obama

African, meaning "crooked." Surname of the 44th President of the United States.

Obed

Hebrew, meaning "servant of God."

Oberon
(abbrev. Obi, Obie)

Old German, meaning "royal bear." The Fairy King in Shakespeare's *A Midsummer Night's Dream*.

Octave
(alt. Octavian, Octavio)

Latin, meaning "eight." An octave is a series of eight notes in a musical scale.

Oda
(alt. Odell, Odie, Odis)

Hebrew, meaning "praise God."

Ogden

Old English, meaning "oak valley."

Oisin

Celtic, meaning "fawn." From an ancient Irish poet.

Ola

Norse, meaning "precious." Ola Nordmann is a personification of Norway, in the same way Uncle Sam represents the USA.

Olaf
(alt. Olan)

Old Norse, meaning "ancestor." The name of the animated snowman in Disney's Frozen.

Oleander

Hawaiian, meaning "joyous."

Oleg
(alt. Olen)

Russian, meaning "holy."

Olin

Russian, meaning "rock."

Oliver
(alt. Olivier; abbrev. Ollie, Olly)

Latin, meaning "olive tree." Associated with the musical Oliver! and Disney's Oliver and Company.

Omar
(alt. Omari, Omarion)

Arabic, meaning "speaker." Actor Omar Epps is known for his roles in TV shows House and Resurrection.

Ora

Latin, meaning "hour."

Oran
(alt. Oren, Orrin)

Gaelic, meaning "light and pale."

Orange

English, from the the fruit and the color.

Orion

Greek, from the Ancient Greek legend of a massive hunter.

Orlando
(alt. Orlo)

Old German, meaning "old land." Famous Orlandos include actor Orlando Bloom, the Shakespearean character Orlando from As You Like It, and the city of Orlando in Florida.

Orpheus

Greek, meaning "beautiful voice." A legendary ancient Greek musician, poet, and prophet.

Orson

Latin, meaning "bear." Film director Orson Welles was known for the movies Citizen Kane and Touch of Evil.

Orville

Old French, meaning "gold town." Associated with popcorn brand Orville Redenbacher.

Osaka

From the Japanese city.

Osborne
(alt. Osbourne)

Norse, meaning "bear god." Associated with Sharon and Ozzy Osbourne's family.

Oscar

Old English, meaning "spear of the gods." The Oscars is the nickname for the Academy Awards.

Oswald

German, meaning "God's power." Oswald the Lucky Rabbit was Walt Disney's first creation.

Otha
(alt. Otho)

German, meaning "wealth."

Othello

Old German, meaning "wealth." From the Shakespearean character and play.

Otis

German, meaning "wealth." Otis Redding was a legendary singer and several US sports stars share the same given name.

Otten

German, meaning "son of Otto."

Otto

German, meaning "wealthy." Anne Frank's father was called Otto Frank.

Owain

Welsh, meaning "youth."

Owen
(alt. Eoghan, Eoin)

Welsh, meaning "well born and noble" or "little warrior." Famous Owens include actor Owen Wilson. Eoghan and Eoin are the Irish variants.

Oz

Hebrew, meaning "strength." Associated with *The Wizard of Oz*.

Boys' names

Pablo
Spanish, meaning "little." Famous Pablos include artist Pablo Picasso.

Paco
Native American, meaning "eagle." Paco Rabanne is a Spanish fashion designer and brand name. His real first name is Francisco.

Padma
Sanskrit, meaning "lotus."

Padraig
(alt. Podrick)
Irish, meaning "noble." Podrick Payne is a character in *Game of Thrones*.

Panos
Greek, meaning "all holy."

Paolo
Italian, meaning "little."

Paresh
Sanskrit, meaning "supreme standard."

Parker
Old English, meaning "park keeper."

Pascal
Latin, meaning "Easter child." The feminine form is Pascale.

Patrick
(alt. Patrice; abbrev. Paddy, Pat)
Irish, meaning "noble." St. Patrick is the patron saint of Ireland.

Patten
(alt. Patton)
English, meaning "noble." Patton Oswalt is a comedian.

Paul
Hebrew, meaning "small." Paul was one of Jesus's main disciples.

Pavel

Latin, meaning "small."

Pax

Latin, meaning "peace."

Paxton

English, meaning "town of peace."

Payne

Latin, meaning "peasant."

Payton

Latin, meaning "peasant's town."

Pedro

Spanish form of Peter, meaning "rock."

Penn

English, meaning "hill." Penn Jillette is a magician and one half of Penn and Teller.

Percival
(alt. Percy)

French, meaning "pierce the valley." The name of one of the Knights of the Round Table.

Perez

Hebrew, meaning "breach." Famous Perezes include Perez Morton, the lawyer and revolutionary Boston patriot, and professional gossiper Perez Hilton.

Pericles

Greek, meaning "far-famed." Pericles was an influential ancient Greek general and statesman.

Perrin

Greek, meaning "rock."

Perry

English, meaning "rock." Associated with the series *Perry Mason*.

Pervis

English, meaning "purveyor."

Peter
(alt. Pedro, Petros, Pierre, Piers; abbrev. Pete)

Greek, meaning "rock." St. Peter was one of Jesus's disciples in the Bible.

Peyton

Old English, meaning "fighting man's estate." Peyton Manning recently retired from professional football.

Philip
(alt. Phillip; abbrev. Phil, Pip)

Greek, meaning "lover of horses." Famous Philips include husband of Queen Elizabeth II, Prince Philip, Philip the Apostle, and author Philip Pullman.

Philo

Greek, meaning "love."

Phineas
(alt. Pinchas)

Hebrew, meaning "oracle." A character in the cartoon *Phineas and Ferb*.

Phoenix

Greek, meaning "dark red." In ancient Greek mythology, a phoenix is a bird that has the power to regenerate itself from its ashes.

Pierce
(alt. Pierson)

Meaning "son of Piers."

Placido

Latin, meaning "placid." Placido Domingo is a famous tenor opera singer.

Pradeep

Hindi, meaning "light."

Pranav

Sanskrit, meaning "spiritual leader."

Presley

Old English, meaning "priest's meadow." Made famous by legendary singer Elvis Presley.

Preston

Old English, meaning "priest's town." Preston Burke is a character from *Grey's Anatomy*.

Primo

Italian, meaning "first." Also a slang term for "excellent."

Primus

Latin, meaning "first." Often used as a name for villains in Marvel comic books.

Prince

English, from the word "prince." Associated with singer and guitarist Prince.

Prospero

Latin, meaning "prosperous." Prospero is the protagonist in Shakespeare's play *The Tempest*.

Pryce
(alt. Prize)

Old French, meaning "prize."

Pryor

English, meaning "first." Famous Pryors include legendary comedian Richard Pryor.

Psalm

Old English, meaning "hymn." The name of Kim Kardashian-West's fourth child.

Ptolemy

Greek, meaning "aggressive" or "warlike."

Boys' names

Qabil
(alt. Quabil, Quadim)
Arabic, meaning "able."

Quadir
Arabic, meaning "powerful."

Quaid
Irish, meaning "fourth."

Quemby
Norse, meaning "from the woman's estate."

Quentin
(alt. Quinten, Quintin, Quinton, Quintus)
Latin, meaning "fifth." Director Quentin Tarantino has been behind numerous successful movies, including *Kill Bill* and *Django Unchained*.

Quillan
Gaelic, meaning "sword."

Quillon
Gaelic, meaning "club."

Quincy
Old French, meaning "estate of the fifth son." Quincy Jones is a music mogul.

Quinlan
Gaelic, meaning "fit, shapely, and strong."

Quinn
Gaelic, meaning "counsel." Quinn is a character from *Glee*.

 Boys' names

Radames

Slavic, meaning "famous joy." A character in the Verdi opera *Aida*.

Raekwon

Hebrew, meaning "God has healed." Associated with Raekwon of Wu-Tang Clan.

Rafael

(alt. Rafe, Rafer, Raffi, Raphael)

Hebrew, meaning "God has healed." One of the archangels in the Bible.

Ragnar

Old Norse, meaning "judgment warrior." Ragnar Lodbrok was a legendary Norse ruler from the Viking era.

Raheem

(alt. Rahim)

Arabic, meaning "merciful and kind."

Rahm

Hebrew, meaning "mercy."

Rahul

(alt. Raoul, Raul)

Indian, meaning "efficient." Rahul was the Buddha's son.

Raiden

(alt. Rainen)

From the Japanese god of thunder.

Rainer

Old German, meaning "deciding warrior."

Raj

Sanskrit, meaning "kingdom," and Polish, meaning "heaven."

Rajesh

(alt. Ramesh)

Indian, meaning "ruler of kings."

Raleigh

Old English, meaning "deer's meadow." Made famous by the explorer Sir Walter Raleigh.

Ralph

Old English, meaning "wolf." Famous Ralphs include actor Ralph Fiennes, fashion brand Ralph Lauren, and character Ralph from *The Simpsons*.

Ram

English, from the word for a male sheep.

Ramiro

Germanic, meaning "powerful in battle." Popular name for baby boys in Argentina.

Ramsey
(alt. Ramsay)

Old English, meaning "wild garlic island." Gordon Ramsay is a celebrity chef.

Randall
(alt. Randal, Randolph, Randy)

Old German, meaning "wolf shield." Can be traced back to the poem "Lord Randall" in 1882.

Raniel

English, meaning "God is my happiness."

Ranjit

Indian, meaning "influenced by charm."

Rannoch

Gaelic, meaning "fern." Also the name of an area in the Scottish Highlands.

Rashad

Arabic, meaning "good judgment."

Rashid
(alt. Rasheed)

Indian, meaning "rightly guided." Ar-Rashid, meaning "The Guide," is one of Allah's names in the Islamic tradition.

Rasmus

Greek, meaning "beloved."

Raven

English, from the word for the large, black bird.

Ravi

Hindi, meaning "sun."

Ray

English, from the word "ray." Famous Rays include singer Ray Charles. Other well-known Rays were actually given the name Raymond.

Raymond
(alt. Rayner; abbrev. Ray)

English, meaning "advisor." Title character of the sitcom *Everybody Loves Raymond*. Actors Ray Winstone and Ray Liotta are both Raymonds.

Raz

Israeli, meaning "secret" or "mystery."

Reagan

(abbrev. Reggie)

Irish, meaning "little king." Ronald Reagan was the 40th President of the United States.

Reginald

(abbrev. Reg, Reggie)

Latin, meaning "regal." Singer Sir Elton John's birth name is Reginald Kenneth Dwight.

Regis

Latin, meaning "of the king."

Reid

Old English, meaning "by the reeds."

Reilly

(alt. Riley)

Irish, meaning "courageous."

Remus

Latin, meaning "swift." Famous Remuses include Romulus and Remus of the ancient Roman myth, and the *Harry Potter* character Remus Lupin.

Rémy

French, meaning "from Rheims."

Renatus

(alt. Renat, Renate, Renato, Rene)

Latin, meaning "rebirth."

Reno

Latin, meaning "renewed." Also the name of the city in Nevada.

Reuben

Spanish, meaning "a son." The name of a sandwich containing corned beef, Swiss cheese, and sauerkraut.

Reuel

Hebrew, meaning "friend of God."

Rex

Latin, meaning "king." The kings of ancient Rome were called Rex, before it became a republic.

Rey

Spanish, meaning "king"; Telugu, meaning "friend."

Reynold

Latin, meaning "king's advisor."

Rhodes

German, meaning "where the roses grow." Also the name of the Greek island.

Rhodri

Welsh, meaning "ruler of the circle."

Rhys

(alt. Reece, Riece)

Welsh, meaning "enthusiasm." Famous Rhyses include actors Jonathan Rhys Meyers and Rhys Ifans.

Richard

(alt. Ricardo, Rikardo; abbrev. Dick, Dickie, Richie, Rick, Ricki, Ricky, Ritchie)

Old German, meaning "powerful leader." Famous Richards include 37th President of the United States Richard Nixon, and actor Richard Gere.

Ridley

English, meaning "cleared wood." Director Sir Ridley Scott is known for the films *Gladiator* and *Thelma & Louise*.

Rigby

English, from the place in Lancashire. Often associated with the Beatles' song "Eleanor Rigby."

Riky

Irish Gaelic, meaning "courageous."

Ringo

English, meaning "ring." Ringo Starr was the drummer with the Beatles.

Rio

Spanish, meaning "river." *Rio* is a song by Duran Duran and associated with the Brazilian city Rio de Janeiro.

Riordan

Gaelic, meaning "bard."

Rishi

Sanskrit, meaning "scribe."

Roald

Scandinavian, meaning "ruler." Roald Dahl is the author of *Charlie and the Chocolate Factory* and many other children's books.

Robert

(alt. Roberto; abbrev. Bob, Bobby, Dobby, Rob, Robbie)

Old German, meaning "bright fame." Famous Roberts include actors Robert de Niro and Robert Pattinson, and legendary singers Bob Dylan and Bob Marley.

Robin

English, from the word for the small, flame-breasted bird. Famous Robins include comedian Robin Williams, singer Robin Thicke, and outlaw legend Robin Hood.

Robinson

English, meaning "son of Robin." The eponymous hero of the novel *Robinson Crusoe*.

Rocco

(alt. Rocky)

Italian, meaning "rest." Also the name of Madonna's son.

Roderick

(abbrev. Rod, Roddy)

German, meaning "famous power." A character from the TV series *The Following*.

Rodney
(abbrev. Rod, Roddy)
Old German, meaning "island near the clearing."

Rodrigo
Spanish form of Roderick, meaning "famous power." Famous Rodrigos include Spanish composer Joaquin Rodrigo.

Roger
Old German, meaning "spear man." Famous Rogers include athlete Sir Roger Bannister, The Who singer Roger Daltrey, and tennis pro Roger Federer.

Roland
(alt. Rowland)
Old German, meaning "renowned land."

Rolf
Old German, meaning "wolf."

Rollie
(alt. Rollo)
Old German, meaning "renowned land."

Roman
Latin, meaning "from Rome." Associated with the Roman people.

Romeo
Latin, meaning "pilgrim to Rome." Made famous by Shakespeare's play *Romeo and Juliet*. Also the name of David and Victoria Beckham's second son.

Ronald
(alt. Ron, Ronnie)
Norse, meaning "mountain of strength." Ron Weasley is a character in the *Harry Potter* series.

Ronan
Gaelic, meaning "little seal."

Rory
English, meaning "red king." Rory Calhoun was an actor. Golfer Rory McIlroy has won the US Open.

Ross
(alt. Russ)
Scottish, meaning "cape."

Rowan
(alt. Roan, Rohan)
Gaelic, meaning "little red one." Rowan Atkinson is a comedian and comic actor, and also the voice of Zazu in *The Lion King*.

Roy
Gaelic, meaning "red." Famous Roys include singer Roy Orbison.

Ruben
Hebrew, meaning "son."

Rudolph
(alt. Rudy)

Old German, meaning "famous wolf." The name of Santa's legendary reindeer.

Rufus

Latin, meaning "red-haired." Actor Rufus Sewell is known for his role in *A Knight's Tale*.

Rupert

Variant of Robert, meaning "bright fame." Actor Rupert Grint is known for his role in the *Harry Potter* series.

Russell

Old French, meaning "little red one." Comedian Russell Brand is known for his role in *Arthur*.

Rusty

English, meaning "ruddy."

Ryan

Gaelic, meaning "little king." Famous Ryans include actors Ryan Gosling and Ryan Reynolds, and comedian Ryan Stiles.

Ryder

English, meaning "horseman."

Rye

English, from the word "rye."

Ryker

From Richard, meaning "powerful leader." *Ryker's Island* is a fictional prison facility in Marvel Comics stories.

Rylan

English, meaning "land where rye is grown."

Ryley

Old English, meaning "rye clearing."

 Boys' names

Saber
(alt. Sabre)
French, meaning "sword."

Sagar
African, meaning "ruler of the water."

Sage
English, meaning "wise." Can also refer to the herb.

Sakari
Native American, meaning "sweet."

Salim
(alt. Saleem)
Arabic, meaning "secure." The Salim Khan family are a Bollywood dynasty.

Salvador
Spanish, meaning "savior." Famous Salvadors include artist Salvador Dali.

Salvatore
Italian, meaning "savior." There have been dozens of the Italian, Sicilian, or New York mafia called Salvatore.

Samir
Arabic, meaning "pleasant companion."

Samson
Hebrew, meaning "son of Sam." The biblical Samson had extraordinary strength.

Samuel
(alt. Sam, Sama, Sammie, Sammy)
Hebrew, meaning "God is heard." Famous Samuels include a prophet from the Bible, actor Samuel L. Jackson, and author Samuel Langhorne Clemens (known as Mark Twain).

Sandeep
(alt. Sundeep)
Hindi, meaning "lighting the way."

Sanjay
Hindi, meaning "victory." Sanjay Gupta is a well-known TV doctor.

Santana
Spanish, meaning "saint." Associated with guitarist Carlos Santana.

Santiago
Spanish, meaning "Saint James." Also the name of the capital city of Chile.

Santino
Spanish, meaning "little Saint James."

Santo
(alt. Santos)
Latin, meaning "saint."

Sasha
(alt. Sacha, Sascha)
Russian, derived from Alexander, meaning "defending men." Sasha can be used for boys or girls.

Sawyer
English, meaning "one who saws wood." Associated with the novel *Tom Sawyer*.

Scott
(alt. Scottie)
English, meaning "from Scotland." Scott Dixon is an IndyCar champion, and cartoonist Scott Adams created *Dilbert*.

Seamus
Irish variant of James, meaning "he who supplants." Seamus Heaney is a Nobel Prize-winning poet.

Sean
(alt. Shaun, Shawn)
Variant of John, meaning "God is gracious." Famous Seans include actors Sean Penn and Sean Connery.

Sebastian
(alt. Sébastien; abbrev. Basti, Seb)
Greek, meaning "revered." The name of the crab character in Disney's *The Little Mermaid*.

Sergio
(alt. Serge)
Latin, meaning "servant."

Old name, new fashion

Augustus	Norris
Bertrand	Percival
Edgar	Reginald
Felix	Sebastian
Gilbert	Theodore
Hector	Winston
Jasper	

Seth

Hebrew, meaning "appointed." Famous Seths include actors Seth MacFarlane and Seth Greene.

Severus

Latin, meaning "severe." Severus Snape is a character in the *Harry Potter* series.

Seymour

English, from the place name in northern France. Famous Seymours include Principal Seymour Skinner of *The Simpsons*, and the late actor Philip Seymour Hoffman.

Shane

Variant of Sean, meaning "God is gracious." Famous Shanes include actors Shane West and Shane Harper.

Sharif

Arabic, meaning "honored." Also a name for descendants of one of Muhammad's grandchildren.

Shea

Gaelic, meaning "admirable."

Shelby

Norse, meaning "willow." Associated with the Mustang car.

Sherlock

English, meaning "fair-haired." The name of the lead character in Sir Arthur Conan Doyle's "Sherlock Holmes" novels.

Sherman

Old English, meaning "shear man."

Shmuel

Hebrew, meaning "his name is God."

Shola

Arabic, meaning "energetic."

Sidney
(alt. Sid, Sydney)

English, meaning "wide meadow." Actor Sidney Poitier is known for his roles in *Guess Who's Coming to Dinner* and *In The Heat of the Night*.

Sigmund

Old German, meaning "victorious hand." Associated with neurologist Sigmund Freud.

Silvanus
(alt. Silvio)

Latin, meaning "woods." An Ancient Roman deity of woods and fields.

Simba
(alt. Sim)

Swahili, meaning "lion." Associated with the character from Disney's *The Lion King*.

Simon
(alt. Simeon)

Hebrew, meaning "to hear." Famous Simons include music producer Simon Cowell and actor Simon Pegg.

Sinbad

Persian, meaning "Lord of Sages." Fictional merchant adventurer.

Sindri

Norse, meaning "dwarf."

Sipho

African, meaning "the unknown one."

Sire

English, from the word used to address reigning kings or nobility.

Sirius

Hebrew, meaning "brightest star." Sirius Black is a character from the *Harry Potter* series.

Skipper

English, meaning "ship captain."

Skyler

Dutch, meaning "guarded" or "scholar."

Solomon

Hebrew, meaning "peace." One of the most important kings in the Bible and the Torah.

Sonny

American English, meaning "son." Singer Sonny Bono was half of Sonny and Cher.

Soren

Scandinavian, meaning "brightest star."

Spencer

English, meaning "guardian." Famous Spencers include actor Spencer Tracy and reality TV star Spencer Pratt.

Spike

English, from the word "spike." Director Spike Lee is known for *Do the Right Thing* and *4 Little Girls*.

Stanford

English, meaning "stone ford." Made famous by Stanford University.

Stanley
(alt. Stan)

English, meaning "stony meadow." Famous Stanleys include director Stanley Kubrick, actor Stanley Tucci, and comic book writer Stan Lee.

Stavros

Greek, meaning "cross."

Stellan

Latin, meaning "starred."

Steno

German, meaning "stone."

Stephen
(alt. Stefan, Stefano, Steffan, Steven; abbrev. Steve, Stevie)

English, meaning "crowned." Famous Stephens include author Stephen King, physicist Stephen Hawking, and actor Stephen Fry.

Stewart
(alt. Stuart)

English, meaning "steward." Stewart Copeland was the American drummer in The Police.

Stoney

English, meaning "stone like."

Storm

English, from the word "storm."

Sven

Norse, meaning "boy." The name of the reindeer in Disney's *Frozen*.

Syed
(alt. Sayyid)

Arabic, meaning "lucky." Associated with the character from *Lost*.

Sylvester

Latin, meaning "wooded." The name of the cartoon cat.

Boys' names

Tacitus

Latin, meaning "silent, calm." Also the name of an ancient Roman historian.

Tad

English, from the word "tadpole."

Taj

Indian, meaning "crown." Made famous by the Indian palace the Taj Mahal.

Takashi

Japanese, meaning "praiseworthy."

Takoda

Sioux, meaning "friend to everyone."

Talbot
(alt. Tal)

English, meaning "command of the valley." Aristocratic name.

Tamir

Arabic, meaning "tall and wealthy."

Tanner

Old English, meaning "leather-maker."

Taras
(alt. Tarez)

Scottish, meaning "crag." Taras was the son of Poseidon in ancient Greek mythology.

Tarek
(alt. Tarik)

Arabic, meaning "to strike."

Tarian

Welsh, meaning "shield."

Tariq

Arabic, meaning "morning star."

Tarquin

Latin, from the Roman clan name. Tarquin Hall is a poet.

Tarun

Hindi, meaning "young."

Tatanka

Hebrew, meaning "bull." Legendary Native American leader Sitting Bull's Western name was Tatanka Lyotake.

Tate

English, meaning "cheerful." Actor Tate Donovan is known for his role in the TV series *Damages*.

Taurean

English, meaning "bull-like." Also used to describe people born under the Taurus star sign.

Tavares

English, meaning "descendant of the hermit."

Tave
(alt. Tavian, Tavis, Tavish)

French, from Gustave, meaning "royal staff"; in Nordic cultures it can mean "guarantor."

Taylor
(alt. Tay)

English, meaning "tailor." Famous Taylors include actor Taylor Lautner and singer Taylor Hanson.

Tennessee

Native American, meaning "river town." Also the name of the state.

Terence
(alt. Terrill, Terry)

English, meaning "tender." Actor Terence Stamp is known for his roles in *Billy Budd* and *The Collector*.

Tex

English, meaning "Texan."

Thane
(alt. Thayer)

Scottish, meaning "landholder." Actor Thane Bettany is the father of actor Paul Bettany.

Thatcher
(alt. Thaxter)

Old English, meaning "roof thatcher."

Thelonious

Latin, meaning "ruler of the people." Thelonious Monk was an influential jazz pianist and composer.

Theodore
(abbrev. Ted, Teddy, Theo)

Greek, meaning "God's gift." Theodore Roosevelt was the 26th President of the United States.

Theophile

Latin, meaning "beloved of God," also "one who loves God."

Theron

Greek, meaning "hunter."

Thierry

French variant of Terence, meaning "tender." Made famous by soccer star Thierry Henry.

Thomas
(alt. Thom, Tom, Tomlin, Tommy)

Aramaic, meaning "twin." Famous Thomases include inventor Thomas Edison and children's character Thomas the Tank Engine.

Thomson
(alt. Thomsen)

English, meaning "son of Thomas." "Thomsen" means "twin" in Aramaic.

Thor

Norse, meaning "thunder." Thor was a hammer-wielding deity in Norse mythology.

Tiago

From Santiago, meaning "Saint James." Also used as a shortened form of Santiago.

Tiberius

English, meaning "from the river Tiber."

Tibor

Latin, from the river Tiber; Hungarian, meaning "a short meeting."

Tieman
(alt. Tiemann)

Gaelic, meaning "lord."

Tilden
(alt. Till)

English, meaning "fertile valley."

Timothy
(alt. Tim, Timmie, Timmy, Timon)

Greek, meaning "God's honor." Famous Timothys include actors Timothy Dalton, Timothy Spall, and Christopher Timothy.

Tito
(alt. Titus, Tizian)

Latin, meaning "defender." Associated with singer Tito Jackson, from the Jackson Five.

Tobias
(alt. Toby)

Hebrew, meaning "God is good."

Todd
(alt. Tod)

English, meaning "fox." Famous Tods include Todd Flanders in *The Simpsons* and Todd Alquist in *Fargo*.

Tonneau

French, meaning "barrel."

Torey

Norse, meaning "Thor."

Torin

Gaelic, meaning "chief."

Torquil

Gaelic, meaning "helmet"; Scandinavian, from Thor the god of thunder and lightning.

Toshi

Japanese, meaning "reflection."

Travis

French, meaning "crossover." Famous Travises include actor Travis Fimmel and drummer Travis Barker.

Trevor
(alt. Tvevin)

Welsh origin, meaning "great settlement." Comedian Trevor Noah currently hosts *The Daily Show*.

Trey
(alt. Tyree)

French, meaning "three." Sometimes used as a nickname for a third-born child.

Tristan
(alt. Tristram)

Celtic from the romantic hero in the tale of Tristan and Isolde. Also one of the Knights of the Round Table.

Troy

Gaelic, meaning "descended from the soldier." Troy was a legendary city in ancient Greece.

Tudor

Variant of Theodore, meaning "God's gift." Also the name of the British dynasty which included Henry VIII and Elizabeth I.

Tyler

English, meaning "tile maker."

Tyrell

French, meaning "puller." Associated with House Tyrell from *Game of Thrones*.

Tyrone

Gaelic, meaning "Owen's county."

Tyson

English, meaning "son of Tyrone." Mike Tyson is widely regarded as one of the best heavyweight boxers of all time, as well as the most ferocious and controversial.

U

Boys' names

Uberto
(alt. Umberto)
Italian, variant of Hubert, meaning "bright or shining intellect."

Udo
German, meaning "power of the wolf."

Ulf
German, meaning "wolf." Also the name of a Danish Viking chief.

Ulrich
German, meaning "noble ruler."

Ultan
Irish, meaning "from Ulster."

Ulysses
Greek, meaning "wrathful." Made famous by the mythological voyager from ancient Greece.

Upton
English, meaning "high town."

Urho
Finnish, meaning "brave."

Uri
(alt. Uriah, Urias)
Hebrew, meaning "my light." Famous Uris include magician Uri Geller.

Uriel
Hebrew, meaning "angel of light." One of the archangels in the Bible.

Usher
English, from the word "usher." Associated with the R&B star Usher.

Uzi
Hebrew, meaning "my strength." A type of submachine gun.

Uzzi
(alt. Uzziah)
Hebrew, meaning "the Lord is my strength." Found in the Bible.

V

Boys' names

Vadim

Russian, meaning "scandal maker." Vadim the Bold was a legendary warrior in Eastern Europe during the ninth century.

Valdemar

German, meaning "renowned leader."

Valente

Latin, meaning "valiant."

Valentine

(alt. Valentin, Valentino; abbrev. Val)

English, from the word "valentine." St. Valentine's Day is named after Valentinus, who was said to have healed the broken heart of his jailer's daughter.

Valerio

Italian, meaning "to be strong."

Van

Dutch, meaning "son of." Famous Vans include the band Van Halen, singer Van Morrison, and the brand of shoe.

Vance

English, meaning "marshland." Vance Astrovik is the real name of the comic book hero Justice.

Vangelis

Greek, meaning "good news." Vangelis is a modern Greek composer.

Varro

Latin, meaning "strong."

Varun

Hindi, meaning "water god." Shortened form of Varuna, who is the Hindu god of all water.

Vasilis
(alt. Vasilly)
Greek, meaning "kingly."

Vaughan
Welsh, meaning "little."

Vernell
French, meaning "green and flourishing."

Verner
German, meaning "army defender." The German form of Werner, although Verner is a more common spelling in Europe.

Vernon
(alt. Vernie)
French, meaning "alder grove." Vernon Dursley is a character in the *Harry Potter* series.

Versilius
Latin, meaning "flier."

Vester
Latin, meaning "wooded." Associated with the guitar maker.

Victor
(alt. Vic, Viktor)
Latin, meaning "champion." Author Victor Hugo wrote *Les Miserables*.

Vidal
(alt. Vidar)
Spanish, meaning "life-giving." Vidal Sassoon is famed as a hairstylist.

Vijay
Hindi, meaning "conquering."

Vikram
Hindi, meaning "sun."

Ville
French, meaning "town."

Vincent
(abbrev. Vin, Vince, Vinnie)
English, meaning "victorious." Famous Vincents include actor Vince Vaughn, artist Vincent van Gogh, and soccer player turned actor Vinnie Jones.

Virgil
Latin, meaning "staff bearer." From the ancient Roman poet of the same name.

Vito
Spanish, meaning "life." Vito Corleone is a character from *The Godfather*.

Vittorio
Italian, meaning "victory."

Vitus
Latin, meaning "life." Associated with St. Vitus, or the medcial condition Saint Vitus Dance.

Vivian

(alt. Vyvian; abbrev. Viv)

Latin, meaning "lively." Used as a name for boys and girls.

Vladimir

Slavic, meaning "prince." Famous Vladimirs include Russian President Vladimir Putin, and legendary warrior Vladimir the Impaler—also known as Dracula.

Volker

German, meaning "defender of the people."

"Bad boy" names

Ace	Conan
Arnie	Guy
Axel	Rhett
Bruce	Spike
Buzz	Tyson

Von

Norse, meaning "hope." In Germany, "von" also means "of" or "from," and is used to denote origin, such as Ulrich von Liechtenstein.

W

Boys' names

Wade

English, meaning "to move forward" or "to go." Wade Robson is a contemporary dance choreographer.

Waldemar

German, meaning "famous ruler."

Walden

English, meaning "valley of the Britons." Famed as the title of the book by Henry Thoreau.

Waldo

Old German, meaning "rule." "Where's Waldo" is a popular children's book character.

Walker

English, meaning "a fuller."

Wallace

English, meaning "foreigner" or "stranger." One of the cartoon duo *Wallace and Gromit*.

Wally

German, meaning "ruler of the army."

Walter
(alt. Walt)

German, meaning "ruler of the army." Famous Walters include *Breaking Bad*'s Walter White, and the movie *The Secret Life of Walter Mitty*.

Ward

English, meaning "guardian."

Wardell

Old English, meaning "watchman's hill."

Warner

German, meaning "army guard." Made famous as the name of the movie studio Warner Brothers.

Warren

German, meaning "guard" or "the game park." Warren Buffett is a business tycoon and philanthropist.

Warwick

Old English, meaning "buildings near the weir." Associated with actor Warwick Davis.

Washington

English, meaning "clever" or "clever man's settlement." George Washington was the first President of the United States.

Wassily
(alt. Vasily))

Greek, meaning "royal" or "kingly." Wassily Kandinsky was an abstract artist.

Watson

English, meaning "son" or "son of Walter." Dr. Watson is a character from the "Sherlock Holmes" stories.

Waverley
(alt. Waverly)

English, meaning "quaking aspen."

Waylon

English, meaning "land by the road." Associated with country singer Waylon Jennings.

Wayne

English, meaning "a cartwright." Famous Waynes include comedian Wayne Brady and rapper Lil Wayne.

Webster

English, meaning "weaver."

Weldon

English, meaning "from the hill of well" or "hill with a well."

Wells

English, meaning "from the hill of well" or "hill with a well."

Wendell
(alt. Wendel)

German, meaning "spring."

Werner

German, meaning "army guard." Werner Heisenberg was a Nobel prize winner and inspiration for the alter ego of Walter White in *Breaking Bad*.

Weston

English, meaning "from the west town."

Wheeler

English, meaning "wheel maker."

Whitley

English, meaning "white wood."

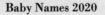
Whitman

Old English, meaning "white man." Made famous by author and poet Walt Whitman.

Whitney

Old English, meaning "white island."

Wilber

(alt. Wilbur)

Old German, meaning "bright will." Wilbur Wright helped invent the first powered airplanes.

Wilder

English, meaning "wild and uncontrolled".

Wiley

Old English, meaning "beguiling" or "enchanting."

Wilford

Old English, meaning "the ford by the willows." Associated with actor Wilford Brimley.

Wilfred

(alt. Wilfredo, Wilfrid; abbrev. Wilf)

English, meaning "to will peace."

Wilhelm

(alt. Willem)

German, meaning "strong willed warrior." The "Wilhelm Scream" is a movie sound effect used in hundreds of movies.

Wilkes

(alt. Wilkie)

Old English, meaning "strong willed protector" or "strong and resolute protector." John Wilkes Booth was the assassin of President Lincoln.

William

(abbrev. Bill, Billy, Will, Willie, Willy)

English (Teutonic), meaning "strong protector" or "strong willed warrior." Famous Williams include William Shakespeare, Prince William, and rapper Will.i.am.

Willis

English, meaning "server of William." Actor Bruce Willis is known for his roles in *Die Hard* and *The Fifth Element*.

Willoughby

Old Norse and Old English, meaning "from the farm by the trees."

Wilmer

English (Teutonic), meaning "famously resolute." Actor Wilmer Valderrama is known for his role in *That 70's Show*.

Wilmot

English, meaning "resolute mind."

Wilson

English, meaning "son of William." Famous Wilsons include legendary R&B singer Wilson Pickett.

Wilton

Old Norse and English, meaning "from the farm by the brook/ streams."

Windell
(alt. Wendell)

German, meaning "wanderer" or "seeker." Actor Windell Middlebrooks was known for his role in the TV series *Scrubs*.

Windsor

Old English, meaning "river bank" or "landing place." The British Royal family is known as the House of Windsor.

Winfield

English, meaning "from the field of Wina."

Winslow

Old English, meaning "victory on the hill." Associated with the sitcom *Family Matters*.

Winston

English, meaning "from Wine's town." Sir Winston Chruchill was prime Minister of Great Britain during World War II.

Winter

Old English, meaning "to be born in the winter."

Winthrop

Old English, meaning "village of friends."

Winton

Old English, meaning "a friend's farm."

Wirrin

Aboriginal, meaning "a tea tree."

Wistan

Old English, meaning "battle stone" or "mark of the battle."

Wittan

Old English, meaning "farm in the woods" or "farm by the woods."

Wolf
(alt. Wolfe)

English, meaning "strong as a wolf." A wild animal in the dog family.

Wolfgang

Teutonic, meaning "the path of wolves." The composer Mozart's chosen name was Wolfgang Amadeus Mozart.

Wolfrom

Teutonic, meaning "raven wolf."

Wolter

Dutch, a form of Walter meaning "ruler of the army."

Woodburn

Old English, meaning "a stream in the woods."

Woodrow

English, meaning "from the row of houses by the wood." Woodrow Wilson was the 28th President of the United States.

Woodward

English, meaning "guardian of the forest."

Woody

American English, meaning "path in the woods." Famous Woodys include filmmaker Woody Allen and the character of Woody from the *Toy Story* series.

Worcester

Old English, meaning "from a Roman site." A tangy sauce of the same name.

Worth

American English, meaning "worth much" or "wealthy place" or "wealth and riches."

Wren

Old English, meaning "tiny bird."

Wright

Old English, meaning "to be a craftsman" or "from a carpenter." Wilbur and Orville Wright were the inventors of powered aircraft.

Wyatt

Teutonic, meaning "from wood" or "from the wide water." Famous Wyatts include director Rupert Wyatt, Wild West sheriff Wyatt Earp, and comedian Wyatt Cenac.

Wynn
(alt. Wyn)

Welsh, meaning "very blessed" or "the fair blessed one"; Old English, meaning "friend."

 Boys' names

Xadrian

American English, a combination of X and Adrian, meaning "from Hadria."

Xanthus

Greek, meaning "golden haired."

Xavier

Latin, meaning "to the new house."

Xenon

Greek, meaning "the guest." One of the noble gases.

Xerxes

Persian, meaning "ruler of the people" or "respected king." Name of a king who attempted to invade the Greek mainland, but failed.

Xylander

Greek, meaning "man of the forest."

Y

Boys' names

Yaal
Hebrew, meaning "ascending" or "one to ascend."

Yadid
Hebrew, meaning "the beloved one."

Yadon
Hebrew, meaning "against judgment." Associated with the Pokémon character.

Yahir
Spanish, meaning "handsome one."

Yair
Hebrew, meaning "the enlightening one" or "illuminating." The spelling Jair appears in the Bible.

Yakiya
Hebrew, meaning "pure" or "bright."

Yanis
(*alt. Yannis*)
Greek, a form of John meaning "gift of God."

Yarden
Hebrew, meaning "to flow downward."

Ye
Chinese, meaning "bright one" or "light."

Yehuda
Hebrew, meaning "to praise and exalt." Often translated as Judah, who was a son of Jacob in the Bible.

Yered
Hebrew, a form of Jared, meaning "descending."

Yerik
Russian, meaning "God-appointed one."

Yervant

Armenian, meaning "king of people."

Yitzak
(alt. Yitzaak)

Hebrew, meaning "laughter" or "one who laughs."

Ynyr

Welsh, meaning "to honor."

Yobachi

African, meaning "one who prays to God" or "prayed to God."

Yogi

Japanese, meaning "one who practices yoga" or "from yoga." Made famous by the cartoon character Yogi Bear.

Yona

Native American, meaning "bear"; Hebrew, meaning "dove." A name used to refer to ancient people who spoke Greek.

York

Celtic, meaning "yew tree" or "from the farm of the yew tree." Also an historic city in the UK.

Yosef

Hebrew, meaning "added by God" or "God shall add." Hebrew form of Joseph.

Yuri

Aboriginal, meaning "to hear"; Japanese, meaning "one to listen"; Russian, a form of George meaning "farmer."

Yves

French, meaning "miniature archer" or "small archer." Fashion brand YSL was founded by Yves Saint Laurent.

Z

 Boys' names

Zachariah
(alt. Zac, Zach, Zachary)
Hebrew, meaning "remembered by the Lord" or "God has remembered." Famous Zachs include actors Zach Braff and Zach Galifianakis.

Zad
Persian, meaning "my son."

Zadok
Hebrew, meaning "righteous one." "Zadok the Priest" is a well-known coronation anthem and has been sung at every crowning of a king or queen in the UK since 1727.

Zador
Hungarian, meaning "violent demeanor." Zador was the priest who anointed Solomon in the Bible.

Zafar
Arabic, meaning "triumphant."

Zaid
African, meaning "increase the growth" or "growth."

Zaide
Yiddish, meaning "the elder ones." Also the name of an unfinished opera by Mozart.

Zain
(alt. Zane)
Arabic, meaning "the handsome son." Actor Billy Zane is known for his roles in *Titanic* and *The Phantom*.

Zaire
African, meaning "river from Zaire." Zaire is the old name for Democratic Republic of the Congo.

Zarek
Persian, meaning "God protect our king." Associated with the Marvel comic book character.

Zayn

Arabic, meaning "masculine beauty."
Made famous by singer Zayn Malik.

Zuma

Arabic, meaning "peace."

A name for all seasons

Spring	Summer	Fall	Winter
Alvern	Augustus	Aki	Aquilo
Attwell	Balder	Akiko	Caldwell
Avir	Cain	Demitrius	Colden
Bradwell	Dax	Dionysus	Crispin
Jarek	Leo	Forrest	Darke
Kell	Sky	George	Eirwen
Marcus	Somers	Goren	Gennaio
Rain	Sunny	Hunter	Jack
Tamiko	Theros	Red	Mistral

Part Three

Girls' names A–Z

Baby names vary widely in spelling and pronunciation. To simplify things, this book usually lists each name only once: under the most common initial and spelling. If a name has a common alternate spelling with a different initial, it may also be listed under that letter.

 Girls' names

A'mari

Variation of the Swahili or Muslim name Amira, meaning "princess."

Aanya

Sanskrit, meaning "the inexhaustible." Also variation of the Russian name Anya.

Aaryanna

Derivative of the Latin and Greek name Ariadne, meaning "the very holy one."

Abigail

(alt. Abagail, Abbigail, Abigale, Abigayle; abbrev. Abbey, Abbie, Abby, Abi)

Hebrew, meaning "my father's joy." Found in the Bible. The biblical Greek version of the name is Abigaia. Also the name of several Hawaiian princesses.

Abilene

(alt. Abelena, Abilee)

Latin and Spanish, meaning "hazelnut."

Abra

Female variation of Abraham. Also Sanskrit, meaning "clouds."

Abril

Spanish for the month of April; Latin, meaning "open."

Acacia

Greek, meaning "point" or "thorn." Also a species of flowering trees and shrubs.

Acadia

Greek, meaning "paradise." Originally, a French colony in Canada.

Ada
(alt. Adair, Adia)

Hebrew, meaning "adornment." Ada Lovelace is widely credited for being the world's first computer programmer, in the 19th century.

Adalee

German, meaning "noble." Also a contraction of Ada and Lee.

Adalia

Hebrew, meaning "God is my refuge." A genus of ladybug.

Addison
(alt. Addisyn, Addyson; abbrev. Addie, Addy, Adi)

English, meaning "son of Adam." Can be used for girls or boys.

Adelaide
(alt. Adalyn, Adalynn, Adelaida, Adeline, Adelina, Adelyn; abbrev. Addie, Addy, Adi)

Old German, meaning "noble kind." Popular after the rule of William IV and Queen Adelaide of England in the 19th century. Adeline Whitney was a children's author in that period.

Adele
(alt. Adela, Adelia, Adell, Adella, Adelle)

German, meaning "noble" or "nobility." Made famous by the singer Adele.

Aden
(alt. Addien)

Hebrew, meaning "decoration."

Aderyn

Welsh, meaning "bird." Also the name of several places in Wales.

Adesina

Yoruba, meaning "she paves the way." Usually given to a first-born daughter.

Adina
(alt. Adena)

Hebrew, meaning "high hopes" or "precious." Found in the Bible.

Adira

Hebrew, meaning "noble" or "powerful." Also the north Italian city.

Adley

English, meaning "son of Adam." Can be used for girls or boys.

Adrienne
(alt. Adriane, Adriana, Adrianna, Adrianne)

Greek, meaning "from the city of Hadria," or Latin meaning "dark." A feminine form of Adrian.

Aegle

Greek, meaning "brightness" or "splendor." The name of several characters in ancient Greek mythology.

Aerin

Variant of Erin, meaning "peace-making." Taken from J. R. R. Tolkien's novels.

Aerith

Modern American, from the video game *Final Fantasy VII*.

Aero
(alt. Aeron)

Greek, meaning "flight."

Aerolynn

Combination of the Greek Aero, meaning "water," and the English Lynn, meaning "waterfall."

Africa

Celtic, meaning "pleasant," as well as the name of the continent.

Afsaneh

Iranian, meaning "a fairy tale."

Afsha

Persian, meaning "one who sprinkles light."

Afton

Originally a name of a river in Scotland.

Agatha
(abbrev. Aggie)

From St. Agatha, the patron saint of bells, meaning "good." Made famous by mystery novelist Agatha Christie.

Aglaia

Greek, meaning "brilliance." One of the three ancient Greek graces.

Agnes

Greek, meaning "virginal" or "pure." St. Agnes of Rome is the patron saint of girls.

Agrippina

Latin, meaning "born feet first." The name of several influential women of ancient Rome.

Aida

Arabic, meaning "reward" or "present." The title of an opera by Giuseppe Verdi.

Aidanne
(alt. Aidan, Aidenn)

Gaelic, meaning "fire."

Ailbhe

Irish, meaning "noble" or "bright."

Aileen
(alt. Aelinn, Aleen, Aline, Alline)

Gaelic variant of Helen, meaning "light."

Ailith
(alt. Ailish)

Old English, meaning "seasoned warrior."

Ailsa

Scottish, meaning "pledge from God." Also the name of a Scottish island.

Aina

Scandinavian, meaning "forever."

Aine
(alt. Aino)

Celtic, meaning "happiness." The Celtic goddess of summer.

Ainsley
(alt. Ansley)

Scottish/Gaelic, meaning "one's own meadow." Ainsley Hayes is a character in *West Wing*. Can be used for girls or boys.

Aisha
(alt. Aeysha)

Arabic, meaning "woman"; Swahili, meaning "life." Aisha was one of the prophet Muhammad's wives.

Aishwarya

Arabic, meaning "woman." Aishwarya Rai Bachchan is a famous Bollywood actor.

Aislinn
(alt. Aislin, Aisling, Aislyn, Alene, Allene)

Irish Gaelic, meaning "dream." A tribute to aisling, which was an old poetic genre in Ireland.

Aiyanna
(alt. Aiyana)

Native American, meaning "forever flowering."

Aja

Hindi, meaning "goat."

Akela
(alt. Akilah)

Hawaiian, meaning "noble"; Hindi, meaning "alone." Akela is the wolf leader from *The Jungle Book*.

Akilina

Greek or Russian, meaning "eagle."

Akiva

Hebrew, meaning "protect and shelter."

Alaina
(alt. Alana, Alane, Alani, Alanna, Alayna, Aleena, Allannah, Allyn)

Feminine form of Alan, originating from the Greek for "rock" or "comely." Also a spelling alternative for Eleanor.

Alana
(alt. Alanna, Allannah)

Gaelic, meaning "beauty;" Hawaiian, meaning "beautiful offering"; Old German, meaning "precious."

Alanis
(alt. Alarice)

Greek, meaning "rock" or "comely." Associated with singer Alanis Morissette.

Alba

Latin for "white." Also the Gaelic name for Scotland.

Alberta
(alt. Albertha, Albertine)

Feminine form of Albert, from the Old German for "noble, bright, famous." Also a province in Canada.

Albina

Latin, meaning "white" or "fair." Name of an Etruscan goddess of the dawn.

Alda

German, meaning "old" or "prosperous." St. Alda was an Italian mystic in the 11th century.

Aldis

English, meaning "battle seasoned."

Aleta
(alt. Aletha)

Greek, meaning "footloose." Queen Aleta Ellis is a character from *The Legend of Prince Valiant*.

Alethea
(alt. Aletheia)

Greek, meaning "truth."

Alexandra
(alt. Alejandra, Alejandrina, Alejhandra, Aleksandra, Alessandra, Alexandrea, Alexandria, Aliandra; abbrev. Alex, Alexa, Alexi, Alexia, Alexina, Ali, Allie, Ally, Lexi, Lexie, Sandra, Sandy, Sasha, Sascha, Shura, Sondra, Xandra, Zandra)

Feminine form of Alexander, from the Greek interpretation of "man's defender." Also one of the ancient Greek goddess Hera's names. Perhaps the name with the most short forms, from many languages, which are often used as names in their own right.

Alexis
(alt. Alexus, Alexys)

Greek, meaning "helper." Alexis was an ancient Greek poet of comedy.

Aleydis

Variant of Alice, meaning "nobility." Alternative name for St. Alice of Scharbeek, the patron saint of the blind and paralyzed.

Alfreda

Old English, meaning "elf power." The modern spelling of AElfthryth of Crowland.

Alibeth

Variant of Elizabeth, meaning "pledged to God." Popular name during the Middle Ages.

Alice
(alt. Alika, Aliki, Alize, Alyce, Alys, Alyse)

English, meaning "noble" or "nobility." Made famous by the novel *Alice in Wonderland*.

Alicia
(alt. Ahlicia, Alecia, Alesha, Alesia, Alessia, Alizia, Alisha, Alycia, Alysha, Alysia)

Latin, originally derived from Alice, meaning "nobility." Famous Alicias include singer Alicia Keys, actor Alicia Silverstone, and the birth name of singer Pink.

Alida
(alt. Aleida)

Latin, meaning "small-winged one."

Alima
Arabic, meaning "cultured."

Alina
(alt. Alena, Aleana)

Slavic form of Helen, meaning "light."

Alison
(alt. Allison, Allisyn, Allyson, Alyson; abbrev. Ali, Allie, Ally)

Variant of Alice, meaning "nobility." Originally the name was Alis in the Middle Ages, with the suffix "on," which means "little."

Alivia
Variant of Olivia, meaning "olive tree."

Aliya
(alt. Aaliyah, Aleah, Alia, Aliah, Aliyah)

Arabic, meaning "exalted" or "sublime." Aliya bint Ali was the last queen consort of Iraq.

Alla
Variant of Ella or Alexandra. Also a possible reference to Allah.

Allegra
Italian, meaning "joyous."

Allura
French, from the word for entice, meaning "the power of attraction."

Alma
Latin for "giving nurture"; Italian for "soul"; Arabic for "learned." Also commonly written as Alma Mater, meaning "nourishing mother" or "fostering mother."

Almeda
(alt. Almeta)

Latin, meaning "ambitious."

Almera
(alt. Almira)

Feminine form of Elmer, from the Arabic for "aristocratic"; Old English meaning "noble."

Alohi
Variant of the Hawaiian greeting Aloha, meaning "love and affection."

Alona
(alt. Alora)

Hebrew, meaning "oak tree."

Alpha

The first letter of the Greek alphabet, usually given to a firstborn daughter.

Alta

Latin, meaning "elevated."

Altagracia

Spanish, meaning "grace." Alta Gracia is also a city in Argentina.

Althaea
(alt. Altea, Altha, Althea)

Greek, meaning "healing power." Althaea was a prominent character in ancient Greek mythology.

Alva

Spanish, meaning "blonde" or "fair-skinned." In Norway and Sweden it is considered the female form of Alf, which means "elf."

Alvena
(alt. Alvina)

Old English, meaning "elf friend." In Old German it is the feminine form of Adelwin, meaning "noble friend."

Alvia
(alt. Alyvia)

Variant of Olivia, meaning "olive tree," or Elvira, from the ancient Spanish city.

Alyssa
(alt. Alisa, Alissa, Allyssa, Alysa)

Greek, meaning "rational." Associated with the alyssum flower.

Amadea

Feminine form of Amadeus, meaning "God's love."

Amalia

German, meaning "work"; Hebrew, meaning "labor of love."

Amana

Hebrew, meaning "loyal and true." Also a genus of tulips.

Amanda
(alt. Amandine; abbrev. Mandy)

Latin, meaning "much loved." Famous Amandas include actors Amanda Bynes and Amanda Seyfried.

Amara
(alt. Amani)

Greek, meaning "lovely forever." Actor Amara Miller is known for her role in TV show *The Descendants*.

Amarantha

Contraction of Amanda and Samantha, meaning "much loved listener."

Amari
(alt. Amaris, Amasa, Amata, Amaya)

Hebrew, meaning "pledged by God."

Amaryllis

(alt. Ameris)

Greek, meaning "fresh." Also a flower.

Amber

French, from the semiprecious stone of the same name. Famous Ambers include actor Amber Heard and model Amber Rose.

Amberly

Contraction of Amber and Leigh, meaning "stone" and "meadow."

Amberlynn

Contraction of Amber and Lynn, meaning "stone" and "waterfall."

Amelia

(alt. Aemilia, Amelie)

Greek, meaning "industrious." Famous Amelias include flying legend Amelia Earhart and two Princess Amelias of Great Britain. Amelie is the French variant and the title of a movie.

America

From the country and continents of the same name. Associated with *Ugly Betty* actor America Ferrera.

Amethyst

Greek, from the precious, mulberry-colored stone of the same name.

Amina

Arabic, meaning "honest and trustworthy."

Aminta

Greek, meaning "defender."

Amira

(alt. Amiya, Amiyah)

Arabic, meaning "a high-born girl"; Hebrew, meaning "rich princess."

Amity

Latin, meaning "friendship and harmony." Also a name of a faction in the *Divergent* series.

Amory

Variant of the Spanish name Amor, meaning "love."

Amy

(alt. Aimee, Amee, Ami, Amie, Ammie, Amya)

Latin, meaning "beloved." Famous Amys include actor Amy Adams and singer Amy Winehouse. Aimee is the French form, used by actor Aimee Garcia, singer Aimee Mann, and Aimee Osbourne of the Osbourne family.

Ana-Lisa

Contraction of Anna and Lisa, meaning "grace" or "consecrated to God."

Anafa

Hebrew, meaning "heron."

Ananda

Hindi, meaning "bliss." One of Buddha's disciples.

Anastasia
(alt. Athanasia)

Greek, meaning "resurrection." Grand Duchess Anastasia of Russia was killed in 1918, following the Russian Revolution.

Anat

Jewish, meaning "water spring." Anat is an important Semitic goddess.

Anatolia

Greek, meaning "east sunrise." From the eastern Greek town of the same name.

Andrea
(alt. Andreia, Andria, Andrine, Andrina)

Feminine form of Andrew, from the Greek term for "a man's woman." Famous Andreas include writers Andrea Levy and Andrea Dworkin.

Andromeda

Greek, meaning "leader of men." From the heroine of an ancient Greek legend.

Anemone

Greek, meaning "breath." Also a flowering plant.

Angela
(alt. Angel, Angeles, Angelia, Angelle, Angie)

Greek, meaning "messenger from God" or "angel." Famous Angelas include actors Angela Lansbury and Angela Bassett.

Angelica
(alt. Angelina, Angeline, Angelique, Angelise, Angelita, Anjelica, Anjelina)

Latin, meaning "angelic." Famous Angelicas include actor Anjelica Huston and *Rugrats* character Angelica Pickles.

Anise
(alt. Anisa, Anissa)

French, from the licorice-flavored plant of the same name.

Aniston

English, meaning "town of Agnes."

Anita
(alt. Anitra)

Derived from Ann, Hannah, or Anahita (the Iranian water goddess), depending on the language. Famous Anitas include singer Anita Baker and *West Side Story* character Anita.

Anna
(alt. Ana)

Derived from Hannah, meaning "grace." A prophetess in the Bible.

Annabel
(alt. Anabel, Anabelle, Annabell,
Annabella, Annabelle, Amabel)

Contraction of Anna and Belle,
meaning "grace" and "beauty."

Annalise
(alt. Annalee, Annalisa, Anneli,
Annelie, Annelise)

Contraction of Anna and Lise,
meaning "grace" and "pledged to
God."

Anne
(alt. Ann)

Originally a French form of Anna,
meaning "grace," but used in England
for many hundreds of years. Famous
Annes include actor Anne Hathaway
and two wives of Henry VIII.

Annemarie
(alt. Annamae, Annamarie, Annelle,
Annmarie)

Contraction of Anna and Mary,
meaning "grace" and "star of the
sea." The name of actor Anne-Marie
Duff.

Annette
(alt. Annetta)

Hebrew, derived from Hannah,
meaning "grace." Associated with
actors Annette Funicello and Annette
Bening.

Annis

Greek, meaning "finished or
completed." The Black Annis
is a blue-faced witch in English
mythology.

Annora

Latin, meaning "honor."

Anoushka
(alt. Anousha)

Russian variation of Ann, meaning
"grace."

Anthea
(alt. Anthi)

Greek, meaning "flower-like." Also
another name for the ancient Greek
goddess Hera.

Antigone

In ancient Greek mythology,
Antigone was the daughter of
Oedipus.

Antoinette
(alt. Antonetta, Antonette, Antonietta;
abbrev. Toni)

Feminine form of Anthony,
meaning "invaluable grace." French
queen consort Marie Antoinette
was executed during the French
Revolution fo 1789.

Antonia
(alt. Antonella, Antonina)

Latin, meaning "invaluable." A very
popular name in ancient Rome.

Anwen

Welsh, meaning "very fair."

Anya

(alt. Aanya, Aniya, Aniyah, Aniylah, Anja)

Russian, meaning "grace."

Aoife

Gaelic, meaning "beautiful joy." Associated with goddess Esuvia.

Apollonia

Feminine of Apollo, the Greek god of the sun. St. Apollonia is the patron saint of dentistry.

Apple

From the name of the fruit. Famous Apples include technology company Apple Inc., and Gwyneth Paltrow's daughter.

April

(alt. Avril)

Latin, meaning "opening up." Also the fourth month, which has associations with the goddess Venus.

Aquilina

(alt. Aqua, Aquila)

Spanish, meaning "like an eagle." Associated with St. Aquilina.

Ara

Arabic, meaning "brings rain." Also a star constellation. Can be used for girls or boys.

Arabella

(alt. Arabelle; abbrev. Bel, Bella)

Latin, meaning "answered prayer." The name of an opera by Richard Strauss.

Araceli

(alt. Aracely)

Spanish, meaning "altar of Heaven."

Araminta

Contraction of Arabella and Aminta, meaning "answered prayer" and "defender."

Arcadia

Greek, meaning "paradise." The daughter of ancient Roman Emperor Arcadius.

Ardelle

(alt. Ardell, Ardella)

Latin, meaning "burning with enthusiasm." Ardelle Kloss is a figure skater.

Arden

(alt. Ardis, Ardith)

Latin, meaning "burning with enthusiasm." Made famous by the cosmetics company Elizabeth Arden.

Arella

(alt. Areli, Arely)

Hebrew, meaning "angel."

Aretha

Greek, meaning "woman of virtue."
Aretha Franklin was a legendary soul singer.

Aria

(alt. Ariah, Arya)

Italian, meaning "melody." Arya Stark is a character in *Game of Thrones*.

Ariadne

Both Greek and Latin, meaning "the very holy one." In ancient Greek mythology, Ariadne was the daughter of King Minos.

Ariana

(alt. Ariane, Arianna, Arienne)

Welsh, meaning "silver."

Ariel

(alt. Ariela, Ariella, Arielle)

Hebrew, meaning "lioness of God." Ariel is the main character in Disney's *The Little Mermaid*.

Arlene

(alt. Arleen, Arline; abbrev. Arlie, Arly)

Gaelic, meaning "pledge." Associated with actor Arlene Dahl.

Armida

Latin, meaning "little armed one." Taken from the character of Armida in *Gerusalemme liberata* by Italian poet Torquato Tasso.

Artemisia

(alt. Artemis, Arti, Artie)

Greek/Spanish, meaning "perfect." Artemisia was a legendary female ancient Persian naval commander.

Arwen

Welsh, meaning "fair" or "fine." Arwen is a key Elven figure in *The Lord of the Rings*.

Ashanti

Geographical area in Africa. Also the name of the popular R&B singer Ashanti.

Ashby

English, meaning "ash tree farm."

Ashley

(alt. Ashlee, Ashleigh, Ashli, Ashlie, Ashly)

English, meaning "ash tree meadow." Famous Ashleys include actor Ashley Judd, and singers Ashley Tisdale and Ashlee Simpson. Can be used for girls or boys.

Ashlynn

(alt. Ashlyn)

Irish Gaelic, meaning "dream."

Ashton

(alt. Ashtyn)

Old English, meaning "ash tree town." Can be used for girls or boys.

Asia

Name of the continent. Also a name for an Oceanid in ancient Greek mythology.

Asma
(alt. Asmara)

Arabic, meaning "highstanding."

Aspen
(alt. Aspynn)

Name of the tree. Also the Colorado city famous for its ski resort.

Assumpta
(alt. Asumpta, Assunta)

Italian, meaning "raised up."

Asta
(alt. Asteria, Astor, Astoria)

Greek or Latin, meaning "starlike."

Astrid

Old Norse, meaning "beautiful like a God." Astrid Lundgren is the author of *Pippi Longstocking*.

Atara

Hebrew, meaning "diadem" or "crown." Also a genus of butterfly.

Athena
(alt. Athenais)

Greek, meaning "wise." Athena was the ancient Greek goddess of wisdom, mathematics, and arts and crafts.

Aubrey
(alt. Aubree, Aubriana, Aubrie)

French, meaning "elf ruler."

Audrey
(alt. Audra, Audrie, Audrina, Audry)

English, meaning "noble strength." St. Etheldreda was known as St. Audrey, and was a seventh-century English princess. Made famous by Hollywood icon Audrey Hepburn.

Augusta
(alt. August, Augustine)

Latin, meaning "worthy of respect."

Aura
(alt. Aurea)

Greek or Latin, meaning either "soft breeze" or "gold." An aura is the perceived field of energy surrounding people and objects in various spiritual beliefs.

Aurelia
(alt. Aurelie)

Latin, meaning gold. The mother of Julius Caesar.

Aurora
(alt. Aurore)

Latin, meaning "dawn." In ancient Roman mythology, Aurora was the goddess of sunrise.

Austine
(alt. Austen, Austin)

Latin, meaning "worthy of respect."

Autumn

Latin, from the name of the harvest season.

Ava
(alt. Avia, Avie)

Latin, meaning "like a bird." Associated with actor Ava Gardner.

Avalon
(alt. Avalyn, Aveline)

Celtic, meaning "island of apples." Avalon is the mythological island in the King Arthur legend.

Axelle

Greek, meaning "father of peace."

Aya
(alt. Ayah)

Hebrew, meaning "bird."

Ayanna
(alt. Ayana)

Yoruba, meaning "beautiful flower."

Ayesha
(alt. Aisha, Aysha)

Persian, meaning "small one."

Azalea

Latin, meaning "dry earth." Also the name of a flowering shrub.

Names of First Ladies

Barbara (Bush)
Edith (Roosevelt)
Elizabeth (Ford)
Grace (Coolidge)
Hillary (Clinton)
Jacqueline (Kennedy)
Martha (Washington)
Mary (Lincoln)
Melania (Trump)
Michelle (Obama)
Nancy (Reagan)

Azalia

Hebrew, meaning "aided by God."

Aziza

Hebrew, meaning "mighty"; Arabic meaning "precious." Female variation of Aziz.

Azure
(alt. Azaria)

French, meaning "sky-blue." Refers to the bright blue color of the sky on a clear day.

Girls' names

Babette
(alt. Babe)

French version of Barbara; Greek meaning "foreign." Babette Cole is the author of children's books *Mommy Laid an Egg* and *Princess Smartypants*.

Bailey
(alt. Baeli, Bailee)

English, meaning "law enforcer."

Bambi
(alt. Bambina)

Shortened version of the Italian "bambina," meaning "child." Made famous by the Disney movie *Bambi*.

Barbara
(alt. Barbra; abbrev. Barb, Barbie)

Greek, meaning "foreign." Famous Barbaras include journalist Barbara Walters, and singer and actor Barbra Streisand.

Basma

Arabic, meaning "smile."

Bathsheba

Hebrew, meaning "daughter of the oath." Bathsheba was a key biblical figure, and mother of King Solomon.

Bay
(alt. Bae, Baya)

From the edible plant the bay leaf, or the geographical name for a large inlet of water.

Beata

Latin, meaning "blessed."

Beatrice
(alt. Beatrix, Beatriz, Bee, Bellatrix; abbrev. Bea)

Latin, meaning "bringer of gladness." Beatrice is a character in Shakespeare's *Much Ado About Nothing*. Princess Beatrice is ninth in line to the British throne.

Belinda
(alt. Belen, Belina)

Contraction of Belle and Linda, meaning "beautiful." Well-known Belindas include singer Belinda Carlisle.

Bella
(alt. Béla)

Latin, meaning "beautiful." Bella (Isabella) Swan is the main female character in the *Twilight* series.

Belle
(alt. Bell)

French, meaning "beautiful." Popularized by the Disney princess in *Beauty and the Beast*.

Belva

Latin, meaning "beautiful view." The inspiration for one of the characters in the musical *Chicago* was real-life murderer Belva Gaertner.

Bénédicta
(alt. Benedetta; abbrev. Bennie)

Latin, the feminine form of Benedict, meaning "blessed." Associated with Benedicta Henrietta of the Palatinate.

Benita
(alt. Bernita; abbrev. Bennie)

Spanish, meaning "blessed."

Berit
(alt. Beret)

Scandinavian, meaning "splendid" or "gorgeous."

Bernadette
(alt. Bernadine; abbrev. Bernie)

French, meaning "courageous." St. Bernadette was known for her visions of the Virgin Mary.

Bernice
(alt. Berenice, Berniece, Burnice)

Greek, meaning "she who brings victory." The name of Herod's daughter in the Bible.

Bertha
(alt. Berta, Berthe, Bertie)

German, meaning "bright." There are four saints called Bertha, all from the Middle Ages.

Beryl

Greek, meaning "pale, green gemstone." The name of a precious mineral.

Bess
(alt. Bessie)

Shortened form of Elizabeth, meaning "consecrated to God." Queen Elizabeth I's nickname was Good Queen Bess.

Beth

Hebrew, meaning "house." Also shortened form of Elizabeth, meaning "consecrated to God."

Bethany
(alt. Bethan)

Hebrew, referring to a geographical location in the Bible.

Bethel

Hebrew, meaning "house of God."
A city in the Bible.

Bettina

(alt. Battina, Betiana, Betina, Bettine; abbrev. Betty, Ina, Tina)

Latin, derived from Benedetta or German derived from Elizabeth. Bettina Bush was the voice for *Rainbow Brite*.

Betty

(alt. Betsy, Bette, Bettie, Bettye)

Originally a shortened version of Elizabeth, meaning "consecrated to God," now often used as a name in its own right. Famous Bettys include cartoon character Betty Boop, actor Betty Grable, and glamor model Bettie Page.

Beulah

Hebrew, meaning "married."
The name of the place that exists between Earth and Heaven.

Beverly

(alt. Beverlee, Beverley)

English, meaning "beaver stream." Made famous by Beverly Hills, CA, and actor Beverley Mitchell.

Beyoncé

American English, made popular by the singer.

Bianca

(alt. Blanca)

Italian, meaning "white." Bianca is a character from Shakespeare's *Othello*.

Bijou

French, meaning "precious ring."

Billie

(alt. Bill, Billy, Billye)

Originally used for girls as a shortened version of Wilhelmina, meaning "determined." Now used almost universally as a standalone name, made popular by jazz singer Billie Holiday who chose it as her stage name, and tennis legend Billie Jean King.

Bina

Hebrew, meaning "knowledge."

Birdie

(alt. Birdy)

English and Swedish, meaning "little bird."

Birgit

(alt. Birgitta)

German, meaning "power and strength." Used as a variation of Bridget.

Blaer

Icelandic, meaning "light breeze."

Blair

Scottish Gaelic, meaning "flat, plain area." Well-known Blairs include actor Blair Underwood.

Blake
(alt. Blakely, Blakelyn)

English, meaning either "pale skinned" or "dark." Associated with actor Blake Lively. Can be used for girls or boys.

Blanche
(alt. Blanch)

French, meaning "white or pale." Famous Blanches include the characters of Blanche Devereaux in *The Golden Girls*, and Blanche DuBois in *A Streetcar Named Desire*.

Bliss

English, meaning "intense happiness."

Blithe

English, meaning "joyous."

Blodwen

Welsh, meaning "white flower." The name of a Welsh opera.

Blossom

English, meaning "flowerlike." *Blossom* was a 1990s sitcom.

Blythe
(alt. Bly)

English, meaning "happy and carefree." Blythe Danner starred in sitcom *Will and Grace* and is the mother of actor Gwyneth Paltrow.

Bobbi
(alt. Bobbie, Bobby)

Shortened version of Roberta, meaning "bright fame." Associated with cosmetics brand Bobbi Brown.

Bonita
(alt. Bo)

Spanish, meaning "pretty." "La Isla Bonita" is a song by Madonna.

Bonnie
(alt. Bonny)

Scottish, meaning "fair of face." One half of the outlaw duo Bonnie and Clyde.

Brandy
(alt. Brandee, Brandi, Brandie)

Dutch, meaning "burnt wine." Name of the liquor.

Brea
(alt. Bree, Bria)

Shortened form of Brianna, meaning "strong." Also the name of an ancient Irish god.

Brenda

Old Norse, meaning "sword."

Brianna
(alt. Breana, Breann, Breanna, Breanne, Brenna, Brenyn, Briana, Brianne, Bryanna)

Irish Gaelic, meaning "strong."

Bridget
(alt. Bridgett, Bridgette, Brigette, Brigid, Brigitta, Brigitte)

Irish Gaelic, meaning "strength and power." Famous Bridgets include actors Bridget Fonda and Brigitte Bardot, and the novel and movie *Bridget Jones's Diary*.

Brier
(alt. Briar)

French, meaning "heather." Sleeping Beauty's pseudonym is Briar Rose in the Disney movie.

Brit
(alt. Britt, Britta)

Celtic, meaning "spotted" or "freckled." Name of actor Britt Ekland.

Britannia

Latin, meaning "Britain." Britannia is the female personification of Great Britain.

Brittany
(alt. Britany, Britney, Britni, Brittani, Brittanie, Brittney, Brittni, Brittny)

Latin, meaning "from Britain." Famous Brittanys include the French province, singer Britney Spears, and actor Brittany Murphy.

Bronwen
(alt. Bronwyn)

Welsh, meaning "fair breast." The spelling of Bronwen is more common for girls, and Bronwyn for boys.

Brooke
(alt. Brook)

English, meaning "small stream." Brooke Shields is an actor and model. Can be used for girls or boys.

Brooklyn
(alt. Brooklynn)

Name of a New York borough. Associated with model Brooklyn Decker.

Brunhilda
(alt. Brunhilde, Brynhildr)

German, meaning "armor-wearing fighting maid." Brynhildr was an important character in Old German mythology.

Bryn
(alt. Brynn)

Welsh, meaning "mount" or "hill."

Bryony
(alt. Briony)

English, from bryonia, the name of a European vine.

Buffy

American English alternative of Elizabeth, meaning "consecrated to God." The protagonist of the sci-fi series *Buffy the Vampire Slayer*.

Girls' names

Cadence
(alt. Candenza)
Latin, meaning "with rhythm." Also used beginning with K.

Cai
Vietnamese, meaning "feminine."

Caitlin
(alt. Cadyn, Caitlann, Caitlyn, Caitlyn, Kaitlin)
Greek, meaning "pure." Catelyn Stark is a central character from *Game of Thrones*. Caitlyn Jenner is a former Olympian athlete and member of the Jenner/Kardashian clan. Also spelt with a K, as for Kaitlin Doubleday.

Calandra
Greek, meaning "lark." A small Mediterranean bird.

Calantha
(alt. Calanthe)
Greek, meaning "lovely flower."

Caledonia
Latin, meaning Scotland.

Calla
Greek, meaning "beautiful." Associated with the calla lily.

Callie
(alt. Caleigh, Cali, Calleigh, Cally)
Greek, meaning "beauty." Callie Khouri is a screenwriter.

Calliope
(alt. Kalliope)
Greek, meaning "beautiful voice." From the muse of epic poetry in Greek mythology.

Callista
(alt. Calista, Callisto, Kallista)
Greek, meaning "most beautiful." Best-known as the name of actor Calista Flockhart.

Camas

Native American, from the root and bulb of the same name.

Cambria

Welsh, from the alternate name for Wales.

Camden
(alt. Camdyn)

English, meaning "winding valley." Also an area of London, England.

Cameo

Italian, meaning "skin." Associated with the notion of a cameo role in film or television.

Cameron
(alt. Camryn)

Scottish Gaelic, meaning "bent nose." Used for boys and girls. Actor Cameron Diaz has starred in many Hollywood hits.

Camilla
(alt. Camelia, Camellia, Camila, Camille, Camillia)

Latin, meaning "spiritual serving girl." Made famous by model Camilla Alves, and Camilla, Duchess of Cornwall, who is married to Prince Charles.

Candace
(alt. Candice, Candis, Kandace)

Latin, meaning "brilliant white." Famous Candaces include basketball player Candace Parker, and Candace Bushnell, author of *Sex and the City*.

Candida

Latin, meaning "white."

Candra

Latin, meaning "glowing."

Candy
(alt. Candi, Kandy)

Shortened form of Candace, meaning "brilliant white." Also a name for sweets or confectionery.

Caoimhe

Celtic, meaning "gentleness." Has many different pronounciations, including "Kyva" and "Keeva," depending on where in Ireland you hear it.

Caprice

Italian, meaning "ruled by whim." Made famous by model and actor Caprice.

Cara

Latin, meaning "darling." Cara Delevingne is a model and Cara Black a bestselling mystery novelist.

Carey
(alt. Cari, Carie, Carri, Carrie, Cary)
Welsh, meaning "near the castle."
Famous Careys include actor Carey
Mulligan and singer Mariah Carey.

Carina
(alt. Corina)
Italian, meaning "dearest little one."
Also the name of a star constellation.

Carissa
(alt. Carisa)
Greek, meaning "grace."

Carla
(alt. Charl, Karla)
Feminine of the Old Norse Carl,
meaning "free man." Supermodel
and singer-songwriter Carla Bruni-
Sarkozy is married to former French
president Nicolas Sarkozy.

Carlin
(alt. Carleen, Carlene)
Gaelic, meaning "little champion."

Carlotta
(alt. Carlota)
Italian, meaning "free man." Carlotta
is a character from *The Phantom of
the Opera*.

Carly
*(alt. Carlee, Carley, Carli, Carlie, Karly,
Karlie)*
Feminine form of the German
Charles, meaning "man." Famous
Carlys include singers Carly Simon
and Carly Rae Jepson, and model
Karlie Kloss.

Carmel
(alt. Carmela, Carmelita, Carmella)
Hebrew, meaning "garden." American
Carmelita Jeter is an Olympic medal-
winning 100-meter sprinter.

Carmen
(alt. Carma, Carmina)
Latin, meaning "song." The opera
Carmen was composed by Georges
Bizet.

Carol
*(alt. Carole, Carrol, Carroll, Caryl,
Karol)*
Originally the short form of Caroline,
meaning "man." Famous Carols
include actor Carol Burnett.

Caroline
*(alt. Carolann, Carolina, Carolyn,
Carolynn)*
German, meaning "man." A feminine
form of Charles. Caroline Kennedy is
the daughter of John F. Kennedy.

Carrington
English, meaning "Charles's town."

Carys
(alt. Cerys)

Welsh, meaning "love."

Casey
(alt. Casy, Casie, Kasey)

Irish Gaelic, meaning "watchful."
Used for girls and boys.

Cassandra
(alt. Casandra, Cassandre, Kassandra;
abbrev. Cassie)

Greek, meaning "one who
prophesies doom" or "entangler
of men." Cassandra was a seer in
ancient Greek mythology.

Cassia
(alt. Casia, Casie, Cassie)

Greek, meaning "cinnamon."

Cassidy

Irish, meaning "clever."

Catherine
(alt. Catalina, Catarina, Caterina,
Catharine, Cathleen, Cathrine,
Cathryn; abbrev. Cate, Cathy, Cathie,
Caity, Caty)

Greek, meaning "pure." Famous
Catherines include Catherine,
Duchess of Cambridge, actor
Catherine Zeta Jones, and Russia's
Catherine the Great. Cathleen is the
Irish variant of Catherine, and Catalina
the Spanish version. All variations and
abbreviations can also be spelled with
an initial K.

Cayley
(alt. Cayla, Caylee, Caylen)

Gaelic, meaning "slim" and "fair."

Cecilia
(alt. Cecelia, Cecile, Cecilie, Cecily,
Cicely, Cicily)

Latin, meaning "blind one."

Celena

Greek, meaning "goddess of the
moon." Also a spelling variation for
Selena.

Celeste
(alt. Celestina, Celestine)

Latin, meaning "heavenly."
Associated with actor Celeste Holm.

Celine
(alt. Celia, Celina)

French version of Celeste, meaning
"heavenly." Associated with singer
Celine Dion.

Cerise

French, meaning "cherry." The color
cerise is a deep, pink-red shade.

Chanah
(alt. Chana)

Hebrew, meaning "grace." Also a
spelling variation for Hannah.

Chance

Middle English, meaning "good
fortune."

Chandler
(alt. Chandell)

English, meaning "candle maker." Can be used for girls or, more commonly, boys.

Chandra
(alt. Chanda, Chandry)

Sanskrit, meaning "like the moon." Chandra is a god of the moon in Hinduism.

Chanel
(alt. Chanelle)

French, meaning "pipe." Name of the French fashion house founded by designer Coco Chanel.

Chantal
(alt. Chantel, Chantelle, Chantilly)

French, meaning "stony spot."

Chardonnay

French, from the wine variety of the same name.

Charis
(alt. Charice, Charissa, Charisse)

Greek, meaning "grace." One of the graces in ancient Greek mythology.

Charity

Latin, meaning "brotherly love."

Charlene
(alt. Charleen, Charline)

German, meaning "man." Associated with actor Charlene Tilton.

Charlize

French form of Charlotte, meaning "little and feminine". Made famous by actor Charlize Theron.

Charlotte
(alt. Charnette, Charolette; abbrev. Charlie, Charley, Charly, Lottie)

French, meaning "little and feminine." Famous Charlottes include Princess Charlotte, author Charlotte Bronte, and the novel *Charlotte's Web* by E. B. White.

Charmaine

Latin, meaning "clan." Derived from Charmain, a favorite servant of Cleopatra.

Chastity

Latin, meaning "purity."

Chava
(alt. Chaya)

Hebrew, meaning "beloved."

Chelsea
(alt. Chelsee, Chelsey, Chelsi, Chelsie)

English, meaning "port or landing place." Famous Chelseas include comedian Chelsea Handler and advocate Chelsea Clinton.

Cher

French, meaning "beloved." Made famous by the singer Cher.

Cherie
(alt. Cheri, Cherise)
French, meaning "dear."

Cherish
(alt. Cherith)
English, meaning "to treasure." The title of a song by Madonna.

Chermona
Hebrew, meaning "sacred mountain."

Cherry
(alt. Cherri)
French, meaning "cherry fruit."

Cheryl
(alt. Cheryle)
English, meaning "little and womanly." Famous Cheryls include dancer Cheryl Burke from *Dancing With The Stars*.

Chesney
English, meaning "place to camp." More commonly used for boys.

Cheyenne
(alt. Cheyanne)
Native American, from the tribe of the same name in Wyoming.

Chiara
(alt. Ceara, Chiarina, Ciara)
Italian, meaning "light." Associated with the singer Ciara.

China
From the country of the same name.

Chiquita
Spanish, meaning "little one."

Chloe
(alt. Cloe)
Greek, meaning "pale green shoot." Famous Chloes include actors Chloe Grace Moretz and Chloe Sevigny, and author Toni Morrison—whose birth name was Chloe Wofford.

Chloris
(alt. Cloris)
Greek, meaning "pale." Made famous by actor and comedian Cloris Leachman.

Christabel
(alt. Christobel)
Latin and French, meaning "fair Christian." The title of a poem by Samuel Taylor Coleridge.

Christina
(alt. Christine, Christen, Christene, Christian, Christiana, Christiane, Christin, Cristina; abbrev. Chris, Chrissy, Christa, Christie, Christy, Crissy, Cristy)
Greek, meaning "anointed Christian." Famous Christinas include singer Christina Aguilera and actors Christina Ricci and Christine Taylor.

Chuma
Aramaic, meaning "warmth."

Cierra
(alt. Ciera)

Irish, meaning "black."

Cinderella

French, meaning "little ashgirl."
Subject of the children's fairy tale.

Cinnamon

Greek, from the exotic spice of the
same name.

Citlali
(alt. Citlalli)

Nahuatl, meaning "star." An ancient
Aztec name.

Citrine

Latin, from the gemstone of the same
name.

Claire
(alt. Clara, Clare, Claira)

Latin, meaning "bright." Associated
with actor Claire Danes.

Clarabelle
(alt. Claribel)

Contraction of Clare and Isobel,
meaning "bright" and "consecrated
to God." Clarabelle is a Disney cow
cartoon character.

Clarissa
(alt. Clarice, Clarisse)

Variation of Claire, meaning "bright."
The title character from the 1990s'
sitcom Clarissa Explains It All.

Clarity

Latin, meaning "lucid."

Claudia
(alt. Claudetta, Claudette, Claudie,
Claudine)

Latin, meaning "lame." The first
female president of Haiti was
Claudette Werleigh. Claudia Schiffer
is a German supermodel.

Clematis

Greek, meaning "vine." A type of
flowering plant.

Clementine
(alt. Clemency, Clementina, Clemmie)

Latin, meaning "mild and merciful."
Also the small orange fruit.

Cleopatra

Greek, meaning "her father's
renown." Famed as an ancient
Egyptian queen.

Clio
(alt. Cleo, Cliona)

Greek, from the ancient Greek muse
of the same name.

Clodagh

Irish, meaning "river."

Clotilda
(alt. Clothilda, Clothilde, Clotilde)

German, meaning "renowned
battle." St. Clotilde was known for
her works of charity.

Clover

English, from the flower of the same name.

Coby

Diminutive of Jacob, meaning "supplanter." More commonly used as a boy's name.

Coco

Spanish, an abbreviation of *socorro*, meaning "help." Name of the French fashion designer Coco Chanel.

Cody

English, meaning "pillow."

Colleen
(alt. Coleen)

Irish Gaelic, meaning "girl." Colleen Camp is an actor.

Collette
(alt. Colette)

Greek/French, meaning "people of victory." Sidonie-Gabrielle Colette was the author of *Gigi*.

Constance
(alt. Constanza, Constantina, Konstance; abbrev. Connie)

Latin, meaning "steadfast." Oscar Wilde's wife was Constance Lloyd. Famous Connies include actors Connie Britton and Connie Nielsen, and journalist Connie Chung.

Consuelo
(alt. Consuela)

Spanish, meaning "comfort." Originally from the Virgin Mary, who was known as Our Lady of Consolation in Spanish.

Cora
(alt. Kora)

Greek, meaning "maiden."

Coral
(alt. Coralie, Coraline, Corelia, Corene)

Latin, from the marine life of the same name.

Corazon

Spanish, meaning "heart" or "darling."

Cordelia
(alt. Cordia, Cordie)

Latin, meaning "heart." Famous fictional Cordelias include characters in Shakespeare's *King Lear* and TV's *Buffy the Vampire Slayer*.

Corey
(alt. Cori, Corrie, Cory)

Irish Gaelic, meaning "the hollow."

Corin
(alt. Corine)

Latin, meaning "spear."

Corinne
(alt. Corinna, Corrine)

French version of Cora, meaning "maiden." Associated with singer Corinne Bailey Rae.

Corliss
English, meaning "cheery."

Cornelia
Latin, meaning "like a horn." The name of several influential women of ancient Rome.

Cosette
French, meaning "people of victory." Name of a key character in Victor Hugo's *Les Misérables*.

Cosima
(alt. Cosmina)

Greek, meaning "order." One of the clones in *Orphan Black*.

Courtney
(alt. Cortney)

English, meaning "court-dweller." Famous Courtneys include actor Courtney Cox and singer Courtney Love.

Creola
French, meaning "American-born, English descent." Associated with the Creole language and people.

Crescent
French, meaning "increasing."

Cressida
From the Trojan heroine in Greek mythology of the same name.

Crystal
(alt. Christal, Chrystal, Cristal, Krystal)

Greek, meaning "ice." A kind of manufactured precious stone.

Csilla
Hungarian, meaning "defenses."

Cyd
Shortened form of Sidney, meaning "wide island." Cyd Charisse was a dancer and actor.

Cynara
Greek, meaning "thistly plant."

Cynthia
(abbrev. Cinda, Cindi, Cindy, Cyndi)

Greek, meaning "goddess from the mountain." Famous Cynthias include actor Cynthia Nixon and designer Cynthia Rowley. Famous Cindys include 1980s supermodel Cindy Crawford and singer Cindi Lauper.

Cyra
Persian, meaning "sun." Also a genus of ladybugs.

Cyrilla
Latin, meaning "lordly." Also a type of flowering plant.

D

Girls' names

Dacey
Irish Gaelic, meaning "from the south."

Dada
Yoruba, meaning "curly haired." Also associated with the art movement Dadaism.

Daenerys
Literary, created by author George R. R. Martin in book series *A Song of Ice and Fire*, and TV series *Game of Thrones*.

Dagmar
German, meaning "day's glory." Dagmar was the stage name of Virginia Egnor.

Dagny
Nordic, meaning "new day."

Dahlia
Scandinavian, from the flowering plant of the same name.

Daisy
(alt. Daisey, Dasia)
English, meaning "eye of the day." A flowering plant.

Dakota
Native American, meaning "allies." Associated with actor Dakota Fanning, and the states of North and South Dakota.

Dalia
(alt. Daliah, Dalila)
Hebrew, meaning "delicate branch." A Lithuanian goddess.

Dallas
Scottish Gaelic, from the village of the same name. Also the city in Texas.

Damaris

Greek, meaning "calf." Found in the Bible.

Damita

Spanish, meaning "little noblewoman."

Dana

(alt. Dania, Danna, Dayna)

English, meaning "from Denmark"; Persian, meaning "a perfect and valuable pearl."

Danae

Greek, from the mythological heroine of the same name.

Danica

(alt. Danika)

Latin, meaning "from Denmark." Famous Danicas include racing driver Danica Patrick, and actor and author Danica McKellar.

Danielle

(alt. Danelle, Daniela, Daniella, Danila, Danita, Danyell; abbrev. Dani, Danni)

The feminine form of the Hebrew Daniel, meaning "God is my judge." Famous Danielle's include actor Danielle Fischel.

Daphne

(alt. Dafne, Daphna)

Greek, meaning "laurel tree." Daphne was a water nymph in Greek mythology.

Dara

Hebrew/Persian, meaning "wisdom." Found in the Bible.

Darby

(alt. Darbi, Darbie)

Irish, meaning "park with deer."

Darcy

(alt. Darcey, Darci, Darcie)

Irish Gaelic, meaning "dark." Famous Darcys include ballerina Dame Darcey Bussell.

Daria

Greek, meaning "rich." Associated with cartoon series *Daria*.

Darla

English, meaning "darling." Made famous by the child star Darla Hood.

Darlene

(alt. Darleen, Darline)

American English, meaning "darling." Darlene Gillespie is a member of the *Mickey Mouse Club*.

Daryl

(alt. Darryl)

Old English, and possibly also Old French, meaning "loved." Daryl Hannah is an actor.

Davina

Hebrew, meaning "loved one." Davina Claire is a character in *The Vampire Diaries*.

Dawn
(alt. Dawna)

English, meaning "to become day."

Daya

Hebrew, meaning "bird of prey." A form of teaching in the Sikh religion.

Deanna
(alt. Dayana, Deana, Deanna, Deanne, Deena, Dena)

English, meaning "girl from the valley." Famous Deannas include singer and actor Deanna Durbin.

Deborah
(alt. Debbra, Debra, Debrah; abbrev. Debbi, Debbie, Debby, Debi)

Hebrew, meaning "bee." A prophetess in the Bible.

December

Latin, meaning "tenth month."

Dee
(alt. Dea)

Welsh, meaning "swarthy." Also a shortened form of many names beginning with "De-."

Deidre
(alt. Deidra, Deirdre)

Irish, meaning "raging woman."

Deja
(alt. Dejah)

French, meaning "already." The French term for "already seen" is "déjà vu."

Delaney
(alt. Delany)

Irish Gaelic, meaning "offspring of the challenger."

Delia

Greek, meaning "from Delos." Associated with the ancient Greek island of Delos.

Delilah
(alt. Delina)

Hebrew, meaning "seductive." Famous Delilahs include the lover of Samson in the Bible, and the songs "Delilah" by Tom Jones and "Hey There Delilah" by Plain White T's.

Della
(alt. Dell)

Shortened form of Adele, meaning "nobility." Donald Duck's twin sister is called Della Duck.

Delores
(alt. Deloris)

Spanish, meaning "sorrows."

Delphine
(alt. Delpha, Delphia, Delphina, Delphinia)

Greek, meaning "dolphin."

Delta

Greek, meaning "fourth child." Also the fourth letter of the Greek alphabet.

Demelza

Cornish, from the hamlet of the same name in Cornwall in the UK. Made popular by the *Poldark* character.

Demetria

(alt. Demetrice, Dimitria)

Greek, from the mythological heroine of the same name.

Demi

French, meaning "half." Famous Demis include actor Demi Moore.

Denise

(alt. Denice, Denisa, Denisse)

French, meaning "to be devoted to Bacchus." Name of the actor Denise Richards.

Desdemona

Greek, meaning "wretchedness." Desdemona is Othello's love interest in Shakespeare's *Othello*.

Desiree

(alt. Desirae, Des'ree)

French, meaning "much desired." Associated with singer Des'ree.

Desma

Greek, meaning "blinding oath."

Destiny

(alt. Destany, Destinee, Destiney, Destini)

French, meaning "fate." Associated with the former girl group Destiny's Child.

Deva

Hindi, meaning "God-like." Deva is also a name for several Buddhist, Hindu, and New Age spiritual entities or people.

Devin

(alt. Devinne)

Irish Gaelic, meaning "poet." More commonly used as a boys' name.

Devon

English, from the county of the same name. Also feminine variant of Devin, meaning "poet."

Diamond

English, meaning "brilliant." One of the hardest and most valuable substances on Earth.

Diana

(alt. Dian, Diane, Dianna, Dianne)

Roman, meaning "divine." Made famous by the late Diana, Princess of Wales.

Diandra

Greek, meaning "two males."

Dilys

Welsh, meaning "reliable."

Dimona

Hebrew, meaning "south." A town in the Bible.

Names for triplets

Abel, Bela, Elba (anagrams)
Aidan, Diana, Nadia (anagrams)
Amber, Jade, Ruby (jewels)
Amy, May, Mya (anagrams)
April, May, June (months)
Ava, Eva, Iva (similar)
Daisy, Lily, Rose (flowers)
Jay, Raven, Robin (birds)
Leah, Lianne, Liam (similar)
Olive, Violet, Sage (colors)
River, Rain, Summer (nature)

Dinah
(alt. Dina)
Hebrew, meaning "justified." Found in the Bible.

Dionne
Greek, from the mythological heroine of the same name. Famous Dionnes include singers Dionne Warwick and Dionne Bromfield, and the infamous Dionne quintuplets.

Divine
Italian, meaning "heavenly." Associated with divinity or Dante's *Divine Comedy*.

Dixie
French, meaning "tenth." Also an old term for the South.

Dodie
Hebrew, meaning "well-loved." Dodie Smith was the author of *101 Dalmations*.

Dolores
(alt. Doloris)
Spanish, meaning "sorrows."

Dominique
(alt. Domenica, Dominica, Domonique)
Latin, meaning "Lord." The name of a song by Soeur Sourire.

Donata
Latin, meaning "given."

Donna
(alt. Dona, Donnie)
Italian, meaning "lady." Famous Donnas include singer Donna Summer and actor Donna Reed.

Dora
Greek, meaning "gift." The title character in *Dora the Explorer*.

Doran
Irish Gaelic, meaning "fist" or "stranger."

Dorcas
Greek, meaning "gazelle." Found in the Bible.

Doreen
(alt. Dorene, Dorine)

Irish Gaelic, meaning "brooding"; Greek, meaning "gift."

Doris
(alt. Dorris)

Greek, from the place of the same name. Made famous by singer and actor Doris Day.

Dorothy
(alt. Dorathy, Doretha, Dorotha, Dorothea, Dorthy; abbrev. Dolly, Dottie, Dotty)

Greek, meaning "gift of God." Most commonly associated with Dorothy from *The Wizard of Oz*.

Dorrit
(alt. Dorit)

Greek, meaning "gift of God." *Little Dorrit* is a novel by Charles Dickens.

Dory
(alt. Dori)

French, meaning "gilded." Associated with Dory from *Finding Nemo* and its sequel *Finding Dory*.

Dove
(alt. Dovie)

English, from the bird of the same name. Used as a symbol of peace.

Dream

English, meaning "rejoice."

Drew

Greek, meaning "masculine." Can be used for girls or boys (as a nickname for Andrew). Made famous by actor Drew Barrymore.

Drusilla
(alt. Drucilla)

Latin, meaning "of the Drusus clan."

Dulcie
(alt. Dulce, Dulcia)

Latin, meaning "sweet."

Dusty
(alt. Dusti)

Old German, meaning "brave warrior." Famous as the name of singer Dusty Springfield.

 Girls' names

Earla

English, meaning "leader."

Eartha

English, meaning "earth." Associated with singer Eartha Kitt.

Easter

Egyptian, from the festival and Pacific island of the same name.

Ebba

English, meaning "fortress of riches." A Top 10 name for girls in Sweden.

Ebony
(alt. Eboni)

Latin, meaning "deep, black wood." Made famous by the song "Ebony and Ivory" by Paul McCartney and Stevie Wonder.

Echo

Greek, meaning "reflected sound." Echo was the name of a nymph in Greek mythology.

Eda
(alt. Edda)

English, meaning "wealthy and happy." An ancient goddess of time and wealth.

Edelmira

Spanish, meaning "admired for nobility."

Eden
(alt. Edie, Eddie)

Hebrew, meaning "pleasure."

Edina

Scottish, meaning "from Edinburgh."

Edith
(alt. Edyth)

English, meaning "prosperity through battle." Edith Wharton was a Pulitzer Prize-winning author.

Edna

Hebrew, meaning "enjoyment."

Edrea

English, meaning "wealthy and powerful." Edrea Vorsal is an opera singer.

Edwina

English, meaning "wealthy friend." Associated with 20th-century socialite Edwina Mountbattten.

Effie

Greek, meaning "pleasant speech." Effie Trinket is a character in *The Hunger Games* series.

Eglantine

French, from the flowering shrub of the same name.

Eileen
(alt. Eibhlín)

Irish, meaning "shining and brilliant." Associated with the song "Come on Eileen" by Dexys Midnight Runners.

Ekaterina
(alt. Ekaterini)

Slavic, meaning "pure."

Elaine
(alt. Elaina, Elayne)

French, meaning "bright, shining light." Elaine Stritch is an actor and singer.

Elba

Italian, from the island of the same name.

Elberta

English, meaning "high-born."

Eldora

Spanish, meaning "covered with gold."

Eleanor
(alt. Alienor, Aliana, Elana, Elanor, Eleanora, Eleanore, Elena, Eleni, Elenor, Elenora, Elina, Elinor, Elinore; abbrev. Elie, Ellie)

Greek, meaning "light." Queen Eleanor of Aquitane was married to England's Henry II and was one of the most influential, wealthy, and powerful women of the Middle Ages.

Electra
(alt. Elektra)

Greek, meaning "shining." Famous as a character in ancient Greek myth.

Elfrida
(alt. Elfrieda)

English, meaning "elf power." Elfrida Andree is a composer.

Eliane
(alt. Eliana)

Hebrew, meaning "Jehovah is God."

Elissa
(alt. Elise)

French, meaning "pledged to God." The other name of Dido, the ancient Roman Queen of Carthage.

Eliza
(alt. Elisha, Elise)

Hebrew, meaning "pledged to God." Made famous by the character Eliza Doolittle from the play *Pygmalion* and film adaptation *My Fair Lady*.

Elizabeth
(alt. Elisabet, Elisabeth, Elizabella, Elsbeth, Elspet; abbrev. Bess, Bessie, Bet, Beth, Betty, Libby, Liz, Lizzie)

Hebrew, meaning "pledged to God." The name of the current Queen of England, Elizabeth II. The previous Queen Elizabeth I was also known as "Good Queen Bess."

Elke
German, meaning "nobility."

Ella
German, meaning "completely."

Elle
(alt. Ellie)

French, meaning "she." Elle Macpherson was one of the original 1980s supermodels, known as "The Body."

Ellen
(alt. Elin, Eline, Ellyn)

Greek, meaning "shining." Associated with comedian and TV host Ellen DeGeneres.

Ellice
(alt. Elyse)

Greek, meaning "the Lord is God."

Elma
(alt. Elna)

Latin, meaning "soul." Elma Napier was an author and pioneering Caribbean politician.

Elmira
(alt. Elmyra)

Arabic, meaning "aristocratic lady." Elmyra Duff is a cartoon character.

Elodie
French, meaning "marsh flower."

Eloise
(alt. Elois, Eloisa, Elouise)

French, meaning "renowned in battle."

Elsa
(alt. Else, Elsie)

Hebrew, meaning "pledged to God." Elsa is a character from Disney's *Frozen*.

Elula
Hebrew, meaning "August."

Elva

Irish, meaning "noble."

Elvina

English, meaning "noble friend."

Elvira
(alt. Elvera)

Spanish, from the place of the same name. Associated with the 1980s film *Elvira, Mistress of the Dark*.

Ember
(alt. Embry)

English, meaning "spark."

Emeline

German, meaning "industrious."

Emerald

English, meaning "green gemstone." A precious stone.

Emery
(alt. Emory)

German, meaning "ruler of work." A dark rock used in the manufacture of nail files.

Emilia

Latin, meaning "rival, eager." Associated with *Game of Thrones* actor Emilia Clarke.

Emily
(alt. Emelie, Emilee, Emilie, Emlyn)

Latin, meaning "rival, eager." Famous Emilys include actor Emily Blunt and author Emily Dickinson.

Emma
(alt. Emme, Emmi, Emmie, Emmy)

German, meaning "embraces everything." Made famous by Jane Austen's novel *Emma*.

Emmanuelle

Hebrew, meaning "God is among us."

Emmeline
(alt. Emmelina; abbrev. Emi, Emme, Emmie, Emmy)

German, meaning "embraces everything." Emmeline Pankhurst was a British activist and suffragette, named by *Time* magazine as "One of the 100 Most Important People of the Twentieth Century."

Ena

Shortened form of Georgina, meaning "farmer."

Enid
(alt. Eneida)

Welsh, meaning "life spirit." Enid Blyton was an English children's novelist.

Enola

Native American, meaning "solitary." Associated with the song "Enola Gay."

Ensley

English, meaning "one's own meadow."

Enya

Irish Gaelic, meaning "fire." Irish singer Enya's birth name was Eithne.

Erica
(alt. Ericka, Erika)

Scandinavian, meaning "ruler forever." Erica Durance is an actor.

Erin
(alt. Eryn)

Irish Gaelic, meaning "from the isle to the west." An old name for Ireland. Erin Brockovich is a legal clerk and activist who was portrayed by Julia Roberts in the eponymous film.

Eris

Greek, from the mythological heroine of the same name. Eris is responsible for chaos, strife, and discord.

Erlinda

Hebrew, meaning "spirited."

Erma

German, meaning "universal."

Ermine

French, meaning "weasel." The fur of a stoat or weasel is known as ermine.

Erna

English, meaning "sincere." A character in Norse mythology.

Ernestine
(alt. Ernestina)

English, meaning "sincere." Ernestine Gilbreth Carey is the author of Cheaper By the Dozen.

Esme

French, meaning "esteemed." Esme Cullen is a character in the Twilight series.

Esmeralda

Spanish, meaning "emerald." Esmeralda is a lead character in The Hunchback of Notre Dame.

Esperanza

Spanish, meaning "hope."

Estelle
(alt. Estela, Estell, Estella)

French, meaning "star." Associated with R&B singer Estelle.

Esther
(alt. Esta, Ester, Etha, Ethna, Ethne)

Persian, meaning "star." A character in the biblical Book of Esther.

Eternity

Latin, meaning "forever."

Ethel
(alt. Ethyl)

English, meaning "noble." Ethel Merman was an actor and singer, best known for rousing musical theater.

Etta
(alt. Etter, Ettie)

Shortened form of Henrietta, meaning "ruler of the house." Famous Ettas include singer Etta James (real name Janesetta), and DC Comic character Etta Candy.

Eudora

Greek, meaning "generous gift." Eudora is a character in Disney's *Princess and the Frog*.

Eugenia
(alt. Eugenie)

Greek, meaning "well born." Princess Eugenie is a granddaughter of Queen Elizabeth II.

Eulalia
(alt. Eula, Eulah, Eulalie)

Greek, meaning "sweetspeaking." Associated with Spanish St. Eulalia.

Eunice
(alt. Unice)

Greek, meaning "victorious." Eunice Kennedy Shriver was JFK's sister and the founder of the Special Olympics.

Euphemia

Greek, meaning " favorable speech."

Eva

Hebrew, meaning "life." Eva Peron was the real-life inspiration for the musical *Evita*.

Evadne

Greek, meaning "pleasing one."

Evangeline
(alt. Evangelina)

Greek, meaning "good news." The very first musical comedy was called *Evangeline*, in 1874.

Evanthe

Greek, meaning "good flower."

Eve
(alt. Evie)

Hebrew, meaning "life." The biblical Eve was the first woman.

Evelina
(alt. Evelia)

German, meaning "hazelnut." An 18th-century novel by Fanny Burney.

Evelyn
(alt. Evalyn, Evelin, Eveline, Evelyne)

German, meaning "hazelnut." Famous Evelyns include singer Evelyn "Champagne" King and deaf virtuoso percussionist Evelyn Glennie.

Everly
(alt. Everleigh, Everley)

English, meaning "grazing meadow."

Evette

French, meaning "yew wood."

Evonne
(alt. Evon)

French, meaning "yew wood." Made famous by Australian tennis pro Evonne Goolagong.

Girls' names

Fabia
(alt. Fabiana, Fabienne, Fabiola, Fabriana)
Latin, meaning "from the Fabian clan."

Fabrizia
Italian, meaning "works with hands."

Faith
English, meaning "loyalty." Famous Faiths include singers Faith Hill and Faith Evans.

Faiza
Arabic, meaning "victorious."

Fallon
Irish Gaelic, meaning "descended from a ruler."

Fanny
(alt. Fannie)
Latin, meaning "from France." The heroine of Jane Austen's *Mansfield Park* is Fanny Price.

Farica
German, meaning "peaceful ruler."

Farrah
English, meaning "lovely and pleasant." Associated with actor Farrah Fawcett and reality TV star Farrah Abraham.

Fatima
Arabic, meaning "baby's nurse."

Faustine
Latin, meaning "fortunate."

Fawn
(alt. Fawne)
French, meaning "young deer." Also the light brown color.

Fay
(alt. Fae, Faye)
French, meaning "fairy." Famous Fays include author Fay Weldon and original *King Kong* actor Fay Wray.

Felicia

(alt. Felecia, Felice, Felicita, Felisha)

Latin, meaning "lucky and happy." Famous Felicias include actors Felicia Day and Felicia Farr, and *American Idol*'s Felicia Barton.

Felicity

Latin, meaning "fortunate."

Fenella

Irish Gaelic, meaning "white shoulder." Made famous by actor Fenella Fielding.

Fenia

Scandinavian, from the mythological giantess of the same name.

Fern

(alt. Fearn, Fearne, Ferne, Ferrin)

English, from the plant of the same name.

Fernanda

German, meaning "peace and courage."

Ffion

(alt. Fion)

Irish Gaelic, meaning "fair and pale" or "foxglove." Very popular name for baby girls in Wales.

Fia

Italian, meaning "flame." Also a nickname for Fiona.

Fifi

Hebrew, meaning "Jehovah increases."

Filomena

Greek, meaning "loved one."

Finlay

(alt. Finley)

Irish Gaelic, meaning "fair-headed courageous one." More commonly used for boys.

Finola

(alt. Fionnula)

Irish Gaelic, meaning "fair shoulder." Associated with actor Finola Hughes.

Fiona

(alt. Fiora)

Irish Gaelic and Scottish, meaning "fair and pale." Princess Fiona is a character in *Shrek*.

Flanna

(alt. Flannery)

Irish Gaelic, meaning "russet hair" or "red hair."

Flavia

Latin, meaning "yellow hair."

Fleur

(alt. Flor)

French, meaning "flower." Fleur Delacour is a character in the *Harry Potter* series.

Flora

Latin, meaning "flower." A fairy
godmother in Disney's *Sleeping
Beauty* (she was the red one).

Florence
*(alt. Florencia, Florene, Florine;
abbrev. Flo, Florrie, Flossie, Floy)*

Latin, meaning "in bloom." Associated
with the Italian city of the same name.

Florida

Latin, meaning "flowery." Also the
southern state.

Frances
*(alt. Francine, Francis; abbrev. Fanny,
Fran, Frankie, Frannie, Franny)*

Latin, meaning "from France."
Famous Franceses include actor
Frances McDormand and playwright
Frances Hodgson Burnett.

Francesca
(alt. Franchesca, Francisca)

Latin, meaning "from France."
Francesca Simon is a children's
author.

Freda
(alt. Freida, Frida, Frieda)

German, meaning "peaceful."
Associated with artist Frida Kahlo.

Frederica

German, meaning "peaceful ruler."
Popular name for modern European
princesses.

Fuchsia

German, from the flower of the same
name.

Girls' names

Gabrielle
(alt. Gabriel, Gabriela, Gabriella; abbrev. Gabbi, Gabby)
Hebrew, meaning "heroine of God." A character in *Xena: Warrior Princess*.

Gaia
(alt. Gaea)
Greek, meaning "the earth." Gaia was the ancient Greek Mother Goddess.

Gail
(alt. Gale, Gayla, Gayle)
Hebrew, meaning "my father rejoices." Gail O'Grady is an actor and producer.

Gal
Hebrew, meaning "wave." Made famous by *Wonder Woman* actor Gal Gadot.

Gala
French, meaning "festive merrymaking."

Galiena
German, meaning "high one."

Galina
Russian, meaning "shining brightly."

Garnet
(alt. Garnett)
English, meaning "red gemstone." Can be used as a twin name alongside Ruby.

Gay
(alt. Gaye)
French, meaning "glad and lighthearted."

Gaynor
Welsh, meaning "white and smooth." Associated with singer Gloria Gaynor.

Gemini

Greek, meaning "twin." The third astrological sign in the Zodiac.

Gemma
(alt. Jemma)

Italian, meaning "precious stone." Well-known Gemmas include actor Gemma Arterton.

Gene

Greek, meaning "well born." Usually a boys' name.

Genesis

Greek, meaning "beginning." Associated with the first book of the Old Testament, and the band Genesis.

Geneva
(alt. Genevra)

French, meaning "juniper tree." A city in Switzerland.

Genevieve
(alt. Genie)

German, meaning "white wave." St. Genevieve is said to have saved Paris.

Georgia
(alt. Georgie)

Greek, meaning "farmer." Also the southern US state and a European country.

Georgina
(alt. Georgene, Georgette, Georgiana, Georgianna, Georgine, Giorgina; abbrev. Giget, Gigi)

Greek, meaning "farmer." Georgina Chapman is an actor and fashion designer. *Gigi* is a novel and a musical.

Geraldine
(abbrev. Geri)

German, meaning "spear ruler." Geraldine Chaplin is an actor and Geri Halliwell is "Ginger Spice" of the Spice Girls.

Gerda

Nordic, meaning "shelter." A character from Hans Christian Andersen's *Snow Queen*.

Germaine

French, meaning "from Germany." Germaine Greer is an author and activist.

Gertrude
(alt. Gertie)

German, meaning "strength of a spear." Made famous by author Gertrude Stein.

Gia
(alt. Ghia)

Italian, meaning "God is gracious."

Gianina
(alt. Giana)

Hebrew, meaning "God's graciousness."

Gilda

English, meaning "gilded." A character from Verdi's opera *Rigoletto*.

Gilia

Hebrew, meaning "joy of the Lord." Also a genus of flowering plants.

Gillian

Latin, meaning "youthful." Famous Gillians include actor Gillian Anderson and author Gillian Cross.

Ginger

Latin, from the root of the same name.

Giovanna

Italian, meaning "God is gracious."

Giselle
(alt. Gisela, Gisele, Giselle, Gisselle)

German, meaning "pledge." Famous Giselles include the romantic ballet, and supermodel Gisele Bündchen.

Gita
(alt. Geeta)

Sanskrit, meaning "song." The *Bhagavad Gita* is an important part of Hindu scripture, and is often simply known as the Gita.

Giulia
(alt. Giuliana)

Italian, meaning "youthful." Associated with TV host Giuliana Rancic.

Gladys
(alt. Gladyce)

Welsh, meaning "lame." Gladys Knight is a singer.

Glenda

Welsh, meaning "fair and good."

Glenna
(alt. Glennie)

Irish Gaelic, meaning "glen."

Gloria
(alt. Glory)

Latin, meaning "glory." Famous Glorias include singers Gloria Estefan and Gloria Gaynor.

Glynda
(alt. Glinda)

Welsh, meaning "fair." Name of the good witch in *The Wizard of Oz*.

Glynis

Welsh, meaning "small glen." Glynis Nunn is a heptathlon athlete.

Golda
(alt. Goldia, Goldie)

English, meaning "gold." Golda Meir is the former Israeli Prime Minister.

Grace
(alt. Graça, Gracie, Gracin, Grayce)

Latin, meaning "grace." The actor Grace Kelly became Princess Grace of Monaco.

Grainne
(alt. Grania)

Irish Gaelic, meaning "love." Also an ancient goddess of corn.

Gratia
(alt. Grasia)

Latin, meaning "blessing." Gratia was the ancient Greek goddess of charm, beauty, and fertility.

Greer
(alt. Grier)

Latin, meaning "alert and watchful."

Gregoria

Latin, meaning "alert."

Greta
(alt. Gretel)

Greek, meaning "pearl." One of the characters in the fairy tale *Hansel and Gretel*.

Gretchen

German, meaning "pearl." Gretchen Mol is an actor.

Griselda
(alt. Griselle)

German, meaning "gray fighting maid."

Gudrun

Scandinavian, meaning "battle."

Guinevere

Welsh, meaning "white and smooth." The legendary Queen consort of King Arthur.

Gwenda

Welsh, meaning "fair and good."

Gwendolyn
(alt. Gwen, Gwendolen, Gwenel)

Welsh, meaning "fair bow." Gwendolyn Brooks is a poet.

Gwyneth
(alt. Gwynneth, Gwynyth)

Welsh, meaning "happiness." Made famous by actor Gwyneth Paltrow.

Gwynn
(alt. Gwyn)

Welsh, meaning "fair blessed."

Gypsy

English, meaning "of the Roman tribe."

Girls' names

Hadassah

Hebrew, meaning "myrtle tree." The Hebrew name for Esther in the Bible.

Hadley

English, meaning "heather meadow." Hadley Richardson was the wife of Ernest Hemingway.

Hadria

Latin, meaning "from Hadria." The name of two ancient cities in Italy.

Hala

Arabic, meaning "halo." A female weather demon in Serbian mythology.

Haley
(alt. Hailee, Hailey, Hailie, Haleigh, Hali, Halie, Haylee, Hayleigh, Hayley, Haylie)

English, meaning "hay meadow." Famous Haleys include singer Haley Reinhart and singer Hayley Mills.

Halima
(alt. Halimah, Halina)

Arabic, meaning "gentle." The prophet Mohammad's foster mother was called Halimah.

Hallie
(alt. Halle, Halley)

German, meaning "ruler of the home or estate." Associated with actor Halle Berry.

Hannah
(alt. Haana, Hana, Hanna)

Hebrew, meaning "grace." Famous Hannahs include actor Hannah Gordon and TV musical comedy *Hannah Montana*.

Harley
(alt. Harlene)

English, meaning "the long field." Used for girls and boys. Made famous by the Harley-Davidson motorbike company.

Harlow

English, meaning "army hill."

Harmony

Latin, meaning "harmony."

Harper

English, meaning "minstrel." Has risen in popularity after its use by Victoria and David Beckham for their daughter Harper Seven.

Harriet
(alt. Harriett, Harriette, Hattie)

German, meaning "ruler of the home or estate." Famous Harriets include activist Harriet Tubman and author Harriet Beecher Stowe.

Haven

English, meaning "a place of sanctuary."

Hayden

Old English, meaning "hedged valley."

Hazel
(alt. Hazle)

English, from the tree of the same name. Also an eye color.

Heather

English, from the flower of the same name. Famous Heathers include actors Heather Graham and Heather Locklear, and model Heather Mills.

Heaven

English, meaning "everlasting bliss."

Hedda

German, meaning "warfare." *Hedda Gabler* is a play by Henrik Ibsen.

Hedwig

German, meaning "warfare and strife." Also Harry Potter's constant owl companion.

Heidi
(alt. Heidy)

German, meaning "nobility." The title of a children's book *Heidi* by Johanna Spyri.

Helen
(alt. Halen, Helena, Helene, Hellen)

Greek, meaning "light." In Greek mythology Helen of Troy was considered to be the most beautiful woman in the world.

Helga

German, meaning "holy and sacred."

Heloise

French, meaning "renowned in war." Heloise d'Argenteuil was a nun and writer.

Henrietta
(alt. Henriette)

German, meaning "ruler of the house." Henrietta Maria of France was queen consort to England's King Charles I.

Long names
Alexandria
Bernadette
Christabelle
Constantina
Evangeline
Gabrielle
Henrietta
Jacqueline
Marguerite
Wilhelmina

Hephzibah
Hebrew, meaning "my delight is in her." Found in the Bible.

Hera
Greek, meaning "queen." Hera is the ancient Greek Queen of the Gods and the goddess of marriage, women, and births.

Hermia
(alt. Hermina, Hermine, Herminia)
Greek, meaning "messenger." A character from Shakespeare's *A Midsummer Night's Dream*.

Hermione
Greek, meaning "earthly." Harry Potter's closest (and smartest) female friend.

Hero
Greek, meaning "brave one of the people."

Hertha
English, meaning "earth." Another name for Nerthus, the goddess of fertility in ancient German mythology.

Hesper
(alt. Hesperia)
Greek, meaning "evening star." The first evening star in ancient Greece.

Hester
(alt. Hestia)
Greek, meaning "star." Hester Prynne is a character from *The Scarlet Letter*.

Hilary
(alt. Hillary)
Greek, meaning "cheerful and happy." Famous Hilarys include actor Hilary Swank and politician Hillary Rodham Clinton.

Hilda
(alt. Hildur)
German, meaning "battle woman." The first female pilot to own a license was Hilda Hewlett.

Hildegarde
(alt. Hildegard)
German, meaning "battle stronghold."

Hildred

German, meaning "battle counselor."

Hilma

German, meaning "helmet."

Hollis

English, meaning "near the holly bushes."

Holly
(alt. Holli, Hollie)

English, from the tree of the same name. Famous Hollys include writer Holly Black and actor Holly Hunter.

Honey

English, meaning "sweet nectar."

Honor
(alt. Honora, Honoria, Honour)

Latin, meaning "woman of worth and respect." Actor Honor Blackman played Bond girl Pussy Galore in *Goldfinger*.

Hope

English, meaning "desire and expectation." One of the three virtues: faith, hope, and charity.

Hortense
(alt. Hortencia, Hortensia)

Latin, meaning "of the garden." The name of Napoleon Bonaparte's mother.

Hulda

German, meaning "loved one." A prophetess in the Bible.

Hyacinth

Greek, from the flower of the same name. A hero in ancient Greek mythology.

I Girls' names

Ianthe
(alt. Iantha)
Greek, meaning "purple flower."

Ida
(alt. Idell, Idella)
English, meaning "prosperous." Ida B. Wells was a prominent African-American civil rights activist and journalist.

Idona
Nordic, meaning "renewal."

Ignacia
Latin, meaning "ardent."

Ila
French, meaning "island." In Hindu mythology, Ila is a character able to change sexes at will.

Ilana
Hebrew, meaning "tree." Famous Ilanas include pianist Ilana Vered and a character in TV series *Lost*.

Ilaria
Italian, meaning "cheerful."

Ilene
American English, meaning "light." Ilene Woods was the voice of Disney's *Cinderella*.

Iliana
(alt. Ileana)
Greek, meaning "Trojan."

Ilona
Hungarian, meaning "light." The name of the Queen of the Fairies in Magyar mythology.

Ilsa
German, meaning "pledged to God." The character played by Ingrid Bergman in *Casablanca*.

Ima
German, meaning "embraces everything."

Iman

Arabic, meaning "faith." Associated with the model, actor and entrepreneur known simply as Iman.

Imelda

German, meaning "all-consuming fight." Imelda Staunton is an Oscar-nominated British actor.

Imogen
(alt. Imogene)

Latin, meaning "last-born."

Ina

Latin, meaning "to make feminine." Famous Inas include author and presenter Ina Garten, childbirth pioneer Ina May Gaskin, and the Ina language of Brazil.

Inaya

Arabic, meaning "taking care."

India
(alt. Indie)

Hindi, from the country of the same name. India Arie is a singer.

Indiana

Latin, meaning "from India." Also the Midwestern state.

Indigo

Greek, meaning "deep blue dye." One of the seven colors of the rainbow.

Indira
(alt. Inira)

Sanskrit, meaning "beauty." Indira Gandhi was the first and only female prime minister of India.

Inez
(alt. Ines)

Spanish, meaning "pure."

Inga
(alt. Inge, Ingeborg, Inger)

Scandinavian, meaning "guarded by Ing."

Ingrid

Scandinavian, meaning "beautiful." Made famous by actor Ingrid Bergman.

Io
(alt. Eye)

Greek, from the mythological priestess and heroine of the same name.

Ioanna

Greek, meaning "grace."

Iola
(alt. Iole)

Greek, meaning "cloud of dawn." Iola Leory by Frances Harper is one of the first published novels by a black female author.

Iolanthe

Greek, meaning "violet flower." The title of a comic opera by Gilbert and Sullivan.

Iona

Greek, from the island of the same name.

Ione

Greek, meaning "violet." Also a genus of orchid.

Iphigenia

Greek, meaning "sacrifice." The ancient Greek victim of slaughter, who became known as the mother of all strong children.

Ira

(alt. Iva)

Hebrew, meaning "watchful."

Irene

(alt. Irelyn, Irena, Irina, Irini)

Greek, meaning "peace." Singer Irene Cara won an Academy Award for Best Original Song.

Iris

Greek, meaning "rainbow." Also a flower and the Greek goddess who travels with the speed of wind from one end of the rainbow to the other, and from sea to sky, and connects the gods with humanity.

Irma

German, meaning "universal."

Isabel

(alt. Isabela, Isabell, Isabella, Isabelle, Isobel, Izabella, Izabelle; abbrev. Izzie, Izzy)

Spanish, meaning "pledged to God." The name of various historical members of European royal families, including Queen Isabella I of Spain. Isabella Swan is the lead character in the *Twilight* series.

Isadora

Latin, meaning "gift of Isis."

Ishana

Hindi, meaning "desire." One of the names for Shiva in the Hindu faith.

Isis

Egyptian, from the goddess of the same name. She was worshipped as the ideal mother and wife, and the goddess of nature and magic.

Isla

(alt. Isa, Isela, Isley)

Scottish Gaelic, meaning "river." Isla Fischer is an actor.

Isolde

Welsh, meaning "fair lady." A character in Richard Wagner's opera *Tristan und Isolde*.

Istas

Native American, meaning "snow."

Ivana
(alt. Iva, Ivanka)

Slavic, meaning "Jehovah is gracious." Associated with model Ivana Trump.

Ivory

Latin, meaning "white as elephant tusks."

Ivy

English, from the plant of the same name. Beyoncé and Jay-Z's daughter is Blue Ivy.

Ixia

South African, from the flower of the same name.

Girls' names

Jacinda
(alt. Jacinta)

Spanish, meaning "hyacinth." Jacinda Barrett is an actor.

Jacqueline
(alt. Jacalyn, Jacklyn, Jaclyn, Jacquelin, Jacquelyn, Jacquline, Jaquelin, Jaqueline; abbrev. Jackie, Jacky, Jacqui)

French, meaning "he who supplants." Famous Jacquelines include actor Jacqueline Bisset, cellist Jacqueline du Pré, First Lady Jacqueline (Jackie) Kennedy Onassis, and singer Jackie Evancho.

Jade
(alt. Jada, Jaida, Jayda, Jayde)

Spanish, meaning "green stone." Associated with TV host Jade McCarthy.

Jaden
(alt. Jadyn, Jaiden, Jayden)

Contraction of Jade and Hayden, meaning "green hedged valley." Used for girls and boys.

Jael

Hebrew, meaning "mountain goat." Found in the Bible.

Jaime
(alt. Jaima, Jaimie, Jami, Jamie)

Spanish, meaning "he who supplants." J'aime is also French for "I love."

Jamila

Arabic, meaning "lovely." Jamila Gavin is a children's author.

Jan
(alt. Jana, Janae, Janay, Jann, Janna, Joana)

Hebrew, meaning "the Lord is gracious"; Arabic, meaning "dear"; Persian, meaning "life."

Jane
(alt. Jayne)

Feminine form of John, meaning "the Lord is gracious." Famous Janes include actors Jane Lynch, Jane Seymour, and Jayne Mansfield.

Janelle
(alt. Janael, Janel, Janell, Jenelle)

American English, derived from Jane, meaning "the Lord is gracious." Janelle Monae is a singer and Janell Burse is a professional basketball player.

Janet
(alt. Janette)

Scottish, meaning "the Lord is gracious." Famous Janets include singer Janet Jackson and Olympic champion swimmer Janet Evans.

Janice
(alt. Janis)

American, meaning "the Lord is gracious." Janice Dickinson is a former supermodel.

Janie
(alt. Janey, Janney, Jannie)

Derived from Jane or short form of Janet, meaning "the Lord is gracious." Famous Janies include Motown songwriter Janie Bradford, country singer Janie Frickie and Janie Hendrix, the sister of musician Jimi.

Janine
(alt. Janeen)

English, meaning "the Lord is gracious." Associated with actor Janine Turner.

Janoah
(alt. Janiya, Janiyah)

Hebrew, meaning "quiet and calm."

January
Latin, meaning "the first month." January Jones is an actor.

Jasmine
(alt. Jasmin, Jazim, Jazmine)

Persian, meaning "jasmine flower." Also the princess in Disney's *Aladdin*.

Jay
Latin, meaning "jaybird."

Jayna
Sanskrit, meaning "bringer of victory."

Jean
(alt. Jeane, Jeanie, Jeanne, Jeannie)

Scottish, meaning "the Lord is gracious." Jean Harlow was a glamorous acting star of the 1930s. Also associated with the sitcom *I Dream of Jeannie*.

Jeana
(alt. Jeanna)

Latin, meaning "queen."

Jeanette
(alt. Jeannette, Janette)
French, meaning "the Lord is gracious." Jeanette MacDonald is an actor.

Jeanine
(alt. Jeannine)
Latin, meaning "the Lord is gracious."

Jemima
Hebrew, meaning "dove." Famous Jemimas include writer Jemima Khan, actor Jemima Kirke, and the children's book character Jemima Puddle-Duck.

Jena
Arabic, meaning "little bird."

Jennifer
(alt. Jenifer; abbrev. Jenna, Jennie, Jenny)
Cornish alternative to Guinevere, meaning "white and smooth." Famous Jennifers include actors Jennifer Lawrence, Jennifer Aniston, Jenna Elfman, Jenna Dewan, and singer Jennifer Hudson.

Jerrie
(alt. Jeri, Jerri, Jerrie, Jerry)
German, meaning "spear ruler." Jerry Hall is a model and actor.

Jerusha
Hebrew, meaning "married." Jerusha Hess is a film maker.

Jeryl
English, meaning "spear ruler." Associated with actor Jeryl Prescott.

Jessamy
(alt. Jessame, Jessamine, Jessamyn)
Persian, meaning "jasmine flower." Also a children's book by Barbara Sleigh.

Jessica
(alt. Jesica, Jessika; abbrev. Jess, Jessa, Jessie)
Hebrew, meaning "He sees." Famous Jessicas include actors Jessica Alba and Jessica Lange, singer Jessie J and the character Jess from *Girls*.

Jesusa
Spanish, meaning "mother of the Lord."

Jette
(alt. Jetta, Jettie)
Danish, meaning "black as coal."

Jewel
(alt. Jewell)
French, meaning "delight." Associated with singer songwriter Jewel.

Jezebel
(alt. Jezabel, Jezabelle)
Hebrew, meaning "pure and virginal." The misbehaving wife of King Ahab in the Bible.

Jill

Latin, meaning "youthful."

Jillian

Latin, meaning "youthful." Jillian Michaels is a personal trainer and TV personality.

Jimena

Spanish, meaning "heard."

Joan

Hebrew, meaning "the Lord is gracious." Famous Joans include St. Joan of Arc, actor Joan Collins, and comedian Joan Rivers.

Joanna

(alt. Joana, Joanie, Joann, Joanne, Johanna, Joni; abbrev. Jo)

Hebrew, meaning "the Lord is gracious." Famous Joannas include actors Joanna Lumley and Joanna Page. Author J. K. Rowling's first name is Joanne.

Jocasta

Italian, meaning "lighthearted." A character in ancient Greek mythology.

Jocelyn

(alt. Jauslyn, Jocelyne, Joscelin, Joslyn; abbrev. Joss)

German, meaning "cheerful." Famous Jocelyns include American socialite Jocelyn Wildenstein, singer Jocelyn Brown, and English soul singer-songwriter Joss Stone.

Jody

(alt. Jodee, Jodi, Jodie)

Shortened form of Judith, meaning "Jewish." Made famous by actor Jodie Foster.

Joelle

(alt. Joela)

Hebrew, meaning "Jehovah is the Lord."

Joie

French, meaning "joy."

Jolene

Contraction of Joanna and Darlene, meaning "gracious darling." The title of a song by Dolly Parton.

Jolie

(alt. Joely)

French, meaning "pretty." Made famous by actor and director Angelina Jolie.

Jonisa
(alt. Jonisha)

Hebrew and French, meaning "God is gracious."

Jordan
(alt. Jordana, Jordin, Jordyn)

Hebrew, meaning "descend." Made famous by singer Jordan Sparks.

Jorgina

Dutch, meaning "farmer."

Josephine
(alt. Josefina, Josephina; abbrev. Jo, Josie, Joss)

Hebrew, meaning "Jehovah increases." Famous Josephines include actor Josephine Baker and author Josephine Bell.

Jovita
(alt. Jovie)

Latin, meaning "made glad." Associated with St. Jovita.

Joy

Latin, meaning "joy." Joy Behar is a comedian.

Joyce

Latin, meaning "joyous." Famous Joyces include author Joyce Carol Oates and actors Joyce Blair and Joyce DeWitt.

Juanita
(alt. Juana)

Spanish, meaning "the Lord is gracious." Associated with the ice maiden Mummy Juanita.

Jubilee

Hebrew, meaning "ram's horn" or "special anniversary." The celebration of an anniversary.

Judith
(alt. Judit; abbrev. Jude, Judi, Judy)

Hebrew, meaning "Jewish." Found in the Bible. Famous Judiths include actors Judy Garland and Judi Dench.

Jules

French, meaning "Jove's child."

Julia
(alt. Juli, Julie)

Latin, meaning "youthful." Famous Julias include actor Julia Roberts, TV chef Julia Childs, and actor and singer Julie Andrews.

Julianne
(alt. Juliana, Juliann, Julianna)

Latin, meaning "youthful." Julianne Moore and Julianna Margulies are both actors.

Juliet
(alt. Joliet, Juliette)

Latin, meaning "youthful." A character in Shakespeare's play *Romeo and Juliet*.

June
(alt. Juna)

Latin, after the month of the same name. The name of several American actors famous in the period 1930–60, and country singer June Carter Cash.

Juniper

Dutch, from the shrub of the same name used in the production of gin.

Juno
(alt. Juneau)

Latin, meaning "queen of heaven." Juno was an ancient Roman goddess of marriage and Rome.

Justice

English, meaning "to deliver what is just." The female spirit of Justice is depicted with balance scales, a blindfold, and a sword.

Justine
(alt. Justina)

Latin, meaning "fair and righteous." Famous Justines include the Christian saint and actor Justine Bateman.

 Girls' names

Kady
(alt. Kadi, Kadie)
Irish Gaelic, meaning "a rhythmic flow of sounds."

Kailani
(alt. Kehlani)
Hawaiian, meaning "sea and sky."

Kala
(alt. Kaela, Kaiala, Kaila)
Sanskrit, meaning "black one." The great ape that saved Tarzan as a baby.

Kali
(alt. Kailey, Kaleigh, Kaley, Kalie, Kalli, Kally, Kaylee, Kayleigh)
Sanskrit, meaning "black one." Also the Hindu goddess of time and change.

Kalila
Arabic, meaning "beloved."

Kalina
Slavic, meaning "flower."

Kama
Sanskrit, meaning "love." Associated with the Hindu goal of intellectual fulfillment.

Kami
Japanese, meaning "lord."

Kamilla
(alt. Kamilah)
Slavic, meaning "serving girl."

Kana
Hawaiian, from the demi-god of the same name who could take the form of a rope that could stretch from Molokai to Hawaii.

Kara
Latin, meaning "dear one." The bracelet worn by Sikhs.

Karen
(alt. Caren, Carin, Caron, Caryn, Karan, Karin, Karina, Karon, Karren; abbrev. Kari)

Greek, meaning "pure." Famous Karens include singer Karen Carpenter, actor Karen Gillan, and TV host and scientist Kari Byron.

Karimah
Arabic, meaning "giving."

Karishma
(alt. Karisma)

Sanskrit, meaning "miracle." Karisma Kapoor is an actor.

Karissa
(alt. Carissa, Korissa)

Greek, meaning "very dear."

Karma
Hindi, meaning "destiny." Karma is the principle of good and bad deeds being returned to you.

Kate
(alt. Kat, Katie, Kathi, Kathie, Kathy, Kati, Katy)

Derived from Catherine or Katherine, meaning "pure." Famous Kates include Princess Kate Middleton and actors Kate Winslet and Kate Hudson.

Katherine
(alt. Katharine, Kathrine, Kathryn, Katrina, Katya, Katyea; abbrev. Kate, Kathy, Katie, Katy, Kay, Kitty)

Greek, meaning "pure." Enduringly popular spelled with either a C or a K.

Kathleen
(alt. Kathlyn)

Greek, meaning "pure." Kathleen Robertson is an actor.

Katniss
From one of the common names of the aquatic plant genus *Sagittaria*. Made famous by the character Katniss Everdeen from *The Hunger Games* trilogy.

Kaya
Sanskrit, meaning "nature"; Turkish, meaning "rock." Also a sweet coconut jam.

Kayla
(alt. Kaylah)

Greek, meaning "pure"; Gaelic, meaning "slim" and "fair."

Kaylee
(alt. Kayley, Kayleigh, Kayli, Kaylin)

Derived from Kayla, meaning "pure." Kayley is a character from *The Magic Sword: Quest for Camelot*.

Keeley
(alt. Keely)

Irish, meaning "battle maid." Keeley Hawes is a British actor.

Keila
Hebrew, meaning "citadel."

Keira
Irish Gaelic, meaning "dark." Name of actor Keira Knightley.

Keisha
(alt. Keesha)

Arabic, meaning "woman." Name of actor Keisha Pulliam.

Kelila

Hebrew, meaning "crown of laurel."

Kelis

American English, meaning "beautiful." Kelis is an R&B singer.

Kelly
(alt. Keli, Kelley, Kelli, Kellie)

Irish Gaelic, meaning "battle maid." Famous Kellys include singer Kelly Clarkson and TV personality Kelly Osbourne.

Kelsey
(alt. Kelcie, Kelsea, Kelsi, Kelsie)

English, meaning "island."

Kendall
(alt. Kendal)

English, meaning "the valley of the Kent."

Kendra

English, meaning "knowing." Kendra Wilkinson is a reality TV star.

Kenna

Irish Gaelic, meaning "handsome."

Kennedy
(alt. Kenadee, Kennedi)

Irish Gaelic, meaning "helmet head." Made famous by the Kennedy family.

Kenya

African, from the eponymous country.

Kenzie

Shortened form of Mackenzie, meaning "son of the wise ruler."

Kerensa

Cornish, meaning "love." Also used as a spelling variation of Karen.

Kerrigan

Irish, meaning "black haired."

Kerry
(alt. Keri, Kerri, Kerrie)

Irish, from the eponymous county.

Khadijah
(alt. Khadejah)

Arabic, meaning "premature baby." Khadija bint Khuwaylid was the first wife of Muhammad and known as the "Mother of Islam."

Khaleesi

Dothraki, meaning "queen." Royal title from Game of Thrones.

Kiana
(alt. Kia, Kianna)

American English, meaning "fibre." Associated with TV personality Kiana.

Kiara

Italian, meaning "light." St. Kiara saved an Irish town from a fire through prayer.

Kiki

Spanish, meaning "home ruler."
"Let's Have a Kiki" is a song by the
Scissor Sisters. Kiki Dee was the stage
name of a pop singer from the 1970s.

Kimberly
(alt. Kimberleigh, Kimberley; abbrev. Kim, Kimmy)

Old English, meaning "royal forest."
Also a town in South Africa. Famous
Kimberlys include reality star Kim
Kardashian and singer Lil' Kim.

Kingsley
(alt. Kinsley, Kynslee)

English, meaning "king's meadow."
Used for boys as well as girls.

Kinsey

English, meaning "king's victory."

Kira

Greek, meaning "lady." The
antagonist in the popular Japanese
anime *Death Note*.

Kiri

Maori, meaning "tree bark." Dame
Kiri Te Kanawa is an opera singer.

Kirsten
(alt. Kirstin; abbrev. Kirstie, Kirsty)

Scandinavian, meaning "Christian."
Kirsten Dunst and Kirstie Alley are
actors and Kirsten Gillibrand is a
politican.

Kizzy

Hebrew, meaning the plant cassia.

Klara

Hungarian, meaning "bright."

Komal

Hindi, meaning "soft and tender."

Kristen
(alt. Kristan, Kristin, Kristine; abbrev. Kri, Krista, Kristi, Kristie, Kristy)

Greek, meaning "Christian." Famous
Kristens include actor Kristen Stewart
and reality TV star Kris Jenner.

Kwanza
(alt. Kwanzaa)

African, meaning "beginning." Also
the name of the African-American
festival in December and January.

Kyla
(alt. Kya, Kylah, Kyle)

Scottish, meaning "narrow spit of
land." The name of actor Kyla Pratt.

Kylie
(alt. Kiley, Kylee)

Irish Gaelic, meaning "graceful."
Associated with the singer Kylie
Minogue.

Kyra

Greek, meaning "lady."

Kyrie

Greek, meaning "the Lord." Also
a prayer sung at the beginning of
Christian masses.

L Girls' names

Lacey
(alt. Laci, Lacie, Lacy)
French, from the town of the same name. Famous Laceys include dancer Lacey Schwimmer.

Ladonna
Italian, meaning "lady." A spelling alternative to Madonna.

Lady
English, meaning "bread kneader." A character from Disney's *Lady and the Tramp*.

Laila
(alt. Layla, Leila, Lejla, Lela, Lelah, Lelia)
Arabic, meaning "night." Famous Lailas include boxer Laila Ali, and the song "Layla" by Eric Clapton.

Lainey
(alt. Laine, Laney)
French, meaning "bright light."

Lakeisha
(alt. Lakeshia)
American English, meaning "woman." A contraction of La and Keisha.

Lakshmi
(alt. Laxmi)
Sanskrit, meaning "good omen." The Hindu goddess of wealth.

Lana
Greek, meaning "light." Famous Lanas include singer Lana Del Rey, and actor Lana Turner.

Lani
(alt. Lanie)
Hawaiian, meaning "heaven and sky."

Lara
Latin, meaning "famous." Famous Laras include actor Lara Flynn Boyle, Tomb Raider star Lara Croft, and an ancient Roman nymph.

Laraine

French, meaning "from Lorraine."

Larissa
(alt. Larisa)

Greek, meaning "light-hearted." Larissa was a nymph in ancient Greek mythology.

Lark
(alt. Larkin)

English, meaning "playful songbird."

Larsen
(alt. Larsan)

Scandinavian, meaning "son of Lars."

Latifa
(alt. Latifah)

Arabic, meaning "gentle and pleasant." Queen Latifah is a rapper and actor.

Latika
(alt. Lotika)

Hindi, meaning "a plant." Also a character in *Slumdog Millionaire*.

Latisha

Latin, meaning "happiness."

Latona
(alt. Latonia)

Latin, from the mythological ancient Roman heroine of the same name who had twin boys with Zeus.

Latoya

Spanish, meaning "victorious one." Name of singer LaToya Jackson.

Latrice
(alt. Latricia)

Latin, meaning "noble."

Laura
(alt. Lora)

Latin, meaning "laurel." Famous Lauras include actor Laura Dern, author Laura Ingalls Wilder, and designer Laura Ashley.

Laurel

Latin, meaning "laurel tree." Also a term used for young women in the Mormon Church.

Lauren
(alt. Lauran, Lauryn Hill, Loren)

Latin, meaning "laurel." Famous Laurens include actors Lauren Bacall and Lauran Grace, and singer-songwriter Lauryn Hill.

Laveda
(alt. Lavada)

Latin, meaning "cleansed."

Lavender

Latin, from the plant of the same name. A character from the *Harry Potter* series.

Laverne
(alt. Lavern, Laverna)

Latin, from the goddess of the same name. Famous Lavernes include Laverne Andrews, of the Andrews Sisters, and sitcom *Laverne & Shirley*.

Lavinia
(alt. Lavina)

Latin, meaning "woman of Rome." In Roman mythology Lavinia is a heroine whose hair caught fire, creating a prophecy.

Lavonne
(alt. Lavon)

French, meaning "yew wood."

Leah
(alt. Lea, Leia)

Hebrew, meaning "weary." Name of musical actor Lea Michele.

Leandra

Greek, meaning "lion man." A character in *Don Quixote*.

Leanne
(alt. Leann, Leanna, Leeann)

Contraction of Lee and Ann, meaning "meadow grace." Famous Leannes include singers LeAnn Rimes and Lee Ann Womack.

Leda

Greek, meaning "gladness." The ancient Greek heroine Leda was seduced by Zeus in the form of a swan.

Lee
(alt. Leigh)

English, meaning "pasture or meadow."

Leilani

Hawaiian, meaning "flower from heaven." Name of actor Leilani Jones.

Leith

Scottish Gaelic, meaning "broad river."

Lena
(alt. Leena, Lina)

Latin, meaning "light." Famous Lenas include actors and filmmakers Lena Dunham and Lena Headey.

Lenna
(alt. Lennie)

German, meaning "lion's strength." The Lenna photograph is a standard test image used in image processing.

Léonie
(alt. Leona, Leone)

Latin, meaning "lioness." Léonie Adams was a 20th-century American poet.

Leonora
(alt. Lenora, Lenore, Leonor, Leonore, Leora)

Greek, meaning "light." Leonora Braham is an opera singer.

Lesley
(alt. Leslee, Leslie)

Scottish Gaelic, meaning "the gray castle." Famous Leslies include actor and dancer Leslie Caron, and singer Leslie Feist. Lesley is more commonly the female spelling and Leslie the male.

Leta

Latin, meaning "glad and joyful."
Leta Hollingworth was a pioneering
child psychologist.

Letha

Greek, meaning "forgetfulness." Also
a type of butterfly.

Letitia
(alt. Leticia, Lettice, Lettie)

Latin, meaning "joy and gladness."
St. Leticia was a Spanish virgin
martyr.

Lexia
(alt. Lexi, Lexie)

Greek, meaning "defender of
mankind." Also a genus of butterfly.

Lia

Italian, meaning "bringer of the
gospel." Lia Williams is an actor.

Liana

French, meaning "to twine around."

Libby
(alt. Libbie)

Originally a shortened form of
Elizabeth, meaning "pledged to
God." Name of singer Libby Holman.

Liberty

English, meaning "freedom." Made
famous by the Statue of Liberty in
New York, NY.

Lida

Slavic, meaning "loved by the
people."

Liese
(alt. Liesel, Liesl)

German, meaning "pledged to God."
Liesl is a character in *The Sound of
Music*.

Lila
(alt. Lilah)

Arabic, meaning "night." In the
Hindu faith, Lila refers to playtime or
pastimes.

Lilac

Latin, from the flower of the same
name. Also the pale purple color.

Lilia
(alt. Lilias)

Scottish, meaning "lily."

Lilith

Arabic, meaning "ghost." In Jewish
mythology Lilith was thought to be a
female demon.

Lillian
(alt. Lilian, Liliana, Lilla, Lillianna)

Latin, meaning "lily." Famous Lillians
include actor Lillian Gish, playwright
Lillian Hellman, and nursing pioneer
Lillian Wald.

Lily
(alt. Lili, Lillie, Lilly)

Latin, from the flower of the same name. Famous Lilys include singer Lily Allen, actor Lily Collins, and model Lily Cole.

Linda
(alt. Lynda)

Spanish, meaning "pretty." Famous Lindas include actor Linda Blair and singer Linda Ronstadt.

Linden
(alt. Lindie, Lindy)

European, from the tree of the same name.

Lindsay
(alt. Lindsey, Linsey, Lynsey)

English, meaning "island of linden trees." Famous Lindsays include actor Lindsay Lohan and skier Lindsay Vonn. Can be used for both girls and boys.

Linette
(alt. Lynette)

Welsh, meaning "idol."

Linnea
(alt. Linnae, Linny)

Scandinavian, meaning "lime or linden tree." An extremely popular name for baby girls in Sweden.

Liora
(alt. Lior)

Hebrew, meaning "I have a light." Also a spelling alternative to Leora.

Lisa
(alt. Leesa, Lise, Liza)

Hebrew, meaning "pledged to God." Famous Lisas include singer Lisa Bonet, actor Lisa Kudrow, and *The Simpsons* character Lisa Simpson.

Lish

Shortened form of Elisha, meaning "my God is salvation."

Lissa

Greek, meaning "bee." Also a shortened form of Melissa.

Lissandra
(alt. Lisandra)

Greek, meaning "man's defender."

Liv

Nordic, meaning "defense." Also a short form of Olivia. Actor Liv Tyler is an original Liv.

Livia

Latin, meaning "olive." Livia Drusilla was the wife of Roman Emperor Augustus.

Logan

Irish Gaelic, meaning "small hollow." Used more commonly for boys.

Lois

German, meaning "renowned in battle." Made famous by *Superman* heroine Lois Lane.

Lolita
(alt. Lola; abbrev. Lollie)

Spanish, meaning "sorrows." The title of a novel by Vladimir Nabokov.

Lona

Latin, meaning "lion." Lona is a moon deity in Hawaiian mythology.

Lorelei
(alt. Loralai, Loralie)

German, meaning "dangerous rock." Associated with the Lorelei myth in Germany.

Lorenza

Latin, meaning "from Laurentium."

Loretta
(alt. Loreto)

Latin, meaning "laurel." Loretta Devine is an actor.

Lori
(alt. Laurie, Lorie, Lorri)

Latin, meaning "laurel." Name of actor Lori Petty.

Lorna

Scottish, from the place of the same name. The title character in R. D. Blackmore's novel *Lorna Doone*.

Lorraine
(alt. Loraine)

French, meaning "from Lorraine." Famous Lorraines include actor Lorraine Bracco, paranormal investigator Lorraine Warren, and playwright Lorraine Hansberry.

Lottie
(alt. Lotta, Lotte)

French, meaning "little and womanly." Also a shortened form of Charlotte.

Lotus

Greek, meaning "lotus flower."

Louise
(alt. Lou, Louie, Louisa, Luisa)

German, meaning "renowned in battle." Famous Louises include actors Louise Fletcher and Louise Lasser.

Lourdes

French, from the town of the same name. Chosen by Madonna for her eldest daughter.

Love

English, meaning "deep affection and attraction."

Lowri

Welsh, meaning "crowned with laurels."

Luanne
(alt. Luann, Luanna)

German, meaning "renowned in battle"; Hawaiian, meaning "enjoyment." Famous Luannes include author Luanne Rice and *Real Housewife* LuAnn de Lesseps.

Lucia
(alt. Luciana)

Italian, meaning "light."

Lucille
(alt. Lucile, Lucilla)

French, meaning "light." Name of actor Lucille Ball.

Lucinda

English, meaning "light." Famous Lucindas include actor Lucinda Jenney and singer Lucinda Williams.

Lucretia
(alt. Lucrece)

Spanish, meaning "light." Important figure in ancient Roman history.

Lucy
(alt. Lucie)

Latin, meaning "light." Associated with the sitcom *I Love Lucy*.

Ludmilla

Slavic, meaning "beloved of the people."

Luella
(alt. Lue)

English, meaning "renowned in battle." Luella Bartley is an English fashion designer.

Lulu
(alt. Lula)

German, meaning "renowned in battle." Name of the singer.

Luna

Latin, meaning "moon." Luna was the personification of the moon in ancient Roman mythology.

Lupita

Spanish, from the town of the same name. Lupita Nyong'o is an Academy Award-winning actor.

Luz

Spanish, meaning "light."

Lydia
(alt. Lidia)

Greek, meaning "from Lydia." Lydia Bennet is one of the five sisters in Jane Austen's *Pride and Prejudice*.

Lynn
(alt. Lyn, Lynna, Lynne)

Spanish, meaning "pretty"; English, meaning "waterfall." Name of the actor Lynn Redgrave.

Lyla

Hebrew, meaning "night."

Lyra

Latin, meaning "lyre." The main female character in Philip Pullman's trilogy *His Dark Materials*.

Girls' names

Mab
(alt. Mabe)

Irish Gaelic, meaning "joy."
Queen Mab is a character from
Shakespeare's *Romeo and Juliet*.

Mabel
(alt. Mabelle, Mable)

Latin, meaning "loveable." Dates
from the fifth century.

Macaria

Spanish, meaning "blessed."

Mackenzie
(alt. Mackenzy, McKenzie)

Irish Gaelic, meaning "son of the
wise ruler." Used for girls and boys.

Macy
(alt. Macey, Maci, Macie)

French, meaning "Matthew's estate."
Famous Macys include department
store Macy's and reality TV star Maci
Bookout.

Mada

English, meaning "from Magdala."
In Hindu mythology, Mada is an
enormous monster who is able to
swallow the universe.

Madden
(alt. Maddyn)

Irish, meaning "little dog." Associated
with the video game series.

Madeline
*(alt. Madaline, Madalyn, Madeleine,
Madelyn, Madilyn; abbrev. Maddi,
Maddie, Madie)*

Greek, meaning "from Magdala."
Associated with Ludwig Bemelmans's
"Madeline" novels.

Madge

Greek, meaning "pearl." Also the
short form of Marjorie and the
nickname of singer Madonna.

Madhuri

Hindi, meaning "sweet girl."

Madison

(alt. Maddison, Madisen, Madisyn)

English, meaning "son of the mighty warrior." Made famous by *Splash* character Madison and President James Madison.

Madonna

Latin, meaning "my lady." Made famous by pop legend Madonna and the Virgin Madonna.

Maeve

Irish Gaelic, meaning "intoxicating." Queen Maeve appears in Irish mythology and Maeve Binchy was an Irish author.

Mafalda

Spanish, meaning "battlemighty." Mafalda Hopkirk is a character in the *Harry Potter* series.

Magali

Greek, meaning "pearl."

Magdalene

(alt. Magdalen, Magdalena)

Greek, meaning "from Magdala." Associated with Mary Magdalene from the Bible.

Maggie

Shortened form of Margaret, meaning "pearl." Famous Maggies include actors Maggie Gyllenhaal and Maggie Grace, and *The Simpsons* character Maggie Simpson.

Magnolia

Latin, from the flowering plant of the same name. Also the name of a movie.

Mahala

(alt. Mahalia)

Hebrew, meaning "tender affection."

Maia

(alt. Maja)

Greek, meaning "mother." An important character in ancient Greek mythology.

Maida

English, meaning "maiden."

Maisie

(alt. Maisey, Maisy, Maizie, Masie, Mazie)

Greek, meaning "pearl." Name of actor Maisie Williams.

Malin

(alt. Maline)

Hebrew, meaning "of Magda." Famous Malins include actor Malin Akerman, singer Malin Berggren, and infamous alleged Swedish witch Malin Matsdotter.

Maliyah
(alt. Malia)

Hawaiian, meaning "beloved." Also the name of one of former President Barack Obama's daughters.

Malka

Hebrew, meaning "queen."

Mallory
(alt. Malorie)

French, meaning "unhappy." The name of children's author Malorie Blackman.

Malvina

Gaelic, meaning "smooth brow."

Mamie
(alt. Mammie)

Shortened form of Margaret, meaning "pearl." Famous Mamies include former First Lady Mamie Eisenhower, actor Mamie Gummer, and infamous midwife Mamie Cadden.

Mandy
(alt. Mandie)

Shortened form of Amanda, meaning "much loved." Famous Mandys include actor Mandy Moore, performer Mandy Miller, and the song "Mandy" by Barry Manilow.

Manisha

Sanskrit, meaning "desire." Manisha is the goddess of wisdom in the Hindu faith.

Mansi

Hopi, meaning "plucked flower."

Manuela

Spanish, meaning "the Lord is among us."

Mara

Hebrew, meaning "bitter." Famous Maras include actors Mara Wilson and Rooney Mara, and author Mara Bergman.

Marcy
(alt. Marci, Marcie, Marcia, Marcela, Marceline, Marcella, Marcelle)

Latin, meaning "war-like." Famous Marcias include actor Marcia Cross and voice actor Marcia Wallace.

Margaret
(alt. Margarete, Margaretta, Margarette, Margret, Margarita, Margeurite; abbrev. Maggie, Margot, Meg)

Greek, meaning "pearl." Famous Margarets include author Margaret Atwood, actor Margaret Rutherford, and former Prime Minister of Great Britain Margaret Thatcher. Margot is the abbreviation of the French form, Marguerite, used by dancer Margot Fonteyn.

Maria
(alt. Mariah)

Latin, meaning "bitter." Famous Marias include tennis pro Maria Sharapova, performer Maria Von Trapp, and singer Mariah Carey.

Marian
(alt. Marianne, Mariam, Mariana, Marion)

French, meaning "bitter grace." Maid Marian is a character from the Robin Hood legend.

Maribel

Hebrew, meaning "beautiful."

Marie

French, meaning "bitter." Famous Maries include French Queen consort Marie Antoinette, physicist Marie Curie, and singer Marie Osmond.

Mariel
(alt. Mariela, Mariella, Marika)

Dutch, meaning "bitter."

Marietta
(alt. Marieta)

French, meaning "bitter." Marietta Stow was a suffragist.

Marigold

English, from the flowering plant of the same name. Associated with the movie *The Best Exotic Marigold Hotel*.

Marilyn
(alt. Marilee, Marilene, Marilynn)

English, meaning "bitter." Made famous by actor and singer Marilyn Monroe.

Marin

American English, from the county of the same name.

Marina
(alt. Marine)

Latin, meaning "from the sea."

Mariposa

Spanish, meaning "butterfly."

Marisa
(alt. Maris, Marissa)

Latin, meaning "of the sea." Famous Marisas include actors Marisa Tomei, Marissa Ribisi, and Marissa Jaret Winokur.

Marisol

Spanish, meaning "bitter sun." Associated with Maria de la Soledad, which is a Spanish title for the Virgin Mary.

Marjolaine

French, meaning "marjoram."

Marjorie
(alt. Margery, Marjory; abbrev. Madge, Marge, Margie, Margit, Margy)

French, meaning "pearl." Famous Marjories include actors Marjorie Reynolds and Marjorie Main, socialite Marjorie Bridges, and autobiographer Margery Kempe.

Marlene
(alt. Marla, Marlen, Marlena)

Hebrew, meaning "bitter." Name of the actor Marlene Dietrich.

Marley
(alt. Marlee)

American English, meaning "bitter." Made famous by singer Bob Marley.

Marlo
(alt. Marlowe)

American English, meaning "bitter."

Marnie
(alt. Marney)

Scottish, meaning "from the sea." Famous Marnies include the character of Marnie from *Girls*, the movie *Marnie* by Alfred Hitchcock, and the birth name of ballerina Dame Darcey Bussell.

Marseille

French, from the city of the same name.

Marsha

English, meaning "war-like." Famous Marshas include singer Marsha Hunt, playwright Marsha Norman, and *Brady Bunch* character Marsha.

Martha
(alt. Marta)

Aramaic, meaning "lady." Found in the Bible.

Martina
(alt. Martine)

Latin, meaning "war-like." Famous Martinas include singer Martina McBride, and tennis pros Martina Hingis and Martina Navratilova.

Marvel

French, meaning "something to wonder at." Also a comic book brand.

Mary

Hebrew, meaning "bitter." Famous Marys include the Virgin Mary and Mary Magdalene from the Bible, and author Mary Shelley.

Masada

Hebrew, meaning "foundation."

Matilda
(alt. Mathilda, Mathilde; abbrev. Tilly)

German, meaning "battlemighty." *Matilda* is a novel by Roald Dahl, and a movie from the book.

Mattea

Hebrew, meaning "gift of God."

Maude
(alt. Maud)

German, meaning "battlemighty." Maude Flanders is a character from *The Simpsons*.

Maureen
(alt. Maura, Maurine)

Irish, meaning "bitter."

Mavis

French, meaning "thrush." Mavis is a character in *Hotel Transylvania*.

Maxine
(abbrev. Maxie)

Latin, meaning "greatest." Maxine Andrews was one of the singing group the Andrews Sisters.

May
(alt. Mae, Maya, Maye, Mayra)

Hebrew, meaning "gift of God." Also the fifth month.

Mckenna
(alt. Mackenna)

Irish Gaelic, meaning "son of the handsome one." Used more commonly for boys.

Medea
(alt. Madea, Meda)

Greek, meaning "ruling." Associated with the Tyler Perry character Madea.

Meg

Shortened form of Margaret, meaning "pearl." Famous Megs include actor Meg Ryan, and the characters of Meg from Disney's *Hercules* and Meg Griffin from *Family Guy*.

Megan
(alt. Meagan, Meghan)

Welsh, meaning "pearl." Famous Megans include actor Megan Fox and the Duchess of Sussex, Meghan Markle.

Mehitabel

Hebrew, meaning "benefited by God."

Mehri

Persian, meaning "kind."

Melanie
(alt. Melania, Melany, Melonie; abbrev. Mel)

Greek, meaning "dark-skinned." Famous Melanies include actor Melanie Griffith and singers Melanie Brown and Melanie Chisholm of the Spice Girls.

Melba

Australian, meaning "from Melbourne." Made famous by Melba toast and the dessert Peach Melba.

Melia
(alt. Meliah)

German, meaning "industrious."

Melina

Greek, meaning "honey." Name of actor Melina Kanakaredes.

Melinda

Latin, meaning "honey."
Philanthropist Melinda Gates is the
wife of Microsoft founder Bill Gates.

Melisande
(alt. Melisende, Melisandre)

French, meaning "bee." Melisandre
is a character from *Game of Thrones*.

Melissa
(alt. Melisa, Mellissa; abbrev. Missy)

Greek, meaning "bee." Famous
Melissas include singer Melissa
Etheridge and actor Melissa Joan Hart.

Melody
(alt. Melodie)

Greek, meaning "song."

Melvina

Celtic, meaning "chieftain."

Menora
(alt. Menorah)

Hebrew, meaning "candlestick."
A Menorah is a candalabrum with
seven branches, used in Jewish
worship; a symbol of Judaism.

Mercedes

Spanish, meaning "mercies."
Made famous by the car company
Mercedes-Benz.

Mercy

English, meaning "mercy."

Meredith
(alt. Meridith)

Welsh, meaning "great ruler."
Meredith Brooks is a singer. Also the
name of the title character Meredith
Grey in *Grey's Anatomy*.

Merle

French, meaning "blackbird." Also
the term for the patterning on the
coat of a dog.

Merry

English, meaning "lighthearted."

Meryl
(alt. Merrill)

Irish Gaelic, meaning "seabright."
The name of actor Meryl Streep and
ice dancer Meryl Davis.

Meta

German, meaning "pearl."

Mia

Italian, meaning "mine." Famous
Mias include actors Mia Farrow
and Mia Wasikowskaa.

Michaela
*(alt. Makaela, Makaila, Makayla,
McKayla, Micaela, Mikaela, Mikaila,
Mikala, Mikayla)*

Hebrew, meaning "who is like
the Lord." The name of gymnast
McKayla Maroney.

Michelle

(alt. Machelle, Mechelle, Michaele, Michal, Michele; abbrev. Micki, Mickie, Micky)

French, meaning "who is like the Lord." Famous Michelles include former First Lady Michelle Obama, and actor Michelle Rodriguez.

Migdalia

Greek, meaning "from Magdala."

Mignon

French, meaning "cute." Also a cut of steak.

Mika

(alt. Micah)

Hebrew, meaning "who resembles God."

Milada

Czech, meaning "my love."

Milagros

Spanish, meaning "miracles." Also a type of Mexican folk charm.

Milan

Italian, from the city of the same name.

Mildred

English, meaning "gentle strength." The title character from the movie and TV series *Mildred Pierce*.

Milena

Czech, meaning "love and warmth."

Miley

American English, meaning "smiley." Name of singer and actor Miley Cyrus.

Millicent

(alt. Milicent; abbrev. Millie, Milly)

German, meaning "high-born power." Famous Millicents include suffragist Millicent Fawcett, British spy Milicent Bagot, and the musical *Thoroughly Modern Millie*.

Mimi

Italian, meaning "bitter." Mimi is a character from Giacome Puccini's opera *La boheme*.

Mina

(alt. Mena)

German, meaning "love"; Persian, meaning "colored glass."

Mindy

(alt. Mindi)

Latin, meaning "honey." Famous Mindys include comedian Mindy Kaling, singer Mindy McCready, and actor Mindy Sterling.

Minerva

Roman, from the goddess of the same name. Minerva was the goddess of wisdom, arts, and defense.

Ming

Chinese, meaning "bright." Associated with the Ming Dynasty in China.

Minnie
(alt. Minna)

German, meaning "helmet." Made famous by Disney's Minnie Mouse.

Mira
(alt. Meera)

Latin, meaning "admirable."

Mirabel
(alt. Mirabella, Mirabelle)

Latin, meaning "wonderful." Also a type of plum.

Miranda
(alt. Meranda)

Latin, meaning "admirable." Famous Mirandas include actors Miranda Richardson and Miranda Hart, and model Miranda Kerr.

Mirella
(alt. Mireille, Mirela)

Latin, meaning "admirable." Mirella Freni is an opera singer.

Miriam

Hebrew, meaning "bitter." A prophetess in the Bible.

Mirta

Spanish, meaning "crown of thorns."

Missy
(alt. Missie)

Shortened form of Melissa, meaning "bee." The name of singer and producer Missy Elliot.

Misty
(alt. Misti)

English, meaning "mist." Associated with Misty from Pokémon.

Mitzi

German, meaning "bitter." Name of actor Mitzi Gaynor.

Miu

Japanese, meaning "beautiful feather."

Moira
(alt. Maira)

Irish, meaning "bitter." Associated with actor Moira Kelly.

Molly
(alt. Mollie)

American English, meaning "bitter." Famous Mollys include actors Molly Ringwald and Molly Sims.

Mona

Irish Gaelic, meaning "aristocratic." The vampire from Mona the Vampire.

Monica
(alt. Monika, Monique)

Latin, meaning "advisor." Famous Monicas include intern Monica Lewinsky, tennis pro Monica Seles, and Friends character Monica Geller.

Monroe

Gaelic, meaning "mouth of the river Rotha." Made famous by singer and actor Marilyn Monroe.

Montserrat
(alt. Monserrate)

Spanish, from the town of the same name. Montserrat Caballe is an opera singer.

Morag

Scottish, meaning "star of the sea." Also the name of the Loch Morar monster in Scotland.

Morgan
(alt. Morgann)

Welsh, meaning "great and bright." Used for girls and boys.

Moriah

Hebrew, meaning "the Lord is my teacher."

Morwenna

Welsh, meaning "maiden." St. Morwenna is the patron saint of Cornwall, England.

Moselle
(alt. Mozell, Mozella, Mozelle)

Hebrew, meaning "savior."

Mulan

Chinese, meaning "wood orchid." Also a Disney movie.

Muriel

Irish Gaelic, meaning "seabright." Name of the novelist Muriel Spark.

Mya
(alt. Maya, Myah)

Greek, meaning "mother." Famous Myas include author Maya Angelou, comedian Maya Rudolph, and the Mayan people of Central America.

Myfanwy

Welsh, meaning "my little lovely one."

Myla

English, meaning "merciful."

Myleene

English, from the Latin Melaine meaning "dark as night."

Myra

Latin, meaning "scented oil." Name of the pioneering lawyer Myra Bradwell.

Myrna
(alt. Mirna)

Irish Gaelic, meaning "tender and beloved." Associated with actor Myrna Fahey.

Myrtle

Irish, from the shrub of the same name. Myrtle Wilson is a character from *The Great Gatsby*.

Girls' names

Nadia
(alt. Nadya)

Russian, meaning "hope." Nadia Comaneci was the first gymnast to be awarded a perfect score of ten in an Olympic event.

Nadine

French, meaning "hope." Name of the socialite Nadine Caridi.

Nahara

Aramaic, meaning "light."

Naima

Arabic, meaning "water nymph."

Nalani

Hawaiian, meaning "serenity of the skies."

Nancy
(alt. Nanci, Nancie; abbrev. Nan, Nanna, Nannie)

Hebrew, meaning "grace." Famous Nancys include former First Lady Nancy Reagan and figure skater Nancy Kerrigan.

Nanette
(alt. Nannette)

French, meaning "grace." Associated with musical *No, No, Nanette*.

Naomi
(alt. Naoma, Noemi)

Hebrew, meaning "pleasant." Found in the Bible. Famous Naomis include actor Naomi Watts, author Naomi Wolf, and supermodel Naomi Campbell.

Narcissa

Greek, meaning "daffodil." Narcissa Malfoy is a character in the *Harry Potter* series.

Nastasia

Greek, meaning "resurrection." Can also refer to a baby born on Christmas Day.

Natalie
(alt. Natalia, Natalya, Nathalie)

Latin, meaning "birth day." Natalie Wood was an actor.

Natasha
(alt. Natasa; abbrev. Nat, Tasha)

Russian, meaning "birth day." A character from Leo Tolstoy's *War and Peace*.

Neda

English, meaning "wealthy." An ancient Greek nymph.

Nedra

English, meaning "underground."

Neema

Swahili, meaning "born of prosperity."

Neka

Native American, meaning "goose."

Nell
(alt. Nelda, Nella, Nellie, Nelly)

Originally a shortened form of Eleanor, meaning "light." The title of a movie. Singer Nelly Furtado was given the name at birth, but Nell Gwynn, mistress of King Charles II, was an Eleanor.

Nemi

Italian, from the lake of the same name.

Neoma

Greek, meaning "new moon."

Nereida

Spanish, meaning "sea nymph."

Nerissa

Greek, meaning "sea nymph." A character in Shakespeare's play *The Merchant of Venice*.

Nettie
(alt. Neta)

Shortened form of Henrietta, meaning "ruler of the house."

Neva

Spanish, meaning "snowy."

Nevaeh

American English, meaning "heaven" (and spelled that way backwards).

Neytiri

Na'vi, meaning "princess." From the *Avatar* film series.

Niamh
(alt. Neve)

Irish, meaning "brightness." An Irish goddess.

Nicola
(abbrev. Nicki, Nicky, Nikki)

Greek, meaning "victory of the people." Famous Nicolas include actor Nicola Peltz and singer Nicola Roberts.

Nicole
(alt. Nichol, Nichole, Nicolette, Nicolle, Nikole)

Greek, meaning "victory of the people." Famous Nicoles include actor Nicole Kidman, socialite Nicole Richie, and singer Nicole Scherzinger.

Nidia

Spanish, meaning "graceful."

Nigella

Irish Gaelic, meaning "champion." Name of British chef Nigella Lawson.

Nikita

Greek, meaning "unconquered." Also a song by Elton John.

Nila

Egyptian, meaning "Nile." Associated with Nila wafers.

Nilda

German, meaning "battle woman."

Nina

Spanish, meaning "girl." Nina Simone was a singer-songwriter and civil rights activist.

Old name, new fashion

Bella	Hazel
Carolyn	Matilda
Clara	Nora
Dorothy	Penelope
Emmeline	Rosalie

Nissa

Hebrew, meaning "sign."

Nita

Spanish, meaning "gracious."

Nixie

German, meaning "water sprite."

Noelle
(alt. Noel)

French, meaning "Christmas." Noelle is usually the feminine form and Noel the masculine form.

Nola
(alt. Nuala)

Irish Gaelic, meaning "white shoulder." Often refers to someone with white or very blonde hair.

Nona

Latin, meaning "ninth."

Nora
(alt. Norah)

Shortened form of Eleanor, meaning "light." The name of screenwriter Nora Ephron, singer Norah Jones, and author Nora Roberts.

Noreen
(alt. Norine)

Irish, meaning "light." Noreen Murray was a scientist who helped develop the vaccine against hepatitis B.

Norma

Latin, meaning "pattern." Marilyn Monroe's birth name was Norma Jean Mortenson.

Normandie
(alt. Normandy)

French, from the province of the same name.

Novia
(alt. Nova)

Latin, meaning "new."

Nydia

Latin, meaning "nest."

Nysa
(alt. Nyssa)

Greek, meaning "ambition." A district in ancient Greek mythology.

Girls' names

Oaklyn
(alt. Oaklynn)
English, meaning "from the oak meadow."

Oceana
(alt. Ocean, Océane, Ocie)
Greek, meaning "ocean."

Octavia
Latin, meaning "eighth."
Famous Octavias include actor Octavia Spencer, and Octavia in Shakespeare's *Antony and Cleopatra*.

Oda
(alt. Odie)
Shortened form of Odessa, meaning "long voyage"; German, meaning "wealth" or "inheritance."

Odele
(alt. Odell)
English, meaning "woad hill." Woad is a dye for the color indigo.

Odelia
Hebrew, meaning "I will praise the Lord." Associated with St. Odelia.

Odessa
Greek, meaning "long voyage."

Odette
(alt. Odetta)
French, meaning "wealthy." Name of the "good" swan in *Swan Lake*.

Odile
(alt. Odilia)
French, meaning "prospers in battle." Name of the "bad" swan in *Swan Lake*.

Odina
Feminine form of Odin, meaning "creative inspiration," from the Nordic god of the same name.

Odyssey

Greek, meaning "long journey."
Title of the epic poem by Homer.

Oksana

Russian, meaning "praise to God."

Ola
(alt. Olie)

Greek, meaning "man's defender."

Olena
(alt. Olene)

Russian, meaning "light."

Olga

Russian, meaning "holy." Name of
the model and actor Olga Kurylenko,
and gymnast Olga Korbut.

Olivia
*(alt. Olivev, Oliviana, Olivié, Ollie;
abbrev. Liv, Livia)*

Latin, meaning "olive." Famous
Olivias include actors Olivia Munn
and Olivia Wilde, and *Scandal*
character Olivia Pope.

Olwen

Welsh, meaning "white footprint."

Olympia
(alt. Olimpia)

Greek, meaning "from Mount
Olympus." Name of actor Olympia
Dukakis.

Oma
(alt. Omie)

Arabic, meaning "leader." In some
communities, Oma refers to a
grandmother.

Omyra

Latin, meaning "scented oil."

Oneida
(abbrev. Ona, Onnie)

Native American, meaning "long
awaited." The name of a tribe.

Onyx

Latin, meaning "veined gem." Also
a semiprecious stone.

Oona
(alt. Oonagh)

Irish, meaning "unity."

Opal

Sanskrit, meaning "gem." Also a
precious stone.

Ophelia
(alt. Ophélie)

Greek, meaning "help." A character
in Shakespeare's *Hamlet*.

Oprah

Hebrew, meaning "young deer."
Name of the legendary TV host
Oprah Winfrey.

Ora
Latin, meaning "prayer." Also a platinum metal.

Orabela
Latin, meaning "prayer."

Oralie
(alt. Oralia)
French, meaning "golden."

Orane
French, meaning "rising."

Orchid
Greek, from the flower of the same name.

Oriana
(alt. Oriane)
Latin, meaning "dawning." One of the many nicknames of Queen Elizabeth I.

Orla
(alt. Orlaith, Orly)
Irish Gaelic, meaning "golden lady."

Orlean
French, meaning "plum." The city of New Orleans in Louisiana.

Orsa
(alt. Osia, Ossie)
Latin, meaning "bear."

Otthid
Greek, meaning "prospers in battle."

Ottilie
(alt. Ottie)
French, meaning "prospers in battle." Name of the opera singer Ottilie Metzger.

Ouida
French, meaning "renowned in battle."

Ozette
Native American, from the village of the same name.

Girls' names

Padma

Sanskrit, meaning "lotus." Padma Lakshmi is an Indian-born American cookery book writer, actor, and TV host.

Paige
(alt. Page)

French, meaning "serving boy." Paige Turco is an actor.

Paisley

Scottish, from the town of the same name. The name of a fabric pattern.

Palma
(alt. Palmira)

Latin, meaning "palm tree."

Paloma

Spanish, meaning "dove." Famous Palomas include singer Paloma Faith and designer Paloma Picasso.

Pamela
(alt. Pamala, Pamella; abbrev. Pam, Pammie)

Greek, meaning "all honey." Famous Pamelas include actors Pamela Anderson and Pamela Adlon, and author Pamela (P. L.) Travers.

Pandora

Greek, meaning "all gifted." Associated with the myth of Pandora's box in ancient Greek mythology.

Pangiota

Greek, meaning "all is holy."

Pansy

French, from the flower of the same name.

Paradisa
(alt. Paradis)

Greek, meaning "garden orchard."

Paris
(alt. Parisa)

Greek, from the mythological hero of the same name. Famous Parises include the French capital and socialite Paris Hilton.

Parker

English, meaning "park keeper." Parker Posey is an actor.

Parthenia

Greek, meaning "virginal."

Parthenope

Greek, from the mythological Siren of the same name. Parthenope Nightingale was sister of nurse Florence Nightingale.

Parvati

Sanskrit, meaning "daughter of the mountain." The Hindu goddess of love and devotion.

Pascale

Latin, meaning "Easter child." Also a boys' name, usually spelt Pascal.

Patience

French, meaning "the state of being patient."

Patricia
(abbrev. Pat, Patsy, Patti, Pattie, Patty, Trisha)

Latin, meaning "noble." Famous Patricias include actors Patricia Arquette and Patricia O'Neal.

Paula

Latin, meaning "small." Famous Paulas include singer Paula Abdul, actor Paula Patton, and chef Paula Deen.

Pauline
(alt. Paulette, Paulina)

Latin, meaning "small."

Paxton

Latin, meaning "peaceful town."

Paz

Spanish, meaning "peace."

Pazia

Hebrew, meaning "golden."

Peace

English, meaning "peace."

Pearl
(alt. Pearle, Pearlie, Perla)

Latin, meaning "pale gemstone."

Peggy
(alt. Peggie)

Greek, meaning "pearl." The name of actor Peggy Lipton and figure skater Peggy Fleming; also associated with the movie Peggy Sue Got Married.

Pelia

Hebrew, meaning "marvel of God."

Penelope
(abbrev. Penni, Pennie, Penny)

Greek, meaning "bobbin worker." Penelope was also the loyal wife of Odysseus in Greek mythology.

Peony

Greek, from the flower of the same name.

Perdita

Latin, meaning "lost." A character in William Shakespeare's play *The Winter's Tale*.

Peri
(alt. Perri)

Hebrew, meaning "outcome." Associated with Peri spirits in Persian mythology.

Perry

French, meaning "pear tree."

Persephone

Greek, meaning "bringer of destruction." The Queen of the Underworld in ancient Greek mythology.

Petra
(alt. Petrina)

Greek, meaning "rock."

Petula

Latin, meaning "to seek." Name of the singer Petula Clark.

Petunia

Greek, from the flower of the same name.

Peyton
(alt. Payton)

Old English, meaning "fighting man's estate." Associated with TV series *Peyton Place*.

Phaedra

Greek, meaning "bright."

Philippa
(abbrev. Pippa)

Greek, meaning "horse lover." Philippa Gregory is an author.

Philomena
(alt. Philoma)

Greek, meaning "loved one." Title of the book and movie *Philomena*.

Phoebe

Greek, meaning "shining and brilliant." Famous Phoebes include actor Phoebe Cates, and *Friends* character Phoebe Buffay.

Phoenix

Greek, meaning "red as blood." The city in Arizona and the mythical bird.

Phyllis
(alt. Phillia, Phyllida, Phylis)

Greek, meaning "leafy bough." Name of the groundbreaking comedian Phyllis Diller.

Pia
Latin, meaning "pious."

Pilar
Spanish, meaning "pillar."

Piper
English, meaning "pipe player." Piper Laurie is an actor. Piper Kerman was the real-life inspiration behind the character Piper Chapman in Netflix hit *Orange is the New Black*.

Plum
Latin, from the fruit.

Polly
Hebrew, meaning "bitter." Associated with the classic Polly Pocket toy.

Pomona
Latin, meaning "apple." The goddess of fruitful abundance in ancient Roman mythology.

Poppy
Latin, from the flower of the same name. Poppy Delevingne is a model.

Portia
(alt. Porsha)

Latin, meaning "from the Portia clan." Portia de Rossi is an actor.

Posy
(alt. Posie)

English, meaning "small flower."

Precious
Latin, meaning "of great worth." Title of the movie *Precious*.

Priela
Hebrew, meaning "fruit of God."

Primrose
English, meaning "first rose."

Princess
English, meaning "daughter of the monarch."

Priscilla
(alt. Priscila)

Latin, meaning "ancient." Actor Priscilla Presley was married to Elvis.

Priya
Hindi, meaning "loved one."

Prudence
(abbrev. Pru, Prudie)

Latin, meaning "caution." Prudence is the mother of all virtues.

Prunella
Latin, meaning "small plum." Prunella Scales is a British actor.

Psyche
Greek, meaning "breath." The name of TV show *Psyche*.

Girls' names

Qianru
Chinese, meaning "pretty."

Qiturah
Arabic, meaning "incense."

Queen
(alt. Queenie)
English, meaning "queen." The name of rapper and actor Queen Latifah.

Quiana
American English, meaning "silky." Name of the model Quiana Grant.

Quincy
(alt. Quincey)
French, meaning "estate of the fifth son."

Quinn
(alt. Quinnie)
Irish Gaelic, meaning "counsel." Quinn is a character from *Glee*.

Quinnlan
Gaelic, meaning "strong and well-made."

 Girls' names

Rachel
(alt. Rachael, Rachelle, Raquel;
abbrev. Rach)

Hebrew, meaning "ewe." Found in
the Bible. Famous Rachel's include
actors Rachel Weisz and Rachel
Bilson, and the *Friends* character
Rachel Green.

Radhika
Sanskrit, meaning "prosperous."

Rae
(alt. Ray)

Feminine form of Ray, meaning
"ray," or shortened form of Rachel,
meaning "ewe." Rae Armantrout is
a poet.

Rahima
Arabic, meaning "compassionate."
Name of smallpox survivor Rahima
Banu.

Raina
(alt. Rain, Raine, Rainey, Rayne)

Latin, meaning "queen."

Raissa
(alt. Raisa)

Yiddish, meaning "rose." Name
of former Russian First Lady Raisa
Gorbacheva.

Raleigh
(alt. Rayleigh)

English, meaning "meadow of roe
deer."

Rama
(alt. Ramey, Ramya)

Hebrew, meaning "exalted."
Associated with the Vishnu's avatars
in the Hindu faith.

Ramona
(alt. Romona)

Spanish, meaning "wise guardian."
Associated with the "Ramona" books,
and the movie *Ramona and Beezus*.

Ramsey
(alt. Ramsay)
English, meaning "raven island."

Rana
(alt. Rania, Rayna)
Arabic, meaning "beautiful thing."

Randy
(alt. Randi)
Shortened form of Miranda, meaning "admirable." More commonly used for boys, as a short form of Randall.

Rani
Sanskrit, meaning "queen."

Raphaela
(alt. Rafaela, Raffaella)
Spanish, meaning "healing God."

Rashida
Turkish, meaning "righteous." Name of actor Rashida Jones.

Raven
(alt. Ravyn)
English, from the bird of the same name. Raven-Symoné is an actor.

Razia
Arabic, meaning "contented."

Reagan
(alt. Reagen, Regan)
Irish Gaelic, meaning "descendant of Riagán." Associated with former President and First Lady Ronald and Nancy Reagan.

Reba
Shortened form of Rebecca, meaning "joined." Name of singer and actor Reba McEntire.

Rebecca
(alt. Rebekah; abbrev. Reb, Reba, Becca, Bex)
Hebrew, meaning "joined." Found in the Bible. Famous Rebeccas include designer Rebecca Minkoff, and actor Rebecca Hall.

Reese
(alt. Reece)
Welsh, meaning "fiery and zealous." Name of actor Reese Witherspoon.

Regina
(abbrev. Geena, Gena, Gina)
Latin, meaning "queen." Famous Reginas include actors Regina Hall and Regina King, and singer Regina Spektor. Geena Davis is an actor.

Reina
(alt. Reyna, Rheyna)
Spanish, meaning "queen."

Rena
(alt. Reena, Rina)
Hebrew, meaning "serene."

Renata
Latin, meaning "reborn." Renata Tebaldi was an Italian opera singer.

Rene

Greek, meaning "peace." Rene Russo is an actor.

Renée
(alt. Renae)

French, meaning "reborn." Name of actor Renée Zellweger.

Renita
(alt. Renira)

Latin, meaning "resistant."

Reshma
(alt. Resha)

Sanskrit, meaning "silk."

Reta
(alt. Retha, Retta)

Portuguese, meaning "straight." Also a shortened form of Margaret.

Rhea

Greek, meaning "earth." Also a type of ostrich-like bird. Name of actor Rhea Perlman.

Rheta

Greek, meaning "eloquent speaker." Flora Rheta Schreiber is an author.

Rhiannon
(alt. Rhian)

Welsh, meaning "witch." A prominent figure in Welsh mythology.

Rhoda

Greek, meaning "rose." Title of the sitcom *Rhoda*.

Rhona

Nordic, meaning "rough island." Rhona Mitra is a model and actor.

Rhonda
(alt. Ronda)

Welsh, meaning "noisy." "Help Me Rhonda" is a song by the Beach Boys.

Ría
(alt. Rie, Riya)

Shortened form of Victoria, meaning "victor."

Ricki
(alt. Rieko, Rika, Rikki)

Shortened form of Frederica, meaning "peaceful ruler." Name of the TV host Ricki Lake.

Rihanna
(alt. Reanna, Rhianna)

Welsh, meaning "witch." Robyn Rihanna fenty is a Barbadian singer and businesswoman.

Riley

Irish Gaelic, meaning "courageous."

Rilla

German, meaning "small brook."

Rima

Arabic, meaning "antelope." Name of the comic book character *Rima the Jungle Girl*.

Riona

Irish Gaelic, meaning "like a queen."

Ripley

English, meaning "shouting man's meadow."

Risa

Latin, meaning "laughter."

Rita

Shortened form of Margaret, meaning "pearl." Famous Ritas include actors Rita Hayworth and Rita Moreno, and singer Rita Ora.

River
(alt. Riviera)

English, from the body of water of the same name.

Roberta
(abbrev. Bobbi, Bobby, Robbie, Robi, Roby)

English, meaning "bright fame." Name of singer Roberta Flack.

Robin
(alt. Robbin, Robyn)

English, meaning "bright fame." Famous Robins include actor Robin Wright Penn, and singers Robyn and Robin Thicke. Used for both girls and boys.

Rochelle
(alt. Richelle, Rochel)

French, meaning "little rock." Name of actor Rochelle Aytes.

Rogue

French, meaning "beggar." Also an "X-Men" character.

Rohina
(alt. Rohini)

Sanskrit, meaning "sandalwood."

Roisin

Irish Gaelic, meaning "little rose."

Rolanda

German, meaning "famous land." Rolanda Watts is a voice actor.

Roma

Italian, meaning "Rome." Also the name of an ancient Roman deity, and a group of nomadic people.

Romaine
(alt. Romina)

French, meaning "from Rome."

Romola
(alt. Romilda, Romily)

Latin, meaning "Roman woman." Name of the actor Romola Garai.

Romy

Shortened form of Rosemary, meaning "dew of the sea." Famous Romys include actor Romy Rosemont and the movie *Romy and Michele's High School Reunion*.

Rona
(alt. Ronia, Ronja, Ronna)

Nordic, meaning "rough island."

Ronnie
(alt. Roni, Ronnie)

English, meaning "strong counsel."

Rosa

Italian, meaning "rose." Made famous by Civil Rights activist Rosa Parks.

Rosabel
(alt. Rosabella)

Contraction of Rose and Belle, meaning "beautiful rose."

Rosalie
(alt. Rosale, Rosalia, Rosalina)

French, meaning "rose garden." Actor Andie MacDowell's birth name is actually Rosalie.

Rosalind
(alt. Rosalinda)

Spanish, meaning "pretty rose." A character in Shakespeare's play *As You Like It*.

Rosalyn
(alt. Rosaleen, Rosaline, Roselyn)

Contraction of Rose and Lynn, meaning "pretty rose."

Rosamund
(alt. Rosamond)

German, meaning "renowned protector." Famous Rosamunds include actor Rosamund Pike and author Rosamunde Pilcher.

Rose
(alt. Rosie, Rosia)

Latin, from the flower of the same name. Famous Roses include actors Rose Byrne and Rose McGowan, and the character of Rose DeWitt Bukater from *Titanic*.

Roseanne
(alt. Rosana, Rosanna, Rosanne, Roseann, Roseanna)

Contraction of Rose and Anne, meaning "graceful rose."

Rosemary
(alt. Rosemarie; abbrev. Rosie, Rosy)

Latin, meaning "dew of the sea." Famous Rosemarys include the late actor Rosemary Clooney and the film *Rosemary's Baby*.

Rosita

Spanish, meaning "rose." Also a character on *Sesame Street*.

Rowena
(alt. Rowan)

Welsh, meaning "slender and fair." Rowena was a powerful and beautiful seductress in ancient Welsh mythology.

Roxanne
(alt. Roxana, Roxane, Roxanna; abbrev. Roxie)

Persian, meaning "dawn." Also a song by The Police. Famous Roxies include the character of Roxie Hart from the musical *Chicago*, and the band Roxy Music.

Rubina
(alt. Rubena)

Hebrew, meaning "behold, a son."

Ruby
(alt. Rubi, Rubie)

English, meaning "red gemstone." Made famous by the song "Ruby Tuesday" by the Rolling Stones.

"Bad girl" names

Delilah	Roxy
Desdemona	Salome
Jezebel	Scarlett
Lilith	Tallulah
Pandora	Trixie

Ruth
(alt. Ruthe, Ruthie)

Hebrew, meaning "friend and companion." Found in the Bible. Famous Ruths include Supreme Court Justice Ruth Bader Ginsburg.

Ryan
(alt. Riaan)

Gaelic, meaning "little king." More commonly used for boys.

Girls' names

Saba
(alt. Sabah)

Greek, meaning "from Sheba."

Sabina
(alt. Sabine)

Latin, meaning "from the Sabine tribe." The title given to political women in ancient Rome.

Sabrina

Latin, meaning "the River Severn." Famous Sabrinas include the movie *Sabrina*, the sitcom *Sabrina, the Teenage Witch*, and the character from *Charlie's Angels*.

Sadie
(alt. Sade, Sadye)

Hebrew, meaning "princess." Sadie Frost is British designer and actor.

Saffron

English, from the reddish-yellow spice of the same name.

Safiyya
(alt. Safiya)

Arabic, meaning "sincere friend." One of Muhammad's wives in the Qur'an.

Sage
(alt. Saga, Saige)

Latin, meaning "wise and healthy." Also an aromatic herb.

Sahara

Arabic, meaning "desert."

Sakura

Japanese, meaning "cherry blossom."

Sally
(alt. Sallie)

Hebrew, meaning "princess." Actor Sally Field has had a long and successful career.

Salome
(alt. Salma)

Hebrew, meaning "peace." A seductress in the Bible.

Samantha
(abbrev. Sam, Sammie, Sammy)

Hebrew, meaning "told by God." Famous Samanthas include TV host Samantha Brown and actors Samantha Lewes and Samantha Morton.

Samara
(alt. Samaria, Samira)

Hebrew, meaning "under God's rule."

Sanaa

Arabic, meaning "brilliance." Also the capital of Yemen.

Sandra
(alt. Saundra; abbrev. Sandy)

Shortened form of Alexandra, meaning "defender of mankind." Famous Sandras include actor Sandra Bullock and the character Sandy from Grease.

Sangeetha
(alt. Sangeeta)

Hindi, meaning "musical."

Sanna
(alt. Saniya, Sanne, Sanni)

Hebrew, meaning "lily."

Santana
(alt. Santina)

Spanish, meaning "holy."

Saoirse

Irish Gaelic, meaning "freedom."

Sapphire
(alt. Saphira)

Hebrew, meaning "blue gemstone." Associated with Push (or Precious) author Sapphire.

Sarah
(alt. Sara, Sarai, Sariah)

Hebrew, meaning "princess." Famous Sarahs include actors Sarah Michelle Gellar and Sarah Hyland, and politician and reality TV star Sarah Palin.

Sasha
(alt. Sacha, Sascha)

Russian, meaning "man's defender." Name of former President Barack Obama's daughter.

Saskia
(alt. Saskie)

Dutch, meaning "the Saxon people"; Danish, meaning "valley of light."

Savannah
(alt. Savanah, Savanna, Savina)

Spanish, meaning "treeless."

Scarlett
(alt. Scarlet)

English, meaning "scarlet." Scarlett O'Hara is the protagonist of Margaret Mitchell's novel *Gone With The Wind*.

Scout

French, meaning "to listen." Also the lead character in Harper Lee's novel *To Kill a Mockingbird*.

Sedona
(alt. Sedonia, Sedna)

Spanish, from the city of the same name.

Selah
(alt. Sela)

Hebrew, meaning "cliff"; Hebrew, meaning "stop and listen."

Selby

English, meaning "manor village."

Selena
(alt. Salena, Salima, Salina, Selene, Selina)

Greek, meaning "moon goddess." Famous Selenas include singers Selena Gomez and Selena Quintanilla-Perez (known simply as Selena), and actor Selena Royle.

Selma

German, meaning "Godly helmet." Name of actor Selma Blair.

Seneca

Native American, meaning "from the Seneca tribe."

Sephora

Hebrew, meaning "bird"; Greek, meaning "beauty."

September

Latin, meaning "seventh month." The ninth month.

Seraphina
(alt. Serafina, Seraphia, Seraphine)

Hebrew, meaning "ardent."
St. Serafina was known for her strong faith despite illness and suffering.

Serena
(alt. Sarina, Sereana)

Latin, meaning "tranquil." Name of tennis pro Serena Williams.

Serenity

Latin, meaning "serene." Also a sci-fi movie.

Shakira

Arabic, meaning "thankful." Name of the singer Shakira.

Shania
(alt. Shaina, Shana, Shaniya)

Hebrew, meaning "beautiful." Name of the singer Shania Twain.

Shanice

American English, meaning "from Africa." Name of the singer Shanice.

Shaniqua
(alt. Shanika)

African, meaning "warrior princess."

Shanna

English, meaning "old."

Shannon
(alt. Shannan, Shanon)

Irish Gaelic, meaning "old and ancient." Shannon Elizabeth is an actor.

Shantal
(alt. Shantel, Shantell)

French, from the place of the same name.

Shanti
(alt. Shantih)

Hindi, meaning "peaceful."

Sharlene

German, meaning "man."

Sharon
(alt. Sharen, Sharona, Sharron)

Hebrew, meaning "a plain." Famous Sharons include reality TV star Sharon Osbourne and actors Sharon Stone and Sharon Tate.

Shasta

American English, from the mountain and Native American tribe of the same name.

Shauna
(alt. Sharna, Shawna)

Irish, meaning "the Lord is gracious." Sharna Burgess is a dancer.

Shayla
(alt. Shaylie, Shayna, Sheyla)

Irish, meaning "blind."

Shea

Irish Gaelic, meaning "from the fairy fort." The tree and nut of the same name.

Sheena

Irish, meaning "the Lord is gracious." Name of the singer Sheena Easton.

Sheila
(alt. Shelia, Shila)

Irish, meaning "blind." Name of singer Sheila E.

Shelby
(alt. Shelba, Shelbie)

English, meaning "estate on the ledge."

Shelley
(alt. Shellie, Shelly)

English, meaning "meadow on the ledge." Famous Shelleys include actor Shelley Fabares and Shelley Duvall, and author Mary Shelley.

Shenandoah

Native American, meaning "after an Oneida chief." Also the name of a national park.

Sheridan

Irish Gaelic, meaning "wild man."

Sheryl

(alt. Sherryl; abbrev. Sheri, Sherie, Sherri, Sherrie)

German, meaning "man." Famous Sheryls include singer Sheryl Crow, businesswoman Sheryl Sandberg, and host Sheryl Underwood. Also comedian and host Sherri Shepherd.

Shiloh

Hebrew, meaning "his gift." Name of Angelina Jolie and Brad Pitt's daughter.

Shirley

(alt. Shirlee)

English, meaning "bright meadow." Famous Shirleys include singer Dame Shirley Bassey, actor Shirley MacLaine, and child star Shirley Temple.

Shivani

Sanskrit, meaning "wife of Shiva."

Shona

Irish Gaelic, meaning "God is gracious."

Shoshana

(alt. Shoshanna)

Hebrew, meaning "lily." Shoshanna Shapiro is a character from Girls.

Shura

Russian, meaning "man's defender"; Arabic, meaning "consultation."

Sian

(alt. Sianna)

Welsh, meaning "the Lord is gracious."

Sibyl

(alt. Sybil)

Greek, meaning "seer and oracle." Sibyl was a prophetess in ancient Greek mythology.

Sidney

(alt. Sydney)

English, meaning "from St. Denis." Name of the city in Australia.

Sidonie

(alt. Sidonia, Sidony)

Latin, meaning "from Sidonia."

Siena

(alt. Sienna)

Latin, from the town of the same name.

Sierra

Spanish, meaning "saw."

Sinead

Irish, meaning "the Lord is gracious." Name of singer Sinead O'Connor.

Siobhan

Irish, meaning "the Lord is gracious." Siobhan Fallon Hogan is an actor.

Siren
(alt. Sirena)

Greek, meaning "entangler." In ancient Greek mythology, sirens were beautiful and dangerous creatures who lured sailors to their deaths.

Siria

Spanish, meaning "glowing."

Skye
(alt. Sky)

Scottish, from the island of the same name in Scotland.

Skylar
(alt. Skyla, Skyler)

Dutch, meaning "giving shelter." Skylar White is a character from *Breaking Bad*.

Sloane
(alt. Sloan)

Irish Gaelic, meaning "man of arms." Famous Sloanes include tennis player Sloane Stephens, the infamous Sloane Rangers, and the character of Sloane Sabbith on *Newsroom*.

Great female singers

Adele (Adkins)
Aretha (Franklin)
Billie (Holiday)
Dionne (Warwick)
Dolly (Parton)
Ella (Fitzgerald)
Gladys (Knight)
Jennifer (Hudson)
Judy (Garland)
Nina (Simone)

Signa
(alt. Signe)

Scandinavian, meaning "victory."

Sigrid

Nordic, meaning "fair victory." Sigrid the Haughty was an important figure in ancient Norse mythology.

Silja

Scandinavian, meaning "blind."

Simcha

Hebrew, meaning "joy."

Simone
(alt. Simona)

Hebrew, meaning "listening intently." Famous Simones include singer Nina Simone, and philosopher Simone de Beauvoir.

Socorro

Spanish, meaning "to aid."

Sojourner

English, meaning "temporary stay." Name of 19th-century women's rights and civil rights activist Sojourner Truth.

Solana

Spanish, meaning "sunlight."

Solange

French, meaning "with dignity." Solange Knowles is a singer.

Soledad

Spanish, meaning "solitude."

Soleil

French, meaning "sun."

Solveig

Scandinavian, meaning "woman of the house."

Sonia
(alt. Sonja, Sonya)

Greek, meaning "wisdom." Sonia Kasuk is a designer.

Sophia
(alt. Sofia, Sofie, Sophie)

Greek, meaning "wisdom." Famous Sophias include director Sofia Coppola and actors Sofia Vergara and Sophia Loren.

Sophronia

Greek, meaning "sensible."

Soraya

Persian, meaning "princess."

Sorcha

Irish Gaelic, meaning "bright and shining."

Sorrel

English, from the herb of the same name.

Spirit

Latin, meaning "breath."

Stacey
(alt. Stacie, Stacy)

Greek, meaning "resurrection." Famous Staceys include actors Stacey Keibler and Stacey Dash, and presenter Stacey Dales.

Star
(alt. Starla, Starr)

English, meaning "star." The name of reality TV star Star Jones.

Stella

Latin, meaning "star." Stella McCartney is a British designer.

Stephanie
(alt. Stefanie, Stephani, Stephany, Stephenie; abbrev. Steph)

Greek, meaning "crowned." Famous Stephanies include actor Stephanie Beacham, and author Stephenie Meyer.

Storm
(alt. Stormi, Stormy)

English, from the weather feature. Kylie Jenner's daughter is Stormi.

Sukey
(alt. Sukey, Sukie)

Derived from Susan, meaning "lily."

Sula

American English, meaning "peace" or "little she-bear." Also the novel Sula by Toni Morrison.

Summer

English, from the season of the same name. Summer Glau is an actor.

Sunday

English, meaning "the first day." Nicole Kidman and Keith Urban's daughter is Sunday Rose.

Sunny
(alt. Sun)

English, meaning "of a pleasant temperament."

Suri

Persian, meaning "red rose." Tom Cruise and Katie Holmes's daughter is Suri.

Surya

Hindi, from the sun god of the same name.

Susan
(alt. Susann, Suzan; abbrev. Sue, Susie, Suzy)

Hebrew, meaning "lily." Famous Susans include actor Susan Sarandon, singer Susan Boyle, and suffragist Susan B. Anthony.

Susannah
(alt. Susana, Susanna, Susanne, Suzanna, Suzanne)

Hebrew, meaning "lily."

Svetlana

Russian, meaning "star."

Swanhild

Saxon, meaning "battle swan."

Sylvia
(alt. Silvia, Sylvie)

Latin, meaning "from the forest." Famous Sylvias include authors Sylvia Plath and Sylvia Day, and singer Sylvia Robinson.

Girls' names

Tabitha
(alt. Tabatha, Tabetha)
Aramaic, meaning "gazelle." Found in the Bible.

Tahira
Arabic, meaning "virginal."

Tai
Chinese, meaning "big."

Taima
(alt. Taina, Tayna)
Native American, meaning "peal of thunder."

Talia
(alt. Tali)
Hebrew, meaning "heaven's dew." Talia Shire is an actor.

Taliesin
Welsh, meaning "shining brow." The name of Welsh poet Taliesin.

Talise
(alt. Talisa, Talyse)
Native American, meaning "lovely water." Talisa Stark is a character from *Game of Thrones*.

Talitha
Aramaic, meaning "young girl."

Tallulah
(alt. Taliyah)
Native American, meaning "leaping water." Famous Tallulahs include actors Tallulah Bankhead and Tallulah Riley, and *Bugsy Malone* character Tallulah.

Tamara
(alt. Tamera)
Hebrew, meaning "palm tree." Famous Tamaras include actors Tamara Taylor and Tamera Mowry.

Tamatha
(alt. Tametha)
American English, meaning "dear Tammy."

Tamika
(alt. Tameka)
American English, meaning "people."

Tamsin
(abbrev. Tami, Tammie, Tammy)
Hebrew, meaning "twin." Tammy Wynette is the name used by the legendary country singer—her real first name was Virginia.

Tanis
Spanish, meaning "to make famous."

Tanya
(alt. Tania, Tanya, Tonya)
Shortened form of Tatiana, meaning "from the Tatius clan." The name of actor Tanya Roberts and figure skater Tonya Harding.

Tara
(alt. Tahra, Tarah, Tera)
Irish Gaelic, meaning "rocky hill." Famous Taras include actors Tara Reid and Tara Fitzgerald.

Tatiana
(alt. Tatyana)
Russian, meaning "from the Tatius clan." Famous Tatianas include actors Tatyana Ali and Tatiana Maslany, and author Tatiana de Rosnay.

Tatum
English, meaning "lighthearted." Famous Tatums include actors Tatum O'Neal and Channing Tatum.

Tawny
(alt. Tawanaa, Tawnee, Tawnya)
English, meaning "golden brown."

Taya
Greek, meaning "poor one." In several languages the name also means "princess" or "goddess."

Taylor
(alt. Tayler)
English, meaning "tailor." Famous Taylors include singer Taylor Swift and actor Taylor Schilling.

Tea
Greek, meaning "goddess." Tea Leoni is an actor.

Teagan
(alt. Teague, Tegan)
Irish Gaelic, meaning "poet."

Teal
English, from the bird of the same name. Also the blue-green color.

Tecla
Greek, meaning "fame of God."

Temperance
English, meaning "virtue." Temperance Brennan is a character from *Bones*.

Tempest

French, meaning "storm." The Shakespeare play of the same name.

Teresa

(alt. Terese, Tereza, Theresa, Therese)

Greek, meaning "harvest." Famous Teresas include nun Mother Teresa, and the late actor Teresa Graves.

Terri

(alt. Teri, Terrie, Terry)

Derived from the short form of Teresa, meaning "harvest." Actor Teri Hatcher was given this short name at birth.

Tessa

(alt. Tess, Tessie)

Derived from the short form of Teresa, meaning "harvest." Famous Tessas include ice dancer Tessa Virtue and literary heroine *Tess of the D'Urbervilles* by Thomas Hardy.

Thais

Greek, from the mythological heroine of the same name.

Thalia

Greek, meaning "blooming." The name of numerous ancient Greek muses, nymphs, and graces.

Thandie

(alt. Thana, Thandi)

Arabic, meaning "thanksgiving." Thandie Newton is an actor.

Thea

Greek, meaning "goddess." Can be a shortened form of Theodora or Dorothea.

Theda

German, meaning "people." Name of the silent movie actor Theda Bara.

Thelma

Greek, meaning "will." Famous Thelmas include singer Thelma Houston, and the movie *Thelma & Louise*.

Theodora

Greek, meaning "gift of God." The name of numerous ancient Roman figures.

Theodosia

Greek, meaning "gift of God."

Thisbe

Greek, from the mythological heroine of the same name.

Thomasina

(alt. Thomasin, Thomasine, Thomasyn)

Greek, meaning "twin." The birth name of singer Tammi Terrell was Thomasina Montgomery.

Thora

Scandinavian, meaning "Thor's struggle." Name of the actor Thora Birch.

Tia
(alt. Tiana)

Spanish, meaning "aunt." Tia Mowry is an actor.

Tiara

Latin, meaning "jeweled headband."

Tierney

Irish Gaelic, meaning "Lord."

Tierra
(alt. Tiera)

Spanish, meaning "land."

Tiffany
(alt. Tiffani, Tiffanie)

Greek, meaning "God's appearance." Name of the one-hit-wonder singer Tiffany.

Tigris
(alt. Tiggy)

Irish Gaelic, meaning "tiger."

Tilly
(alt. Tilda, Tillie)

Shortened form of Matilda, meaning "battle-mighty."

Timothea

Greek, meaning "honoring God."

Tina
(alt. Teena, Tena)

Shortened form of Christina, meaning "anointed Christian." Famous Tinas include comedian Tina Fey and singer Tina Turner.

Tirion

Welsh, meaning "kind and gentle."

Tirzah

Hebrew, meaning "pleasantness." Found in the Bible.

Titania

Greek, meaning "giant." The Fairy Queen from Shakespeare's play *A Midsummer Night's Dream*.

Toby
(alt. Tobi)

Hebrew, meaning "God is good." Usually a boy's name.

Toni
(alt. Tony)

Latin, meaning "invaluable." Feminine version of Tony, or short form of Antoinette. Famous Tonis include singer Toni Braxton, author Toni Morrison, and choreographer Toni Basil.

Tonia
(alt. Tonja, Tonya)

Russian, meaning "praiseworthy."

Topaz

Latin, meaning "golden gemstone."

Tori
(alt. Tora)

Shortened form of Victoria, meaning "victory." Famous Toris include actor Tori Spelling and singer Tori Amos.

Tova
(alt. Tovah, Tove)
Hebrew, meaning "good."

Tracy
(alt. Tracey, Tracie)
Greek, meaning "harvest." Famous Tracys include singer Tracy Chapman, actor Tracey Ullman, and artist Tracey Emin.

Treva
Welsh, meaning "homestead."

Trilby
English, meaning "vocal trills." Also the name of a style of men's hat.

Trina
(alt. Trena)
Greek, meaning "pure."

Trinity
Latin, meaning "triad." Associated with the Christian Holy Trinity. The lead female character from the film series *The Matrix*.

Trisha
(alt. Tricia)
Shortened form of Patricia, meaning "noble." Name of singer Trisha Yearwood.

Trista
Latin, meaning "sad."

Trixie
Shortened form of Beatrix, meaning "bringer of gladness."

Trudie
(alt. Tru, Trudy)
Shortened form of Gertrude, meaning "strength of a spear."

True
English, meaning "loyal."

Tullia
Roman, meaning "bound for glory."

Twyla
(alt. Twila)
American English, meaning "star." Name of the choreographer Twyla Tharp.

Tyler
English, meaning "tiler." Used for both boys and girls.

Tyra
Scandinavian, meaning "Thor's struggle." Tyra Banks is a model.

Tzipporah
Hebrew, meaning "bird."

U

Girls' names

Ula
(alt. Ulla)
Celtic, meaning "gem of the sea."

Ulrika
(alt. Urica)
German, meaning "power of the wolf."

Uma
Sanskrit, meaning "flax." Uma Thurman is an actor best known for her roles in Quentin Tarantino's *Pulp Fiction* and *Kill Bill*.

Una
Latin, meaning "one."

Undine
Latin, meaning "little wave."

Unique
Latin, meaning "only one."

Unity
English, meaning "oneness."

Uriela
(alt. Uriella)
Hebrew, meaning "God's light."

Ursula
Latin, meaning "little female bear." The villain from Disney's *The Little Mermaid*.

Uta
German, meaning "prospers in battle."

Girls' names

Vada

German, meaning "famous ruler."

Valdis

(alt. Valdiss, Valdys, Valdyss)

Norse, meaning "goddess of the dead," from the mythological goddess of the same name.

Valencia

(alt. Valancy, Valarece)

Latin, meaning "strong and healthy." A city in Spain.

Valentina

Latin, meaning "strong and healthy."

Valentine

Latin, from the saint of the same name.

Valerie

(alt. Valarie, Valeria, Valery, Valorie; abbrev. Val, Vale, Valia, Vallie)

Latin, meaning "to be healthy and strong." Famous Valeries include actors Valerie Bertinelli and Valerie Harper, and the song "Valerie" by The Zutons.

Vandana

Sanskrit, meaning "worship."

Vanessa

(alt. Vanesa)

Greek, meaning "butterfly." Famous Vanessas include actor Vanessa Hudgens and singer Vanessa Williams.

Vanity

Latin, meaning "self-obsessed."

Vashti

Persian, meaning "beauty." A Persian queen in the Bible.

Veda

Sanskrit, meaning "knowledge and wisdom."

Vega

Arabic, meaning "falling vulture."

Velda

German, meaning "ruler."

Vella

American English, meaning "beautiful."

Velma

English, meaning "determined protector." A character from *Scooby Doo*.

Venice
(alt. Venetia, Venita)

Latin, meaning "city of canals." An Italian city.

Venus

Latin, from the Roman goddess of the same name. Venus was the goddess of love, beauty, sex, and fertility.

Vera
(alt. Verla, Verlie)

Slavic, meaning "faith." Famous Veras include designer Vera Wang, actor Vera Farmiga, and singer Vera Lynn.

Verda
(alt. Verdie)

Latin, meaning "spring-like."

Verena

Latin, meaning "true." Associated with St. Verena.

Verity

Latin, meaning "truth."

Verna
(alt. Vernie)

Latin, meaning "spring green."

Verona

Latin, from the Italian city of the same name.

Veronica
(alt. Verica, Veronique)

Latin, meaning "true image." Famous Veronicas include actors Veronica Lake and Veronica Carlson, and the "Veronica Mars" series and movie.

Veruca

Latin, meaning "wart." Veruca Salt is a character from *Charlie and the Chocolate Factory*.

Vesta

Latin, from the Roman goddess of the same name.

Vicenta

Latin, meaning "prevailing."

Victoria
(abbrev. Tori, Vicki, Vicky, Vikki, Vix)

Latin, meaning "victory." Famous Victorias include designer Victoria Beckham, England's Queen Victoria, and lingerie store Victoria's Secret.

Vida
Spanish, meaning "life."

Vidya
Sanskrit, meaning "knowledge." Refers to learning and knowledge in the Hindu faith.

Vienna
Latin, from the city of the same name in Austria.

Vigdis
Scandinavian, meaning "war goddess."

Vina
(alt. Vena)

Spanish, meaning "vineyard."

Viola
Latin, meaning "violet." Name of the actor Viola Davis.

Violet
(alt. Violetta)

Latin, meaning "purple." The famed nurse and survivor Violet Jessop.

Virginia
(alt. Virgie, Virginie; abbrev. Ginnie, Ginny)

Latin, meaning "maiden." Famous Virginias include author Virginia Woolf, *Raising Hope* character Virginia Chance, and the eastern states of Virginia and West Virginia.

Vita
Latin, meaning "life."

Vittoria
Variation of Victoria, meaning "victory."

Viva
Latin, meaning "alive." Name of the actor Viva.

Vivian
(alt. Vivien, Vivienne, Vyvian)

Latin, meaning "lively." Famous Vivians include actor Vivian Leigh, designer Vivienne Westwood, and photographer Vivian Maier.

Vivica
(alt. Viveca)

Scandinavian, meaning "war fortress." Name of the actor Vivica A. Fox.

Vonda
Czech, meaning "from the tribe of Vandals." Vonda Shepard is a singer.

Girls' names

Waleska

Polish, meaning "beautiful."

Wallis

English, meaning "from Wales." Name of socialite Wallis Simpson, the woman held responsible for the abdication of Great Britain's King Edward VIII.

Wanda

(alt. Waneta, Wanita)

Slavic, meaning "tribe of the vandals." Name of comedian and actor Wanda Sykes.

Wava

English, meaning "way."

Waverly

(alt. Waverley)

Old English, meaning "meadow of aspens."

Wendy

English, meaning "friend." Famous Wendys include host Wendy Williams, the character of Wendy Darling in *Peter Pan*, and the hamburger chain Wendy's.

Whisper

English, meaning "whisper."

Whitley

Old English, meaning "white meadow."

Whitney

(alt. Witney)

Old English, meaning "white island." Famous Whitneys include the late singer Whitney Houston, comedian Whitney Cummings, and dancer Witney Carson.

Wilda

German, meaning "willow tree."

Wilhelmina
(abbrev. Mina, Mine, Minna, Willa, Willy, Wilma)

German, meaning "determined to protect." A popular name with the German royal family.

Willa
(alt. Willene, Willia)

German, meaning "helmet." Willa Cather is an author.

Willow

English, from the tree of the same name. Famous celebrity children called Willow include Willow Smith (Will and Jada Pinkett Smith's daughter) and Willow Hart (Pink and Carey Hart's daughter).

Winifred
(alt. Winnie)

Old English, meaning "holy and blessed." South African activist Winifred "Winnie" Madikizela-Mandela was once married to former South African President Nelson Mandela.

Winona
(alt. Wynonna)

Indian, meaning "first-born daughter." Famous Winonas include actor Winona Ryder and singer Wynonna Judd.

Winslow

English, meaning "friend's hill."

Winter

English, meaning "winter."

Wisteria

English, meaning "flower."

Wren

English, meaning "wren."

Wynne
(alt. Wynn)

Welsh, meaning "white."

X Girls' names

Xanthe
Greek, meaning "blonde." The name of several ancient Greek mythological characters.

Xanthippe
Greek, meaning "nagging."

Xaverie
Greek, meaning "bright."

Xaviera
Arabic, meaning "bright."

Xena
(alt. Xenia)
Greek, meaning "foreigner." The title character from the TV sci-fi series *Xena: Warrior Princess*.

Ximena
Greek, meaning "listening."

Xiomara
Spanish, meaning "battle ready."

Xochitl
Spanish, meaning "flower." Queen Xochitl was a legendary Toltec ruler.

Xoey
Variation of Zoe, meaning "life." Spelling alternative for Zoey or Joey.

Xristina
Variation of Christina, meaning "follower of Christ." Singer Christina Aguilera often spells her name Xristina.

Xylia
(alt. Xylina, Xyloma)
Greek, meaning "from the woods."

Girls' names

Yadira
Arabic, meaning "worthy."

Yael
Hebrew, meaning "mountain goat."
Found in the Bible.

Yaffa
(alt. Yahaira, Yajaira)
Hebrew, meaning "lovely."

Yamilet
Arabic, meaning "beautiful."

Yana
Hebrew, meaning "the Lord is gracious."

Yanira
Hawaiian, meaning "pretty."
A character in ancient Greek mythology.

Yara
Arabic and Persian, meaning "small butterfly." Yara Greyjoy is a character from *Game of Thrones*.

Yareli
Latin, meaning "golden."

Yaretzi
(alt. Yaritza)
Aztec, meaning "forever beloved."

Yasmin
(alt. Yasmeen, Yasmina, Yasmine)
Persian, meaning "jasmine flower."

Yelena
Greek, meaning "bright and chosen."

Yesenia
Arabic, meaning "flower."

Yetta
English, from Henrietta, meaning "ruler of the house."

Yeva

Hebrew variant of Eve, meaning "life."

Ylva

Old Norse, meaning "she wolf."

Yoki
(alt. Yoko)

Native American, meaning "rain." Yoko Ono is an artist and peace activist.

Yolanda
(alt. Yolonda)

Spanish, meaning "violet flower." Name of reality TV star Yolanda Foster.

Yoselin

English, meaning "lovely."

Yoshiko

Japanese, meaning "good child." Princess Yoshiko was an important Empress of Japan.

Ysabel

English, meaning "God's promise." Spelling alternative to Isabel.

Ysanne

Contraction of Isabel and Anne, meaning "pledged to God" and "grace."

Yuki

Japanese, meaning "lucky."

Yuliana

Latin, meaning "youthful."

Yuridia

Russian, meaning "farmer."

Yvette
(alt. Ivette, Ivonne, Yvonne)

French, meaning "yew." Yvette Nicole Brown is an actor.

Z

Girls' names

Zafira
Arabic, meaning "successful."

Zahara
(alt. Zahava, Zahra)
Arabic, meaning "flowering and shining." Name of Angelina Jolie and Brad Pitt's daughter.

Zaida
(alt. Zaide)
Arabic, meaning "prosperous"; Hebrew, meaning "loved grandfather."

Zalika
Swahili, meaning "well born."

Zaltana
Arabic, meaning "high mountain."

Zamia
Greek, meaning "pine cone."

Zaneta
(alt. Zanceta, Zanetah, Zanett, Zanetta)
Hebrew, meaning "a gracious present from God."

Zaniyah
Arabic, meaning "lily."

Zara
(alt. Zaria, Zariah, Zora)
Arabic, meaning "radiance." A fashion brand.

Zaya
(alt. Zayah)
Tibetan, meaning "victorious woman."

Zelda
German, meaning "dark battle." Associated with the hugely successful video game series *Legend of Zelda*.

Zelia
(alt. Zella)
Scandinavian, meaning "sunshine."

Zelma
German, meaning "helmet."

Zemira
(alt. Zemirah)
Hebrew, meaning "joyous melody."
Title of the opera Zemira by
Francesco Bianchi.

Zena
(alt. Zenia, Zina)
Greek, meaning "hospitable."

Zenaida
Greek, meaning "the life of Zeus."
Associated with physician
St. Zenaida.

Zenobia
Latin, meaning "the life of Zeus."
Zenobia was a queen of ancient
Roman Syria.

Zephyr
Greek, meaning "the west wind."

Zetta
Latin, meaning "seven."

Zia
Arabic, meaning "light and splendor."

Zinaida
Greek, meaning "belonging to Zeus."

Zinnia
Latin, meaning "flower."

Zipporah
Hebrew, meaning "bird." Zipporah
was one of Moses' wives in the Bible.

Zita
(alt. Ziva)
Spanish, meaning "little girl."
St. Zita is the patron saint of maids
and domestic servants.

Zizi
(alt. Zizzy)
Hungarian/Hebrew, meaning "God
is my oath."

Zoe
(alt. Zoi, Zoie, Zoey, Zoeya, Zooey)
Greek, meaning "life." Famous Zoes
include actors Zoe Saldana and
Zooey Deschanel.

Zoila
Greek, meaning "life."

Zoraida
Spanish, meaning "captivating
woman."

Zosia
(alt. Zosima)
Greek, meaning "wisdom." Zosia
Mamet is an actor.

Zoya

Greek, meaning "life." Zoya Kosmodemyanskaya was a Soviet Union heroine.

Zula

African, meaning "brilliant."

Zuleika

Arabic, meaning "fair and intelligent." Zuleika was the name of Potiphar's wife in the Bible.

Zulma

Arabic, meaning "peace."

Zuzana

Hebrew, meaning "lily."

Zuzu

Czech, meaning "flower." Susan (Zuzu) is a character in the movie *It's A Wonderful Life*.

A name for all seasons

Spring	Summer	Fall	Winter
April	August	Autumn	January
Kelda	June	Demetria	Neva
May	Persephone	September	Neve
Primavera	Soleil	Theresa	Perdita
Verda	Summer	Tracey	Rainer